Founded in 1807, John Wiley & Sons is the oldest independent publishing company in the United States. With offices in North America, Europe, Asia, and Australia, Wiley is globally committed to developing and marketing print and electronic products and services for our customers' professional and personal knowledge and understanding.

The Wiley Corporate F&A series provides information, tools, and insights to corporate professionals responsible for issues affecting the profitability of their company, from accounting and finance to internal controls and performance management.

Data Sleuth

Using Data in Forensic Accounting Engagements and Fraud Investigations

LEAH WIETHOLTER

WILEY

Published by John Wiley & Sons, Inc., Hoboken, New Jersey.
Published simultaneously in Canada.

For general information on our other products and services or for technical support, please contact our Customer Care Department within the United States at (800) 762-2974, outside the United States at (317) 572-3993 or fax (317) 572-4002.

Wiley also publishes its books in a variety of electronic formats. Some content that appears in print may not be available in electronic formats. For more information about Wiley products, visit our website at www.wiley.com.

Library of Congress Cataloging-in-Publication Data:

Names: Wietholter, Leah, author.
Title: Data sleuth : using data in forensic accounting engagements and
  fraud investigations / Leah Wietholter.
Description: Hoboken, New Jersey : Wiley, [2022] | Series: Wiley corporate
  f&a | Includes index.
Identifiers: LCCN 2021062798 (print) | LCCN 2021062799 (ebook) | ISBN
  9781119834380 (cloth) | ISBN 9781119834403 (adobe pdf) | ISBN
  9781119834397 (epub)
Subjects: LCSH: Forensic accounting. | Fraud investigation.
Classification: LCC HV8079.F7 W54 2022 (print) | LCC HV8079.F7 (ebook) |
  DDC 364.16/3—dc23/eng/20220112
LC record available at https://lccn.loc.gov/2021062798
LC ebook record available at https://lccn.loc.gov/2021062799

Cover Design: Wiley
Cover Image: © DNY59/Getty Images

SKY10033455_022522

For Chris, Sherlock, Irene, and Watson

Contents

Foreword

"**A**ND WE GET TO carry a gun."

They are not quite the first words I heard Leah speak, but they are certainly not far off. Her first comments teasingly ribbed the Big Four accounting firms, "I've never worked an 80-hour week." At the time, I worked for one of them.

Leah was speaking at an event for students studying accounting and finance and led hard into her presentation. After an internship with the Federal Bureau of Investigation (FBI) in Washington, DC, she had gone on to extend her internship into a role on a forensics unit in Oklahoma. She had taken a different path in her studies and was enjoying the chance to share it with others and to inspire others to consider options that may go overlooked for the more traditional. Even then, she was trying to see different ways of doing things. (To be clear to those contemplating an intern with a sidepiece hanging out going through boxes of bank statements, I don't think she personally carried a gun in her internship role, but it was certainly a future job "perk" for agents.)

At the time, I chuckled a bit at her playful audacity. I had been on my own journey and could faithfully say at the time that I had not worked an 80-hour week, despite working for the jokingly villainous Big Four as she had briefly painted them. But I have to admit, her presentation changed my own that would follow. I would have to step up my game.

Looking back, though, I think the spirit behind the person expressed in those two phrases would resonate and only grow as I would get to know her more. Leah is a leader – someone willing to take steps others haven't and someone who looks for ways to bring people along with her on the ride.

Speaking of taking steps, that's actually how we would become friends. In its simplest telling, the story goes that about a dozen people all found their way to an informal ballroom dancing group set up by a mutual friend. Everyone knew someone, but no one knew everyone. And no one knew how to ballroom dance. At all.

For about three months, we would meet up weekly and trade partners and bruised toes and a few laughs and red faces. But we would also trade spots at meals afterward. Then we would trade turns at different people's houses, at volleyball nets, at cookouts, and at '80s themed birthday parties where we learned an introductory version of the Thriller dance. We would exchange conversations on topics more meaningful about purpose and dreams and courage to take next steps. I will always count it a great inspiration that ballroom dancing lessons would connect people in such meaningful ways. Although some wouldn't find a lasting passion for the tango, we would find lasting passion to see each other accomplish the things that mattered to them.

Leah stands out for her customary boldness. After working with a local accounting firm following her time with the FBI, she realized she had the skill, ability, brand, and nerve to chart her own course. Giving it some intentional thought – but not a second one – she started her own business. She recognized that she had value to offer and that there was a niche she could fill. She didn't need a large accounting firm. She didn't need the FBI. In our conversations, she was certainly grateful for all the lessons and the relationships. But she didn't need the "tried and true" structures and career paths. She was perfectly capable to chart her own course. No, it is more than that – it would have been a compromise not to.

Workman Forensics was born.

There are three factors that are common to most fraud that is perpetrated: incentive/pressure, opportunity, and rationalization. How ironically apropos that these would also be key elements in entrepreneurship, and especially in Leah's entrepreneurship for a business to help detect and prevent fraud. Still, there is something more. As much as it takes incentive and rationalization to make a case to step into the unknown and create something new, it is often seeing and grasping the opportunity that separates entrepreneurs. Although the three sides of that triangle are always relevant, they matter only when someone takes action. Maybe we all see opportunities, find incentives, and can rationalize the journey we would take. But few of us ever do.

It is not only seeing the opportunity, but seizing it, that separates Leah from her peers. And it continues to separate her.

This is a good time to insert a quick observation from those ballroom dance days of old. Leah was determined and present, and I like to think she had a good time, though she did not continue past those three months unless cajoled. She had one main struggle along the way: she had a hard time following. She was always ready to lead, and she knew where she wanted to go. And her eyes were set on bigger things.

As I mentioned, she started her forensics business. She signed the lease on a trendy commercial district in midtown Tulsa and signed up to capture the dream she had described along the way.

It took off.

Under her leadership, the business grew to the point that she had more work than she could do alone. But she was undeterred – she would bring disparate people together to accomplish something more than each could do alone. Faithful to her commitment to community, she found ways to bring others along with her. In fact, she would hire some of those very people we met on the dance floor, with skills ranging from education to accounting and others along the way. They didn't need to be great at every aspect, but their combined skills could lead to greater outcomes.

She trained them and used their varied skillsets, all repurposed as part of a cohesive strategy. From that, Leah was already starting to see how the different pieces fit together that would become the basis for the Data Sleuth. She had to be able to separate the forensics process into manageable activities that she could direct others to complete and bring them back together into meaningful analysis. It allowed her business to grow and for her to take people who didn't have a deep forensics background and teach them to perform integral activities for her thriving business.

But Leah didn't stop there. Instead, the realized dream of Workman Forensics gave flight to others. In the world where podcasts were only being conceived, she worked with others to develop a new concept podcast that would make the world of forensic accounting available – and more important, interesting – to the masses. In a whodunnit series called The Investigation Game, both a training curriculum and a podcast, she would innovate a way of teaching that even the certification and training boards recognized led to meaningful education. She is frequently innovating.

I have been privileged to be surrounded by strong women in my life, who have taught me lessons on courage, strength, and resilience. My grandmother opened a cosmetics business in her 40s after co-owning a hardware store and boarding people at our grandparents' home. My aunt ascended various tiers in her career to support nutrition needs of children while simultaneously battling a crippling form of breast cancer, earning her PhD while taking bouts of chemo. My mom would face being a single parent and a caretaker for her own mother who lived a thousand miles away while holding down a full-time job and the grace to still share and give into others' lives with joy and sincerity.

I can't tell if Leah has ever really considered the challenges that she may have uniquely faced in the tango she has been dancing with her own destiny.

Like those old ballroom lessons, I think she has continued to be the first mover in that duo, guiding destiny and seeing clearly her own next steps. And in a larger sense, I see how she continues to find an unconventional path, and to inspire others to join her along the way.

Reflecting on those first comments I remember from her all those years ago, I honestly don't know for sure whether she carries a firearm at this stage of her career. Or whether she would still name it as a key perk in the path she's taken. I like to think that in some ways, she's traded it for a machete – a tool to clear new paths – and is leaving markers to help others join her along the way. Or in another sense, maybe the Data Sleuth Process has opened up an entirely differ-ent arsenal. She's found that in her business, sidekicks carry better ammunition than sidearms.

James Bowie, CPA

Preface

I N 2013, I RECEIVED the recognition of being one of Oklahoma's 40 under 40, sponsored by *Oklahoma Magazine*. As part of this honor, I was asked to attend a photo shoot to publish with my bio for the magazine. To my surprise, when I arrived, there was also a video interview component for which I had not prepared. The interviewer asked, "Where do you see your business in five years?" For a moment I thought, *Hopefully I'm still in business*. I was a little over two years into the entrepreneurship thing and felt as though every day was only about survival. Fortunately, what I heard myself say instead was, "To make forensic accounting accessible to more people."

But let's start at the beginning. When I was 12 years old, I was obsessed with a radio drama, *Adventures in Odyssey*, specifically the episode titled, "A Name, Not a Number." In this episode, the character Tasha Forbes was introduced as a special agent for the National Security Agency. To this point in my life, I had not thought much about careers. If you had asked me then what I wanted to be when I grew up, I would have said I was going to be a teacher. I do think I consciously realized that women could be something other than a mom or a teacher. This episode about Tasha's career as an agent, however, made me realize that I, as a female, could be an investigator. As an avid reader of mystery novels, I determined that I would become an investigator.

I continued with this dream of a career through high school and learned as much as possible about every federal law enforcement agency. Eventually, I decided that the Federal Bureau of Investigation was the agency for me and began to invest in and focus on areas that would increase my chances of becoming an FBI agent. In 2006, I was given the internship of a lifetime as one of the students selected to participate in the FBI's Honors Internship Program in Washington, DC.

My first day in Washington, DC, was a 12-year-old girl's dream coming to life at age 20. Dressed in a black pantsuit and turquoise button-up shirt, I felt smart, strong, and ready to learn all that I could over the 10-week internship. Standing in line with my new internship friends and at least 100 other college-aged students from around the United States, I was ready to go through security to enter the doors of the headquarters of the Federal Bureau of Investigation.

"What's your name?" the security guard asked. "Leah Workman." He asked a second time, this time asking for my driver's license. *This is not a good sign*, I thought. My mind started racing through all the paperwork, background check interviews, polygraph testing and wondered if maybe I had missed completing one of the many federal forms. All the students chatting outside of the J. Edgar Hoover Building in nervous excitement about their first day sounded like a loud, constant buzz, but as soon as the security guard said, "You're not on the list. Please step aside," everything went silent. Blood drained from my face.

The security processing of the interns slowed to a complete stop, and the security guard pulled me out of line. Heads began to turn in my direction as the line stopped moving, and thankfully, before it became even more embarrassing, the internship coordinator for my group stepped forward to save the day. My name had in fact been omitted from the list, and to this day, I still do not know why. After a short discussion with the internship coordinator, the security personnel verified that I was indeed an intern. I was admitted, received my access badge, and was sworn in.

After orientation and exploring DC, my internship group returned to West Virginia for our work assignments. The internship coordinator let us know we would be taking group photos, meeting with management, and receiving our assignments. We made sure to look as professional as possible by wearing suits again that day. As soon as we walked outside to carpool to the office, I realized that I once again was going to be singled out. Everyone was wearing a black suit, and I was wearing a cream suit.

What began as embarrassment and very unwanted attention those first few days of the internship resulted in an incredible pattern that forced me to learn quickly that being the only one or singled out or different did not have to be detrimental. In fact, these uncomfortable moments laid a foundation for a career advantage.

The 10-week internship was just the beginning of my career with the FBI. When I returned to school the following semester, I was not only about to graduate with my accounting degree, but because of a new program, I was able to continue the internship as an actual FBI employee under the direction of an experienced forensic accountant for the following two years. At the end of the two-year assignment, with only one career option in mind, I took the phase 1 assessment to become an FBI special agent. A few weeks later, based on my assessment results, I was not accepted. Devastated, I relived the exam over and over as I felt lost trying to find my next step. The test questions were like that of a personality test coupled with an assessment of my decision-making abilities. Although this is not the intention of the test, I felt as if the FBI was telling me once again, that I, including my personality and decision-making choices, did not fit in.

My lifelong dream career had been denied me, but as it was not the first time, after a brief period of mourning, I decided to do what I heard all "good" accountants do. I applied to work in public accounting. I chose to work in the tax department because I could then at least prepare my own tax returns.

While working for the accounting firm in Tulsa, forensic accounting was becoming a more requested service, and the firm invited me to work on forensic accounting engagements and fraud investigations. While there, I was able to work on several cases including a $3 million embezzlement from a bank, a divorce, and an engagement involving the tracing of millions of dollars of funds. It was really exciting to take what I learned working for law enforcement and under the direction of the FBI forensic accountant and apply it to the private sector. One major problem with this setup remained. In working for a public accounting firm, I still had to prepare tax returns during the busy seasons leading up to the tax deadline. After a couple of years, I started looking for another job. When I found none that interested me, an accounting headhunter suggested, "What would happen if you started your own investigation and forensic accounting business?" In November 2010, I opened Workman Forensics.

Workman Forensics was established to provided forensic accounting and fraud investigation services, and we have continued to provide only these services for over 11 years. I have managed a team as big as 11 employees, and as small as 1– which included only me. In 2014, I realized that the number of hours I was working per week managing deadlines, business development, human resources, and casework was not sustainable. I am grateful to the many team members who have worked with me over the last six years. It is because of their hard work and specialized talents that we were able to begin developing what is now known as the Data Sleuth Process.

Being an entrepreneur and business owner for over 10 years now, I have read so many books and listened to so many podcasts by great leadership and business minds that talk about vision. If I am being honest, after hearing the term "vision" repeatedly, I began to tune it out because my interpretation of the way they defined vision felt materialistic. The goal of a business vision seemed to focus on doing big things to make more money, which is not a bad thing when someone is in business. I just did not want that to be my vision for my business.

In January 2021, I realized that I needed to embrace vision as more than financial goals beginning with the sharing of seemingly enormous ideas and goals I had been cultivating over the last few years. To take it a step further, I chose a word for the year to break down this vision into an action item; the word chosen was "invest." That one-word vision for the year has since resulted in one team member earning her Certified Fraud Examiner's credential. I passed the Certified Public Accountant exam. Another team member is working to earn the Certified in Financial Forensics credential. We are even now in the process of building an escape room experience. As we continue to move forward, I am amazed by the power of the word I once avoided, vision.

It was actually during the strangeness of 2020 that the concepts presented in this book truly emerged with great promise. When all of our referral sources temporarily stopped referring because the courthouse was closed and clients were asking to pause our casework, our team made continuous improvements to the process and continued to ask ourselves, "When we open again, what are the things we will want to use in a better way?" We focused our working hours to improving the Data Sleuth Process to the point where it can be shared with the readers of this book. Through the improvement of this process, we were able to begin the creation of the subset process Find Money in Divorce – a modular course with training videos and workbooks to help spouses find hidden assets and understated income in divorce cases. It was during this time that we created new game-based virtual case studies qualifying for continuing education for The Investigation Game product line.

Even though Workman Forensics may have started as a story about survival, it is now a story of innovation, as we continue to meet and work with professionals all over the world through casework, The Investigation Game trainings, and The Investigation GamePodcast. Our strategic approach to financial investigations using the Data Sleuth Process has changed my business for the better, and I am excited to experience where imagination and vision take us next.

Acknowledgments

THANK YOU TO MY family and friends who support and listen to my ideas.

Thank you to the past and present Workman Forensics team. Without your encouragement, diligence, and continuous improvement, the Data Sleuth Process would not be what it is today.

Thank you to friends, family, and colleagues who reviewed each chapter. I am forever grateful.

CHAPTER ONE

Building a Data Sleuth Team

A T THE INTERSECTION OF the forensic accounting, fraud investigation, and data analysis engagements is the Data Sleuth Process. Born out of necessity from my solo practitioner struggles, the practicality of the Data Sleuth Process is useful for solo practitioners – especially those new to the profession. But the true power of the Data Sleuth Process is realized in a team-centric environment. Most of the skills expected of a solo forensic accountant are those that improve with experience, but in the context of a team, the expectations can be distributed across all of the members instead of relying on one person to be a jack-of-all-trades. Each investigation engagement presents its own unique challenges, and it may feel as though only someone with years of experience can provide a solution; however, with a reliable, duplicative process, a team-centered model can be developed and provide a better work product than had the professional performed the engagement alone.

In the early days of building my practice, I intentionally ignored all of the business professionals who relentlessly talked about scalability being the ultimate business leader's dream with time for vacation and rest. I would think, *You preach this method because you sell products or have recurring client engagements and have never worked an investigation.* I was convinced that the only duplication that had a chance of happening in my business was by finding someone who I trained to be like me. I tried and failed many times, which only reinforced my cynicism about the scalable dream. The responsibilities and requirements of being a forensic accountant or fraud investigator who provides expert testimony require significant career and life investment.

Forensic accounting career opportunities sounded intriguing to team members until they realized the accompanying pressure. They watched as I developed business, while managing client expectations and deadlines, reviewed analyses with extreme scrutiny to reduce the risk of errors being discovered during testimony, and continued study of accounting and legal knowledge. Many team members were happy to play a part in the investigations, but no one wanted to become the forensic accounting expert.

My caseload as a solo practitioner grew so much that I could not physically work each investigation with the level of care needed in the available waking hours of a week. I began hiring team members, but I struggled to find a way to equip team members with the knowledge they needed to make independent decisions to reduce my work. Frustrated with the long hours and my suffering health, I began working with a business coach. During one of the sessions, he asked me, "Leah, if you were at home sick, and I offered to work for you for free, what would you tell me to do? Where would I start?" I stared blankly at him. His response to my seemingly never-ending silence was, "You look like a deer in headlights," and he repeated his previous questions. I finally responded with great frustration in my eyes, "I would tell you to go home, and I'll finish it when I feel better." He continued to increase the pressure and questions because he refused to accept that answer, and eventually, he said, "Fraud schemes and the ways in which people steal money are not infinite. Tell me the first answer that comes to mind when I ask, 'What do you do?'" I blurted, "I find money for people." We both stopped and realized the clarity of that statement. I find money for people. This mental breakthrough planted the seeds for the Data Sleuth Process to grow where it is now shared with investigation professionals around the world.

 THE FIRST TEAM

When my childhood dream of becoming an agent with the Federal Bureau of Investigation seemed to vanish, and public accounting was no longer a means to returning to the FBI, I felt lost. Although I did not realize it at the time, the skills I learned and experience I gained in those first few years of my career were the foundations to opening my own forensic accounting and fraud investigation business in 2010.

One of the factors playing into my decision to leave public accounting was the volume of forensic accounting work I was personally responsible for, including data processing, analysis, and review. Management encouraged the forensic accounting work, but there was no focused development plan for a more robust forensic accounting division. When there was a case requiring full-time hours for months, or a rapidly approaching deadline, I would receive approval to borrow various personnel from the tax department but equipping my ever-changing team to overcome the steep learning curve for them to meaningfully contribute, while also serving as the case manager and lead investigator, was nearly impossible. Regardless of how intelligent or willing the borrowed talent was, with a deadline quickly approaching, it was often easier to work the case alone.

When I decided to open Workman Forensics, I told my manager at the time, "I think I will just take some small cases – maybe even just divorce work – and work from my dining room table for a while. Then I will decide what to do with my life." I assumed I would work alone on cases like I had been in public accounting, but this time, I would have more control over the types and sizes of the investigations. After three months of marketing and meeting litigation attorneys, I was hired by an attorney for a case with a hearing date rapidly approaching. I knew that preparing what was needed to provide expert testimony before the deadline was impossible without help. The amount of time needed to process data in a financial investigation usually correlates to the amount of revenue generated by an organization, and this case was no exception. For each month of bank statements, 20 to 30 double-sided pages had to be scanned and subsequently entered into a spreadsheet. Additionally, if an investigation requires the manual data entry of check payees and memo lines from check images, the data processing could take weeks – especially as a solo practitioner. The client was needing a two-week turnaround on the project, and I knew there were not enough hours for me to singlehandedly process, analyze, and prepare to testify without a team.

Fortunately, during that same week, an unprecedented snowstorm created an opportunity for roommates and friends at my house to enter bank statement data into spreadsheets working around my dining room table. Although I had not had success at the previous firm explaining the analysis needed for financial investigations, I was confident that I could explain to my friends the steps required for the repetitive data entry of bank statements. My friends were the key to success in meeting the deadline as they worked with me to find a process for processing the data. When all of the data had been compiled into spreadsheets, I worked to calculate the loss and finished the analysis. While I worked around the clock to prepare for the hearing testimony, my phone kept ringing with inquiries from potential clients.

My solo journey lasted six months when I realized it was not going to stay that way. Not knowing how one decides to create a team, I decided to hire someone who could relieve my workload by processing data. I felt confident that

I could at least use the process my friends and I created to teach an employee until I discovered my next step. The data processing step being performed by a team member was extremely helpful, but I still had more hours of casework than I wanted to work in a week. That is when I began looking to hire another professional who could be responsible for financial investigations like me. No matter how hard I tried, I could not find someone who remained long term because of the incredible expectations and pressures of a forensic accountant or fraud investigator.

 ## THE FORENSIC ACCOUNTANT

Watching Ben Affleck's character in *The Accountant* at first glance seemed absolutely ridiculous as he performed a financial investigation, worked through Benford's analysis on the walls of the conference room, and faced violent opponents until I stopped to consider the current role and expectations of a forensic accountant. Knowing martial arts and being an impeccable marksman, or markswoman, is not listed on most forensic accountants' curriculum vitae; however, the forensic accounting or fraud investigation career, at the testifying expert level, requires a uniquely broad and, at the same time, intricate set of skills.

The experience needed to gain proficiency in the areas essential for a forensic accountant who also testifies as an expert witness requires tremendous focus and effort. Forensic accounting, especially with technological advances, has the power to find missing money and bring clarity to financial disputes. However, the experience factor is the largest barrier to one's entry into the profession. To truly create value for a client, a forensic accountant must be able to clearly articulate findings in a report and through testimony, which opens the expert up to personal and professional scrutiny by opposing parties.

For the next section, I will be using the terms forensic accountant and investigator to refer to an investigation professional who works a financial investigation or litigation dispute engagement from start to finish as a sole practitioner with the expectation that the professional will testify to her findings.

 ## TECHNICAL AND STRATEGIC

A forensic accountant must be technically accurate and use relevant theories and standards in engagements as these are the primary areas in which opposing counsel and the opposing expert will look to exploit to discredit the work by the forensic accountant. A forensic accountant is expected to be extremely proficient in all areas surrounding the financial facts of the case without overstepping her expertise and experience. This could include accounting standards, audit standards, tax preparation, general business, best practices, and so forth.

For example, early in my career I testified to bank statement evidence showing that an executive had paid his personal credit cards using checks funded by the company. As part of my testimony, I stated that the executive had signed the checks. On cross-examination, the defendant's attorney suggested that I should have examined tax returns instead of bank statements. Knowing that bank statements are best evidence and most reliable when compared to tax returns in this situation, I was able to testify appropriately. The defendant's attorney also argued that I could not testify to his client having signed the checks as I was not a handwriting expert. In my response, I was able to then clarify that the name signed on the signature line of the checks was that of the executive.

While being technically proficient, a forensic accountant creates the greatest value when she can partner with legal counsel to understand the attorney's strategy for a case and advise as to what analyses may or may not be performed to support the theory. This part of the work has gotten easier with experience. In the beginning of my career, I did not know how to separate and simplify the details to address the bigger picture objective of the attorney. With experience, however, I now better understand how an expert can be valuable by absorbing the facts and advising counsel of the pertinent investigation findings. Sometimes, the greatest help to an attorney is advising of the evidence that is contrary to his theory for the case and then work to explain evidence from which the attorney can derive another theory. The navigation between technical proficiency and strategy is challenging both during an investigation and in testifying.

THOROUGH AND EFFICIENT

Other areas in which the balance of two responsibilities of a forensic accounting increases with experience are thoroughness and efficiency. Forensic accounting, over the course of my career, has experienced tremendous improvement in efficiency through technological advancements; however, the inherent complexity of the profession remains. The forensic accountant lives in the tension between being both thorough and efficient. The pressure to be both thorough and efficient exists in not only the relationship with the end-client but also with deadlines often out of the forensic accountant's control.

After being in business for six years, I worked a case involving an embezzlement with a total loss exceeding $3 million. At this point, I was working as a solo practitioner and knew from listening to the client's concerns and attorney's strategy the most efficient, yet thorough, way to investigate the case within the client's budget and the attorney's deadlines. I worked the entire case and prepared a report in 40 hours, over approximately two weeks, for which both a civil lawsuit and federal criminal charges were filed. The ability to manage such a thorough and efficient investigation was a result of years of experience and dedication to the profession.

 ## DETAIL-ORIENTED AND EFFECTIVE COMMUNICATION

The stereotypical accountant is personified as someone who is detail oriented, often working tirelessly to ensure that every penny is reconciled. However, the stress of understanding all of the details resulting in effective communication is tricky. The attention to detail that a forensic accountant delivers involves the very details that have been key in assisting clients and their attorneys settle financial disputes. However, navigating through details to find the gem that resolves arguments and then communicating the significance of the findings effectively and clearly is learned through practice.

When testifying as an expert in a criminal defense matter, there were over 20,000 pages of documents provided by the prosecutor. I personally reviewed all of the documents, as I was a sole practitioner, and discovered an email that clearly supported my client's position. My client claimed that he had no knowledge of one of the transactions for which he had been charged. I wanted to include the email in my trial testimony, but when I tried to explain its significance to my client's counsel, she challenged me to simplify my explanation even further as I would be testifying in front of a jury. With her challenge on this one finding, I reworked my entire testimony outline to communicate a story. Communicating in this way contributed to the legal strategy of the attorney, and my client was found not guilty of all but one count.

In this criminal jury trial case, the defense attorney's strength was communicating stories juries could understand. She was gifted at creating demonstrative open and closing arguments that incorporated illustrations the jury understood and remembered. She wanted me as the expert witness to do the same. A few years later, I was asked to investigate and testify for the defense in a bench trial. My task, after performing the investigation, was to explain my findings related to how the husband's assets were separate from that of his wife. His wife had pled guilty to embezzlement, and the business owner was trying to recover from the loss through the husband's separate assets. Remembering the criminal jury trial, I asked our graphic designer to prepare an illustration of the timing and use of funds between spouses. The attorney I was working with did not normally use illustrations in expert testimony, which led to an awkward testimony. Although I believed the illustration helped clarify the use of funds, the resulting awkward testimony did not accomplish the effective communication I had hoped for with the judge.

From these experiences, even when all the details seem important, I have learned to ask more questions of the attorneys and work with them to strategize about the best way to use the most valuable detailed findings.

ACCOUNTING KNOWLEDGE AND LEGAL KNOWLEDGE

Possessing a broad range of accounting knowledge and basic legal process knowledge is vital for a forensic accountant. A testifying expert in the area of forensic accounting will likely encounter engagements that require an understanding of financial accounting and reporting, tax returns, tax strategy, and audit. At the same time, it is helpful to an attorney if the testifying expert has some knowledge of the legal processes to integrate the expert more efficiently into an existing case. Experience, once again, is truly the best teacher in this area. It can be frustrating to professionals because acquiring the knowledge requires someone hiring them to allow opportunities to learn.

The way that I gained knowledge early on was by asking questions of attorneys. Whether an attorney had hired me to help with a case or not, I tried to meet with anyone who would accept an invitation and to ask them as many questions as possible. Before meeting with an attorney about a case or over lunch introduction, I mentally prepared questions to inquire about their preferred methods in approaching cases and about their best and worst expert witness experiences. The feedback was not consistent, as the attorneys seemed to all have varying experiences, but it was helpful in developing a method for me to become a trusted expert and effective expert witness.

One example of the helpful skills I learned through this inquiry method included understanding the difference between testifying in a bench trial versus a jury trial. In a bench trial, attorneys encouraged me to testify with the judge in mind even though the attorneys were asking the questions in front of me. With this in mind, I began sitting in the witness stand to answer questions slightly turned toward the judge to encourage any clarifying questions the judge might want to ask of me. Additionally, if I do not understand a step in the legal process on a particular case, I ask the client's attorney to explain its purpose so that I can know for future reference.

MEETING DEADLINES AND DEVELOPING BUSINESS

A client often realizes that they need a forensic accountant in response to some type of crisis. Although the fraud scheme, hidden assets, or improprieties occurred over a long period of time, a client wants to know what happened, the resulting loss, and his next steps as soon as possible. The emotional response of a client creates urgency, which results in deadlines for the forensic accountant. Also, it is not uncommon that attorneys will wait until the end of the discovery phase in a lawsuit to engage the forensic accountant. To better understand the reason attorneys will wait to hire an expert, I have tried to identify a pattern; however, I have not identified the root cause in cases other than class action lawsuits. In class action lawsuits, a law firm is typically paying all investigation expenses before collecting, and collection on a case is not guaranteed. It appears the delay in hiring an expert is for the attorney to make sure the expert is truly needed before incurring the expense. Whatever the cause, when an attorney delays the hiring of a forensic accountant, some cases are already scheduled for hearings, trials, or other court deadlines that the forensic account-ant cannot change. When this happens, the forensic accountant must perform the analysis, review, and be ready to testify by the imposed deadline.

When working on cases with tight deadlines, maintaining consistent market-ing and business development is challenging. Business development is especially challenging when deadlines require that weeks, or months, will be spent on one project consuming all the available work hours in a week. When facing the choice between working billable hours and business development, the forensic account-ant is most likely to prioritize meeting the deadlines with a work product that solves problems. Although word will spread about the dependability of a reliable expert, through the demonstration of meeting deadlines, the pressure to sustain business development to secure future work exists.

 FORENSIC ACCOUNTANT PROBLEMS

As mentioned in the opening of this chapter, I determined that finding others like myself who were willing to take on the level of responsibility and investment necessary to become a forensic accountant – who also testified as an expert – was not common. When observing the problems I faced as a sole practitioner, or the professional involved in every level of the details, I understood why few would want to take on this role. These problems included:

- **The Scalability Problem.** The inability to enable others to provide meaning-ful assistance throughout the life of a project in an efficient manner where profit is realized for the firm's owner.

- **The Strategy Problem.** The difficulty in balancing a strategy perspective while focused on all the details in an investigation.
- **The Review Problem.** The insecurity to ensuring a high-quality work product able to be used under the greatest scrutiny.
- **The Sustainability Problem.** The stress of managing highly detailed work that may result in personal credibility and character being attacked, which is not sustainable for all professionals in the long run.

THE SCALABILITY PROBLEM

During my third year of business, entrepreneurship was at the height of trendiness, and an aspiring entrepreneur was especially popular if she could create a scalable business idea and obtain venture capital. To own a scalable business would allow the entrepreneur to earn a lot of money on only few hours of work per week, affording the owner the opportunity to take vacations and to live the life she wanted. Not-for-profit initiatives supporting entrepreneurs were promoted throughout the city. It seemed as if every lunch I attended with other business owners would involve constant conversation around how they were going to grow through scaling in the next few years.

One day, I was invited to share about my business at one of the not-for-profit venture capital events. I thought I had made it clear that I was not looking for investors. The leaders understood, but they needed to fill the second presentation slot, so I agreed to do so. Carefully crafting a six-minute presentation communicating the highlights of my forensic accounting business and the value I looked to create for clients, I ended my presentation and opened the floor for questions. A man sitting in the front row asked, "So what about your business is scalable?" I responded, "Nothing." He preceded to lecture me, and anyone else in the audience listening, as to the benefits of a scalable business. I will admit that I was entirely offended.

Because it was none of his business, I did not respond, but the lack of scaling was not for lack of trying. I had tried to reduce my work hours to enjoy life, but the constant demands of the work and the struggle to duplicate my efforts had convinced me at the time that scaling a forensic accounting practice was impossible. Not to mention, that if an entire business's success was based on the available hours of one expert technician, like a forensic accounting expert, who would want to invest in that business?

Frustrated by the man's comments at the presentation, I continued to work as a sole proprietor; however, I constantly wondered if it was possible to create a scalable model for forensic accounting and fraud investigations – where the clients were served well, the work product was as consistent, and the attorneys would trust a team approach. I ignored these nagging thoughts until a new client's case involved more than I could handle alone. Cautiously and slowly, I began hiring again.

As a new business owner, I was naïve in believing that I could hire smart people to work investigations without any formal training and stay within a reasonable budget. There were a lot of factors I had never considered before, but because I had no formal forensic accounting training and could still navigate messy financial disputes, I expected the same of the people I hired. Forgetting the experiences and opportunities I had been given to learn about the intricacies of financial investigations, I unrealistically expected the talented people I hired to untangle a financial investigation without training and stay on a budget.

As much as my team and I wanted to help every person who contacted our firm, the challenge of running an investigation business in the private sector is earning the revenue necessary to stay in business. Engagement after engagement, we burned through the client's budget without a viable solution. Even though we did not promise the client as to what the solution would entail, we had promised that we would find a solution. I felt so obligated to provide a solution, even if the project budget had been exhausted, I would find myself working all night long to finish the investigation after my team had gone home. The worst part mentally for me, and potentially detrimental to the business, was that I was unable to charge for the time.

 THE STRATEGY PROBLEM

Working cases alone, as part of the public accounting firm and as a sole proprietor, presented a problem – no one was actively engaged enough in the details of the case to brainstorm high-level strategy, to foresee potential complications, or to troubleshoot analysis problems. The lack of others with similar or more experience in the detail review of my analysis greatly contributed to the ever-mounting pressure of the job itself. Inherent to investigations is the constant realization that investigation decisions could result in deposition or trial testimony with unyielding scrutiny. Any issued reports, articles, blogs, podcast interviews, or opinions could be used in court as part of a cross-examination attempt to discredit me, demonstrate a lack of objectivity, or accuse me of advocacy. The constant apprehension that I may not have all of the facts or that errors existed in the work product loomed. Nothing reinforced this uncertainty more than a memory from my time at the FBI.

A case agent held a team briefing in the conference room, which doubled as the break room, to discuss an ongoing investigation. On the whiteboard, he drew a variation of what I now know is the Rumsfeld Matrix that is replicated in Figure 1.1.[1] The case agent used this matrix to explain how he viewed the case he was working and requested ideas from the team. Pointing to each quadrant, he advised of the case facts known and unknown. Then pausing briefly and pointing at the third quadrant, he took a deep breath and said, "I do not know what I do not know."

Anxiety about not knowing what I do not know can be paralyzing, but complete disregard for the quadrant is reckless. Early in my career, I was overly sensitive to the third quadrant of the matrix and was concerned that anything I had ever spoken or written could be taken out of context by an opposing counsel and used against me to a client's detriment. This worry caused me to be slow to offer expert opinions unless it could be proven from multiple perspectives and a lot of supporting data. However, a healthy respect of quadrant three can give an expert an edge. When an investigator incorporates humility into her work, and exercises professional skepticism, it yields a result that is founded on facts rather than the answer a paying client, a pressuring boss, or an influential politician desire. I accept that even though the profession may refer to me as an expert, I do not know

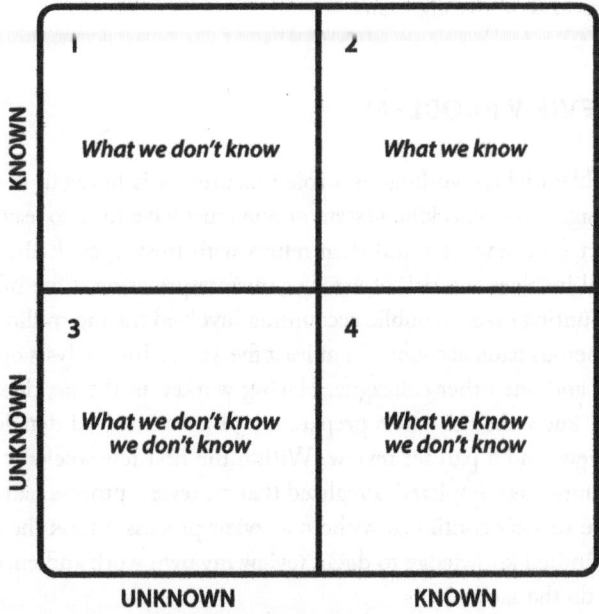

FIGURE 1.1 What we know and don't know matrix.

everything. It is the acceptance and acknowledgment of the third quadrant that keeps me sharp, focused, and continuously improving.

It is also the third quadrant that, I believe, necessitates the involvement of a team in an investigation. I am not suggesting that every expert needs a team composed of employees, and therefore, must run an entire practice or firm. A team can simply be a group of people working together to accomplish a similar goal. For investigations, a team is a group of people – who are not necessarily like-minded – but are committed to uncovering the truth of what happened. The rallying of this group empowers the lead investigator, or testifying expert, to present the evidence in a clear manner. The unity of a team like this contributes to reducing the risk of the unknown in quadrant three. A team of professionals with different backgrounds and perspectives reduces the risk of "not knowing what is unknown" but also helps the lead investigator step away from the details to remind her of the bigger picture.

The year when I was a sole practitioner is one of my least favorite years in this profession. The fear that I overlooked some key piece of evidence or that my analysis results did not reconcile to supporting documents kept me awake at night. Thankfully, relationships with experienced Certified Public Accountants, attorneys, and other investigators provided guidance, mentorship, and perspective in the year I needed them most. Aware that I cannot know everything there is to know, the implementation of a team – formalized as an employee staff or not – is vital to the success of investigations.

 ## THE REVIEW PROBLEM

Another problem when working as a sole practitioner is in detail review. Either one must design a self-checking system or one must have time to leave the analysis and report for a few days and then return with fresh eyes. Either way is not ideal and still involves the risk of error or misinterpretation. One of my earliest forensic accounting cases in public accounting involved tracing millions of dollars through numerous bank accounts for at least five years. The analysts on the project included me and one other colleague. Having worked in the tax department for over a year, I knew the tax return preparation process involved detailed review, a manager review, and a partner review. Within the first few weeks as analysis on various accounts was completed, I realized that no review process had been established. As the analysis continued without a review process, I took the responsibility with my limited knowledge to detail review my own work and encouraged my colleague to do the same.

Within a few months, the results of the analysis were presented in trial. There were several testifying experts, but I was not one on this case. However, through some maneuvering of the opposing counsel, the other side was able to call my colleague and me to the stand. Although we were called as the other side's witnesses, opposing counsel requested that we be treated as hostile witnesses. A hostile witness is one who is adverse to the side who called him to testify. If the judge determines that the witness is hostile, the attorney may ask leading questions as if the witness was under cross-examination.[2] The attorneys in this case were granted this request, and we were ordered to answer questions that likely would not have been allowed under normal circumstances. I was so new to the field; this was my first time to testify with any form of cross-examination. All of my previous testifying experience was in front of a federal grand jury. With every question asked, I desperately hoped they would not uncover a mistake. After testifying for over two days, I breathed a long sigh of relief. Unfortunately, when my colleague took the stand to testify to her work, a large error was revealed. The judge ordered a recess, and my colleague and I worked long into the night to correct the analysis, hopeful that the corrected analysis would be admitted as the attorney for our client questioned my colleague the next morning. Thankfully, the correction was received, and ultimately, our side won the case. Sadly, my extremely talented colleague vowed to never again work on forensic accounting engagements.

Many professionals believe the niche to be exciting and intriguing – maybe because of influence from mystery novels and FBI television shows – but in the end, it is a profession of highly detailed work for which most clients want the professional to testify. If the professional testifies, the highly detailed work product is put under a microscope by the opposing counsel and at least one other highly trained expert. This expert's assignment is to find weaknesses, especially in the areas that the professional did not know that they did not know. The enormous pressure and inspection demand that all work be prepared as if they are going to trial. At a bare minimum, a rigorous review process must be established. Without a proper review process, serious professional risks arise including inaccurate work being discovered in a deposition or trial.

 ## THE SUSTAINABILITY PROBLEM

The enormous pressure, scrutiny, and risk in this field takes its toll on a professional. I experienced severe burnout in the fourth year and eighth year of business. As a result, any criticism, whether from clients, employees, or opposing counsel when testifying, felt too personal. I could no longer compartmentalize negativity as just part of the job. Dealing with clients who would refuse to pay our fees because they did not like the results of the investigation, or because they simply did not want to, began to make me question this profession entirely. Feelings of resentment grew as I wrote paychecks to employees whose work I stayed up all night adjusting to incorporate into a report due the next day. Not to mention the cash flow nightmare I faced in this project-based industry with no recurring clients like in public accounting with tax and audit engagements. When the stress reached an all-time high and began to negatively affect my health and some of my closest relationships, I knew I could not continue in this way. I either had to find a solution or find another career.

 ## DATA SLEUTH SOLUTIONS

The creation and implementation of the Data Sleuth Process over the last five years has provided our team with solutions to reduce burnout, risks, and problems that I faced as the sole professional responsible for investigations. The experiment to create what is now the Data Sleuth Process began with the question, "If I can build a team of people who have experience and proficiency in at least some of the areas required in a financial investigation, can we then make forensic accounting accessible to more professionals and in turn to more clients?" The current status of the Data Sleuth Process development has solved the scalability problem, the strategy problem, the review problem, and the sustainability problem inherent in many forensic accounting practices.

 ## THE SCALABILITY SOLUTION

Beginning to hire a team again brought many challenges, but with the dream of a healthy life, I implemented two practices into my business: I involved employees in creating solutions, and I met frequently with a business coach. In the beginning, incorporation of data analysis software to analyze data sources brought some relief by assigning individual analyses. However, when it was time for me to connect the dots and final review to provide a final report, things seemed to fall apart. In these final steps of the investigation, I would discover that some of the individual analyses did not answer the actual questions of the client. It seemed that additional work was always needed to provide a valuable work product, but we would have only a couple of days remaining before the deadline. The primary cause of this consistent issue was identified as a process problem; we did not have a way for the team to work together to connect the client concerns to the analyses assigned. Because team members did not know why they were performing an analysis, they could not advise as to whether the analysis addressed the client's questions. It was not until I would try to connect the analysis to the client's concerns at the end of the project that the inapplicability of the analysis was discovered.

The members of my team were sharp and were willing to contribute more to the investigation, but I was unable to train them in these important investigation steps. I was frustrated because I was making decisions that I thought were obvious, but my team advised that the decisions seemed logical to me because I had the benefit of experience they did not. We needed to find a way to translate the experience-based process in my head into a process the team could follow.

Before the breakthrough with my business coach, I believed that the number of ways people committed fraud or hid money was infinite. When I was able to understand that there were only a finite number of ways, tackling the process and experience issues to create a process did not seem insurmountable. For the first time in years, I had hope. If there truly were only a finite number of ways people steal money, then I could identify them and advise the team about where to look, making adjustments along the way to allow for the unpredictable parts of investigations. The process of working investigations as a team infinitely improved with this simple breakthrough. We were able to identify that:

- The most common types of investigations we enjoyed working involved embezzlement (corporate fraud), partnership disputes, estate/trusts, and divorce.
- The areas in which most people stole or hid money in these preferred investigations involved analyzing the ways in which money came into an organization, marital estate, or trust and the ways in which money left the same.
- The most common types of data used in the preferred investigations involved bank statements, credit card statements, payroll reports, and accounting records.

We started to build an investigative process focused on our preferred types of investigations that supported our collective strengths. By identifying all of the similarities within the investigations we preferred, we created a standard case planning process that could be replicated. The case planning process allowed communication of the client's concerns so that when analyses were complete, the responsible team member could ask herself, "Does this analysis provide the answer to this client's concern?" If the answer was no, the team member could then get the team together to formulate a new approach. We also recognized that the inputs and data sources might change from case to case, but the strategic planning would allow for adjustments to be made to customize the analysis.

The involvement of the team in the creation and improvement of the process over the years has created incredible buy-in that has not only resulted in a process that serves clients better than when I worked alone, but it has also solved the training problem. When the team is focused in making their areas of contribution to the investigation better, they have a better understanding of the purpose and intention for the decisions being made, which empowers them to make higher-level decisions along the way. The forensic accountant's scalability problem now has a viable solution allowing the incorporation of new team members into a structured process resulting in a consistent, reliable work product.

THE STRATEGY SOLUTION

I learned early on the importance of understanding clients' concerns and an attorney's needs in order to propose strategies to accomplish both. However, the communication of the concerns, expectations, and strategy to my team was difficult, and I often wanted to slip back into the mindset that doing the work on my own was simpler. Knowing this was not going to hold true in the long run, I listened to podcasts and read books about communicating with and growing a team. We incorporated all kinds of personality tests and work style trainings into our team development, but the greatest change came when I decided to no longer personally associate with the analyst role.

We were working on a publicized and controversial investigation for over a year. With drama building as the case lagged on, we hurried to finalize our findings, present the report, and close the matter. During that year, multiple team members had worked on the case, but most of the analysis tasks had been assigned to me at the end. Although I tried to assign pieces to various team members, I was too busy with other parts of the investigation to clearly communicate the purpose of the specific tasks within each analysis. The stress of poor communication on my part and the rapidly approaching deadline resulted in frustration felt by the analysts and me. The analysts worked diligently to find solutions, but they did not know where to begin. Because I was in the middle of the analysis details, managing the client calls, and trying to find a way to piece together a very disjointed case, I was constantly worrying about public backlash if we messed up. With all of this happening at the same time, I was unable to lead from a strategic point of view. Hoping adrenaline would keep me moving, we met the deadline. I presented the findings amid a controversial meeting. Driving from the meeting, I said out loud to myself, "I am no longer an analyst. I have a team, and I need to be the strategist."

I had realized that the weakest area in our developing, yet lacking, process was in planning, but after I removed myself from the analyst role, I had an idea. The next week, a new client hired us for a case, and I gathered the team together for our new case planning process. Before the planning session, I created a list of the client's concerns and my proposed strategies. Then I translated those strategies into what we now call investigation priorities, explained further in Chapter 6. I began the meeting by explaining the case story gathered from my initial client meeting. Then, taking the list of investigation priorities, such as, "Quantify overpayments of payroll to subject," I gave each team member an opportunity to ask questions about the case and to describe an analysis they thought would be appropriate. For each analysis, types of data that would be required to perform the analysis and the corresponding data processing tasks were identified. We repeated this process for every investigation priority.

The most challenging part of hosting a case planning meeting like this was reminding myself to be the facilitator and remain quiet until the end. When all of the investigation priorities had been addressed, I then provided strategic edits to the plan focusing on superfluous or duplicative analyses and identifying multiple uses for the data. At the completion of the edits, each team member advised as to which analyses or data processing task they would most like to complete. The edited case plan was presented to the client for approval, and the tasks were assigned to each team member with a process for subsequent review.

By documenting a case plan and creating work paper templates and processes to reinforce the case plan, we incorporated the requirement that an analyst communicate their findings and the significance of the findings in every analysis work paper. After the analysis was reviewed, the findings were compiled into a findings summary along with any attachments (i.e. exhibits consisting of tables, graphs, or charts further explained in Chapter 11). At this point, we could connect a client's concerns and investigation priorities to all data processing and analysis and the resulting findings. The strategy and problem-solving value that I once brought to the table as an individual expert cannot compare to the implementation of the strategy that we now provide to clients as a team. The communication of the plan for the case allowed me to do only the parts necessary and to capitalize on the individual strengths of team members resulting in a high-quality, consistent work product.

THE REVIEW SOLUTION

The review step, whether detail or final, promotes accuracy; incorporates multiple perspectives; reduces the risk of egregious, simple errors; and upholds consistency in the final work product. The Data Sleuth review solution is built into the process itself. The review step occurs after data processing and before analysis, at the completion of each analysis, after all findings have been compiled, and lastly before the final report is issued. With the team understanding the purpose of an investigation from the case planning meeting, the review step becomes simple. Whoever performs the analysis does not review the same work, and the reviewer can provide insight because she knows the client concerns and the underlying analysis purpose.

The most difficult to scale, or assign to those with less experience, in an investigation are the overall case strategy and testifying pieces. These two areas necessitate the involvement of an experienced professional. As that professional on my current team, without the Data Sleuth Process and review step, I would be tempted rework every analysis to ensure its accuracy, validity, and reliability. To do so is highly inefficient. With the Data Sleuth Process and the imbedded review steps contributing to the quality control of the work product, I can rely on my team and trust the process to find the big oversights. Errors are still a risk, as the process is composed of talented people, but people, nonetheless. However, trusting the input of a team of people is still more reliable than working the entire investigation alone. At this point, I am not sure I could ever go back to working solo because the work we produce now, the money we find for clients, and the clarity we add to situations are truly better than I could have ever created on my own.

 ## THE SUSTAINABILITY SOLUTION

Fortunately, closing shop in those most challenging years was not an option because we had clients to serve and investigations to work. These struggles forced me to plow ahead continuing to believe that a solution existed for my investigation business struggles that also promoted the vision of making forensic accounting accessible to more people. The creative development of the Data Sleuth Process gave me energy to move on in the most difficult years. When I would feel as if creating the process would never work, my team's constant focus on continuous improvement would give me the energy to continue. Workman Forensics does not need a team of people where everyone thinks they know everything. We just need a team of people who bring their unique expertise to serve clients well and to trust the process to do what we cannot do on our own. And this is why, I believe, the Data Sleuth Process creates the sustainability solution for the forensic accounting and fraud investigation professionals.

 NOTES

1. Donald H. Rumsfeld, *Department of Defense News Briefing* (February 12, 2002).
2. Gerald Hill and Kathleen Hill, "Hostile Witness," Publisher Fine Communications, accessed October 24, 2021, https://dictionary.law.com/Default.aspx?selected=884.

CHAPTER TWO

The Data Sleuth Process

T HE USE OF THE Data Sleuth Process for the Workman Forensics team has been focused primarily on engagements involving corporate fraud, embezzlement, partnership disputes, bank fraud, divorce, estate and trust disputes, economic damages, and civil or criminal defense.

Before diving into the specifics of the process itself, it is important for a forensic accountant or investigator to understand the mindset of the Data Sleuth when beginning an engagement including the simultaneous management of client expectations and professional standards of objectivity and conflicts of interest.

The Data Sleuth Process, which created solutions for the struggles and problems described in the previous chapter, is outlined within this chapter.

 ENGAGEMENT TYPES

Serving clients as a consultant or expert witness in the forensic accounting and fraud investigation professions provides opportunities to solve problems and bring clarity to complex financial matters and disputes. We define an end-client as the organization or business that is responsible for paying the fees in the matter. As mentioned in the previous chapter, when we first began creating the Data Sleuth Process, the team identified the types of investigations we preferred working. By identifying the engagement types, we were able to begin creating a structured investigation process. The engagements we identified as being preferred cases are those listed next. There are other types of litigation support or consulting engagements for which forensic accountants and investigators are hired; however, throughout this book, the engagement types and end-clients will be limited to the ones listed here.

Engagements in which the end-clients are typically organizations include:

- Corporate fraud or embezzlement
- Bank or loan fraud
- Partnership or shareholder disputes

Engagements in which the end-clients are typically individuals include:

- Divorce
- Estate and trust disputes
- Civil or criminal defense

Engagements in which the end-clients are attorneys typically include economic damages for class-action lawsuits where a civil fraud claim is being made. An attorney may also be the end-client when the attorney has a contingency fee arrangement with a client as part of a civil lawsuit.

The Case of the Reimbursing Controller

Kevin not only ran a large company, but he was also in the midst of managing a lot of life-changing family situations. Over coffee one morning, a friend and fellow entrepreneur in a similar industry told Kevin of his recent discovery that his controller had stolen over $2 million. Kevin's friend was discovering that it would be nearly impossible to collect the stolen funds, as she had gambled the money away and did not have resources to repay the sum. This conversation left Kevin concerned about his own business, especially considering the recent family distractions, so he called an investigator about his fears. He told the investigator that he trusted his controller, but just needed to be sure she was not stealing money. He could certainly do without that additional stress. In that first phone call, he also emphasized that because he doubted she was actually stealing, he did not want to spend a lot of money.

After learning more about the company operations, controls, and the controller's access, the initial risk examination indicated the company had three primary areas of fraud risk:

- Diverted customer payments
- Unauthorized expenditures from bank accounts and/or credit card accounts by the controller
- Unauthorized expense reimbursements from a project manager

Kevin disagreed with fraud risks one and three and instructed the investigator to limit the scope of the investigation to fraud risk number two. The investigator prepared a case plan emphasizing an exploratory phase to include one-year review of bank accounts, credit cards, and supporting accounting software exports. The investigator explained that if the controller had been stealing funds through expenditures, it was likely that the loss was the greatest in the most recent year. This approach would help keep limit the investigation costs while performing the exploratory phase. If suspicious transactions were identified, the relevant period could always be expanded.

With the client's approval of the case plan, the Data Sleuth engagement began, starting with the bank statements and credit card statements. The transactions for each bank and credit card account were summarized by payee and provided to the client for an initial review. From the bank transactions, Kevin identified several payees he did not recognize and requested they be researched further. All but four payees originally marked for additional research were found to be either normal business or project-specific expenses that benefited the business. Expenditures paid to four payees for which the benefit could not be determined totaled $3,000.

When the one-year analysis results identified only $3,000 of transactions, Kevin did not believe the results of the exploratory phase investigation were accurate. Gathering the bank and credit card statements, data processing, and data analysis on this project occurred over two weeks, and over this time, where Kevin had once trusted the controller, he now believed she was stealing tens of thousands of dollars per year, but at this point, this belief was supported by nothing except fear. Because the analysis results were considerably less than he believed, he insisted the investigator do more. The investigator advised that the team could perform the same analysis for the previous year or that she could interview the controller about the four payees totaling $3,000.

Kevin selected the latter as he did not want to pay the fees associated with the additional year of analysis. The investigator and Kevin agreed that the interview would be informal, nonadmission seeking, and as nonconfrontational as possible. Although Kevin was convinced tens of thousands of dollars were missing, he claimed he still wanted to trust the controller and did not want her to leave for thinking otherwise.

Kevin and the investigator met with the controller in her office. Kevin explained that he had been concerned after he learned about the theft from his friend's company and had requested the investigator review his company records. The controller was not happy about this inquiry but agreed to cooperate. The investigator explained the source of the findings and that she wanted to ask questions regarding a few transactions. As the investigator worked her way down the list of transactions, the controller would look at Kevin and say before answering each question, "I asked you if I could charge this transaction to the credit card and reimburse the company later out of payroll, and you said I could." Her statement would remind Kevin about a previous conversation, he would respond with, "Oh that's right. I did say that." At the conclusion of the transaction questions, the controller provided a spreadsheet of the transactions and the amounts deducted from her paycheck to repay the company along with the remaining balance.

Despite the exploratory phase results and the interview outcome, Kevin was still convinced the controller was stealing tens of thousands of dollars and asked the investigator what remaining analysis could be performed. The investigator referenced the other two fraud risk areas. She explained that the majority of the evidence to date indicated that another employee, the project manager, had a greater risk and opportunity to steal funds than the controller. Kevin decided he was not going to spend more money on the investigation and requested the findings to be written in a report and the case to be closed. It is still unknown what analyses were performed or evidence discovered that resulted in this outcome.

Several months later, the investigator was advised that a friend of Kevin's had quantified hundreds of thousands of dollars the controller had stolen and that the controller had been fired.

Data-Driven Results

Perhaps one of literature's most well-known sleuths, Sherlock Holmes, said it best: "It is a capital mistake to theorize before one has data. Insensibly one begins to twist facts to suit theories, instead of theories to suit facts."[1]

It is not uncommon that a client provides an investigator with his understanding and interpretation of the events that occurred in a dispute. No matter how diligent the client is at collecting information about the dispute or issue at hand, he still retains some sort of bias, and in "The Case of the Reimbursing Controller," friends and family seemed to encourage and amplify Kevin's theories with emotional responses during the investigation instead of evidence.

Although empathy is invaluable in client relationships, maintaining objectivity and allowing facts to uncover the story – rather than finding facts to fit a client's theory – is imperative as it ultimately affects the lives of others and affects the investigator's future reputation.

SIMULTANEOUSLY MANAGING CLIENT EXPECTATIONS AND OBJECTIVITY

The balance between following data and developing an expert opinion within the confines of a client's expectations and timeline is challenging for an investigator. Common tensions faced in client engagements include the following:

- **Client beliefs versus evidentiary support.** When the client believes one series of events happened causing their harm, but the evidence suggests otherwise, clients may believe the investigator is not providing the best customer service or is somehow an adversary to their claims and causes. This not only creates a strain in the once-trusting relationship between the client and investigator but can also cause a client to withhold payment or promote negative feedback about the investigator.

  Practice Management Recommendation: Provide a case plan and contract or engagement letter for a client to review and sign listing the agreed-upon procedures and payment terms for the investigation. Insist that both be completed prior to providing any services.

- **Complete analysis versus client budget.** Sometimes when a client is anxious about a once-trusted employee stealing money from his company, he wants the full-service investigation – until the cost estimate is discussed. At this point, risk based priorities can be presented to create a manageable scope, but the client may choose a priority based on how he feels about an employee and decide to use the case budget on a lower-risk concern. This is difficult for the investigator because had the client opted to spend the budget on the higher risk priority, the results may have been more helpful in addressing the client's concerns.

  Practice Management Recommendation: Although an analysis may be focused on a lower risk priority, if any evidence is obtained concerning a higher risk priority, disclose the information to the client.

- **Client Misconceptions about an Expert.** Although much in the forensic accounting and fraud investigation profession relies on the consultant being an expert, the term "expert" in this context does not denote the ability to know the truth of what happened without compiling and analyzing evidence. When a client begins to tell their story, general ideas and high-level investigation paths may begin to form in the investigator's mind, but the investigator does not know exactly what has happened until she follows the data through the investigative process. Clients often believe an expert can simply "look at the documents" they have and predict the outcome of an investigation. This is antithetical to the foundational concept of an investigation. Similar to the scientific method, a hypothesis may be formed at the beginning, but the scientist does not know if the hypothesis is valid until it is tested. The same is true in an investigation. The investigator is an expert at investigation – not in predicting the future or extrapolating a series of historical events from a couple of documents.

Practice Management Recommendation: Communicate as frequently as possible with the client, and through as many mediums as possible, from the beginning through the end of an engagement about realistic expectations and capabilities.

The Case of the Mistaken Divorcee

Cindy's husband had filed for divorce. They had been business partners for over 14 years and married for 25. After enjoying a comfortable financial living for most of the marriage, it was now time to divide the assets and go their separate ways. Cindy believed her husband was spending more money than she was from the joint accounts as the divorce proceedings lagged on, and she wanted a forensic accountant to determine which spouse owed the other money out of the property settlement. Cindy appeared to know exactly how funds in the business and personal accounts worked and sold her story well.

Obtaining information from the client was slow going at first; then, just two weeks before a hearing concerning property settlement disputes, a flurry of financial data appeared in the forensic accountant's email inbox. The team got to work and quickly began to notice that not only were the data incomplete, they also did not appear to support Cindy's story. In fact, it appeared from the initial analyses that Cindy would need to write a large check to her ex-husband.

Upon seeing this result, the forensic accountant called the attorney immediately to discuss the findings, which were very much the opposite of what he expected. The attorney was in total shock and disbelief and questioned the results. The forensic accountant followed up with a call to client to give her notice prior to the hearing. After learning what the accountant had found, both the attorney and client decided to spin the results in the client's favor by gathering their own evidence and performing their own analysis. The forensic accountant's analysis and report were never presented in court, or to opposing counsel, or used to assist the client in any way.

■ **Attorney objectives versus expert opinion.** Attorneys are often a great source of referrals for consulting investigators and experts – for some consultants, this is his or her primary revenue source. It is not uncommon that an attorney has a desired objective for an expert analysis in mind that will complement his theory for the case. Stress on this relationship is created when the attorney's desired outcome is not the opinion of the expert based on relevant facts and the expert's experience.

Practice Management Recommendation: Document as many conversations as possible with the attorney. Provide the attorney with a copy of the case plan approved by the client. Be specific in reports as to the documents reviewed and related findings. If addendum reports are written subsequent to the issuance of a final report, reference the previous report so that the addendum cannot stand alone.

Don't Be a Hired Gun

Do not start an investigation with a predetermined conclusion in mind. Let the evidence and data drive the results – not the client's opinion, pressure from the attorney, or any other external factors. Excellent, data-driven analysis and opinions always drive referrals and additional engagements. Simply obliging what the client or the attorney wants and fulfilling the expert stereotype of being a "hired gun" will eventually harm an investigator's reputation – even if this strategy appears successful in the short run. If an investigator wants to work the largest, most interesting cases, she should not settle for providing results that are not based on data and best evidence. The large cases are entrusted to investigators who have followed through with smaller data-driven investigations time and again. The forensic accounting and fraud investigation profession is currently not that large, and reputations spread like wildfire. If the investigator cannot handle making objective decisions on the little cases, it is likely to affect being selected for larger cases.

There Is a Middle Ground

Although an expert should not perform tasks and calculations solely to appease the client in contradiction of supporting data, there may be opportunities for a compromise, as providing valuable client service is a significant element of each engagement. For example, whereas one calculation may be the expert's opinion of a loss, an additional calculation can be performed at the instruction of an attorney. The expert may need to testify to both calculations at a hearing or trial, but only one is her opinion. In situations like this, clarity in communication of even the most subtle differences is key to delineating between the opinion and other calculations.

The Case of the Sentencing Hearing

A forensic accountant had been hired to evaluate the loss presented by the federal government in a fraud matter on behalf of the defendant. The defendant was acquitted of all charges except one, for which a sentencing hearing was scheduled. Tedious tracing of the funds related to the one charge was requested, and when finished, the forensic accountant identified that the loss was much less than expected. At this point, the attorney asked the forensic accountant to opine on sentencing guidelines to make the dollar amount charged to his client smaller – and a lesser sentencing for the client. The forensic accountant refused to opine on the sentencing guidelines, as it was outside of her experience; however, she did agree to perform an additional calculation under the attorney's interpretation of the guidelines.

At the hearing, after having presented the traced loss amount, she also testified to the additional calculation. She was careful to testify only as to the calculation performed at the attorney's request and not the application of the sentencing guidelines.

 ## PROFESSIONAL STANDARDS

Maintaining objectivity in the presence of pressure from clients or their counsel is not just a matter of professional reputation and future business development. There is also the fact that professional certifying and licensing organizations provide standards for the professionals they support including accountants, auditors, and fraud investigators. In one form or another, these organizations include within their professional codes a standard of objectivity.

Professional Standards of Objectivity

The Association of Certified Fraud Examiners states in the CFE Code of Professional Standards in Section III.A.3, "Certified Fraud Examiners shall maintain objectivity in discharging their professional responsibilities within the scope of the fraud examination."[2]

The American Institute of Certified Public Accountants (AICPA) states in their Professional Responsibilities under Objectivity:

> [I]n the performance of any professional service, a member must maintain objectivity and integrity, shall be free of conflicts of interest, and shall not knowingly misrepresent facts. A conflict of interest may occur if a member performs a professional service for a client and the member or his or her firm has a relationship with another person, entity,

product or service that could, in the member's professional judgment, be viewed by the client or other appropriate parties as impairing the member's objectivity.[3]

By approaching investigations with objectivity, a forensic accountant or investigator can follow data-driven decisions as they have not become entwined or part of the story. Another standard to observe when working client engagements is to ensure that there are no conflicting interests in the professional's involvement.[4]

Conflicts of Interest

As stated in the AICPA professional standards, in this line of work, a professional must ensure that a conflict of interest with regard to the case does not exist. As part of a prudent client onboarding process, an investigator should have a step in which anyone working on the engagement provides feedback as to any conflicts of interest pertaining to any of the parties in the case or their counsel. This step should also occur prior to learning about the nature of the case and any working theories or strategies.

It is not uncommon for an attorney to jump into the details of the case in requesting assistance from an investigator prior to communicating with the parties involved to the investigator. An awkward conversation results especially when the investigator must inform the attorney, without breaking client confidentiality, that she has already been hired to help the other side. In order to honor client confidentiality, requesting the names of the parties and their counsel early in the conversation is best. Then, if the investigator is aware of a conflict, identify it immediately by simply stating, "I'm sorry, but I have a conflict in this matter." This type of response provides the attorney with what they need to know but does not reveal the specific conflict – such as working with the parties opposing this attorney's client.

Another tricky situation may arise when an investigator reviews the parties and counsel and no conflict is identified; however, later in the case, the investigator discovers that a new attorney has entered an appearance and at the same time is representing the investigator in a matter. When this occurs, it is helpful to communicate it to the end-client immediately. The end-client may decide that they do not trust the relationship and must end the engagement, but getting in front of issues like this is vital for an investigator's relationship with a client who has likely already been lied to, resulting in the case at hand.

Objectivity and Investigating Facts

Although many of the professional standards tend to indicate that objectivity revolves around conflicts of interest, in fraud investigations and forensic accounting engagements, a professional's view of the situation can erode from that of an objective third party to one wrapped up in the client's story. The nature of the work involves working with clients whose trust in others has been broken. They are often fragile, emotional, and working through grief over once-trusting relationships ending abruptly – usually with the client suddenly becoming aware of a situation they never dreamed they would experience. If the investigator is empathetic, it is easy to end up in the story with the client. When this happens, objectivity becomes cloudy, and what the investigator once saw as evidence, or lack of evidence, becomes grasping at straws and formulating theories to help the client instead of uncovering the facts.

It is essential to remember that an investigator, expert, or other professional in these situations is not an advocate. The attorney is the client's advocate. The way an investigator best helps the client is to remain outside of the story. While maintaining empathy, this distance allows the investigator to provide the attorney and client with a simple, clear picture of what actually happened. Whether the client and attorney like the results of the investigation is irrelevant; strategies can be developed from the actual facts and result in much more positive outcomes than by "twist[ing] facts to suit theories."[5]

 ## THE DATA SLEUTH PROCESS

A tool to help investigators maintain objectivity throughout a case is the use of an investigative process. There is no one-size-fits-all investigative process that will apply to all situations, but for the forensic accounting engagements and fraud investigations defined at the beginning of this chapter, Workman Forensics has developed the following Data Sleuth Process that serves as a guide in all such engagements.

The Data Sleuth Process was developed out of necessity as the workload and hiring of staff to perform the work demanded it. The first step in developing the process was to observe which actions, information requests, and analyses were performed in every case, no matter the client's unique situation or story. When these steps were separated out and organized in a linear fashion, a picture of the investigative process began to form. The next step was to identify the data and information inputs that were consistent across the repetitive steps in each case. For example, in the majority of cases worked, bank and credit card statements are requested. These data then undergo a standard analytical workflow to identify outliers and other data findings or indicators pertinent to the case.

As the process was applied to each case, staff could then be assigned based on their personal strengths, interests, and talents. This distribution of work had the added benefit of increased objectivity by creating space between the client's emotional story and the actual data analysis. The client intake part of the process is now handled by an experienced, credentialed forensic accountant case manager while the analysis portion is performed by an experienced, credentialed data analyst. The case manager reviews the analysis to ensure that nuances and concerns of the client are addressed in the analysis, but in this way, the data analyst can view the data from a neutral third-party perspective.

The details of the Data Sleuth Process are continuously refined and improved and will be explained in greater detail throughout the remaining chapters of this book. The overall process has proven successful in numerous forensic accounting engagements and financial investigations performed by Workman Forensics and continues to guide the way we serve clients and work cases. The Data Sleuth Process is illustrated in Figure 2.1.

The Data Sleuth Process illustrated in the figure was developed to assist new investigators and data analysts in applying a careful, methodical approach to investigations. Within an investigation, it is not uncommon that an investigator has one chance to obtain the best evidence, and discretion is often key. However, if a new investigator has never performed an investigation, he will not know which step might trigger an unexpected response and cause evidence to disappear or witnesses to refuse to cooperate.

Some investigators may want to perform background research and then interview the subject to see what they can learn. However, in my experience, if this step is taken too early, the subject is often not helpful because there is no baseline research or data findings indicating to the investigator whether the subject is being truthful or not. Then, when the same investigator returns after data analysis to discuss the findings with the subject, the subject has often retained counsel and is no longer willing to cooperate at all.

In a financial fraud investigation, it may be that the only person who knows what happened is the subject. To jump ahead of the process and interview too early is a critical mistake, and often leads to the best piece of evidence – learning about the scheme from the subject himself – being forfeited, resulting in more fees charged to the end-client and a longer investigation.

The Data Sleuth Process, as illustrated in Figure 2.1, works as a funnel that starts with third-party information gathering and moves toward the subject's connections/influence and ends, if possible, with a subject interview. Figure 2.2 provides an illustration of the process as a funnel for information and data within engagements.

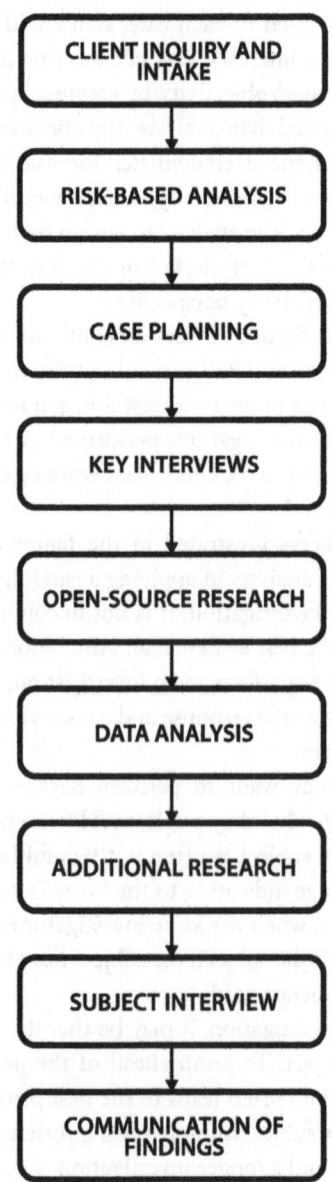

FIGURE 2.1 Illustration of the Data Sleuth Process used by Workman Forensics.

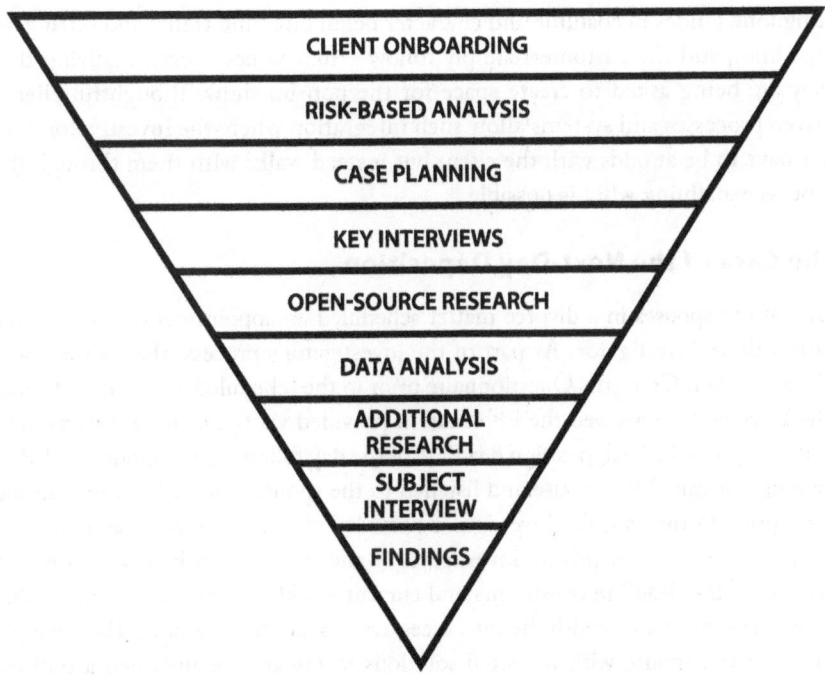

FIGURE 2.2 Funnel representation of information in an engagement.

Client Onboarding

The way in which a client project starts will often dictate the way it ends. Get the client on board with the process from the very first encounter – including the initial inquiry call. This could begin with a simple request that the client schedules a meeting to discuss their case, and even prior to the call, completes a form providing details about their investigation priorities, access to information, legal representation, and any court case references. This allows the investigator taking the initial client call to be prepared to address questions from the potential client; if necessary, the investigator can also be prepared to listen and then politely advise the client as to why they are not the best fit for the concern.

An overworked, exhausted investigator will make mistakes whereas an investigator who uses a process to establish standards can allow the process to set the boundaries without having to "get tough" with clients. A difficult balance in this profession is serving vulnerable clients well while also maintaining professionalism, distance, and time boundaries. Although it may seem like a surprising analogy, Disney World is a great example of how establishing processes, standards, and boundaries can be seamlessly integrated into the overall customer experience. When a pop-up show is about to begin on the streets of the Magic

Kingdom, guides in costume and character begin directing traffic and setting up tape lines, and the customers simply follow – maybe never even realizing that they are being asked to create space for the pop-up show. Thoughtful client-driven processes and systems allow such integration where the investigator does not have to be at odds with the client but instead walks with them through the process explaining what is possible.

The Case of the Next-Day Deposition

One of the spouses in a divorce matter scheduled an appointment to discuss his case with an investigator. As part of the investigator's process, the spouse completed a Client Concerns Questionnaire prior to the scheduled appointment time. The investigator reviewed the information provided via the form and discovered that the spouse had a deposition deadline of the day following the inquiry call. The investigator called the spouse and listened to the spouse's story. Having read the form prior to the call, the investigator provided alternative recommendations – such as hiring a local private investigator – and was able to kindly advise that because of the deadline constraints and current workload, she would not be able to perform the analysis with the care necessary to meet the deadline. These simple steps left the spouse with potential solutions to research, maintained a positive impression of the investigator, and established the boundaries and expectations should the spouse decide he needed her help in the future.

Having a process for client onboarding not only helps filter out the clients who are not a good fit for an investigator, but it also provides the client with an opportunity to slow down and think about what they are wanting out of the engagement. It provides a moment for the client to identify the specific items of concern instead of the whole problem feeling insurmountable and impossible. Encouraging the client to follow this process establishes a starting point for the next step – risk-based analysis and case planning.

Risk-Based Analysis

To connect the client's concerns to the case plan, or scope of the investigation, an investigator needs to perform a risk-based analysis of the client's situation. For fraud investigations in an organization, the investigator should identify the areas within the organization most vulnerable to fraud. For a forensic accounting engagement such as identifying hidden assets for an individual in divorce, a risk analysis should be performed to identify key areas in which the spouse could have hidden assets or understated income. It is the risk-based analysis that allows the investigator to convert the client's concerns into action items and prioritize the action items within the case plan. Risk-based analysis in which the end-client is an organization or individual is explained in greater detail in Chapter 7.

Case Planning

Using the client's concerns from the client onboarding step and the results of the risk-based analysis, the investigative team can then create a plan to address each concern. This process is explained in greater detail in Chapter 6. Within the case plan, each of the client's concerns are translated into an investigation priority to be matched with a corresponding analysis. The analysis identifies the data needed to address the client's concerns.

The case planning step provides a natural checkpoint for the client and investigator to ensure that good communication is happening and that they are both on the same page. It is more efficient for both parties to establish an understanding of the concerns up front. Doing so gives the investigator an opportunity to specify the concerns she can and cannot address. The client in turn learns what is required and can identify if he has enough access to data or information to move forward. When the client sees their concerns, related analyses, and required data in the form of a written plan, they can more accurately understand the estimated fees; this also provides an opportunity for the client to prioritize the areas of concern based on their budget.

Key Interviews

The following approach to interviews is specifically geared toward investigators in private industry. Investigators in law enforcement may have procedures that are required to interview subjects.

To better understand the information available for the analysis planned, an investigator should consider performing interviews of key individuals with knowledge of the issue being investigated. Through discussion with the client, the investigator should identify the parties involved and categorize them as potential witnesses, associates of the subject, and subject(s). Interviews should begin with the parties farthest removed from the subject and subject associates to limit the chances of the subject learning of the investigation prematurely. Throughout the investigation, interviews (formal or informal) will then begin to converge in an ultimate interview of associates of the subject and the subject(s) as illustrated in Figure 2.3.

The key interviews at this stage should be designed to help the investigator learn about the processes and procedures used within a business, systems used, available data, internal controls, business entity setup, and the like. These interviews should not be confrontational in nature and should be for information gathering only.

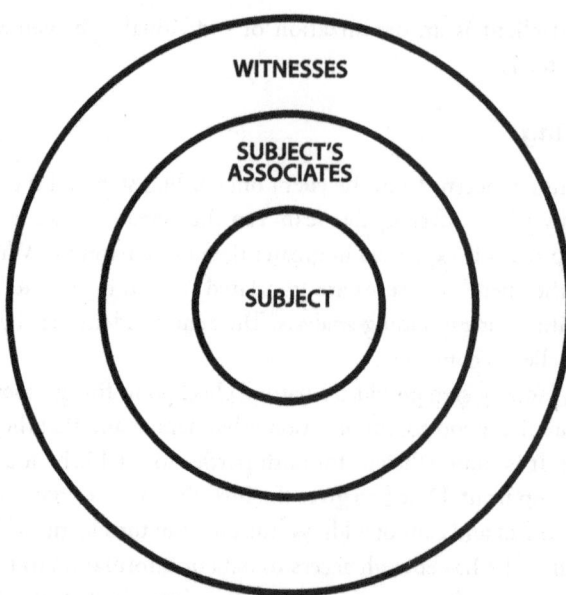

FIGURE 2.3 Illustration of the order of key interviews throughout the Data Sleuth Process.

Open-Source Research

Open-source intelligence (OSINT) has become an expertise owned by private investigators and a niche within this profession. This step in the investigation process, as used by Workman Forensics, is not executed to the level of an OSINT expert or specialist but rather gathers easily accessible information that contributes to the understanding of the subject and facts or circumstances surrounding the client concerns.

Open-source research at this step generally includes the use of public records databases to identify assets owned, business entities registered in various states, judgments, liens, licenses, etc. This step is particularly helpful in creating a list of business entities owned so they can be considered as part of the data analysis step as well as any utilities or bills paid on various homes. Organizing this information and making it readily accessible to other investigators or data analysts working on the case often results in findings that may have been overlooked without it.

The Case of the Missing Inventory

A client discovered inventory normally ordered for the business had been overordered by an employee. They hired an investigator to examine the data to quantify the inventory that had been purchased but never received by the company. The suppliers of the inventory were contacted and provided data exports of all orders from the client company. Examination of the data exports identified various shipping addresses. The orders were then summarized by shipping address and compared to employee addresses discovered as part of public records searches and employee records held by the client company. It was discovered that over one third of the purchases had been shipped directly to an employee's home. These orders were quantified as part of the overall investigation and provided to the client.

Open-source intelligence needs should be identified as part of the case planning process to ensure that when the analysis step is being performed, the research findings are available to incorporate at that time.

Data Analysis

Chapters 9 and 10 are exclusively focused on the area of data analysis in a variety of forensic accounting engagements and fraud investigations. Conceptually, however, this step in the Data Sleuth Process is the critical step in an engagement. Within this step, information gathered from the previous steps is used to quantify the amount of missing or hidden money. It is also in this step that evidence supporting the subject's intent is uncovered.

Results from data analysis within a forensic accounting engagement or fraud investigation will ultimately be organized into a few categories or buckets through client feedback and/or additional research, analysis or inquiry. The three categories that apply to the majority of engagements, as illustrated in Figure 2.4, are as follows:

- Transactions or actions by the subject that benefited the client
- Transactions or actions by the subject that did not benefit the client
- Transactions or actions by the subject for which the appropriate bucket is not determinable

The transactions or actions by the subject identified as not benefiting the client begin to generate the findings and quantification of a loss. For the transactions or actions by the subject for which the appropriate bucket is not determinable, additional research and analysis may be needed, which leads to the next steps in the process.

Other Data Sources and Evidence

With the transactions or actions for which the appropriate data analysis findings bucket cannot be determined, further research may be required. Potential

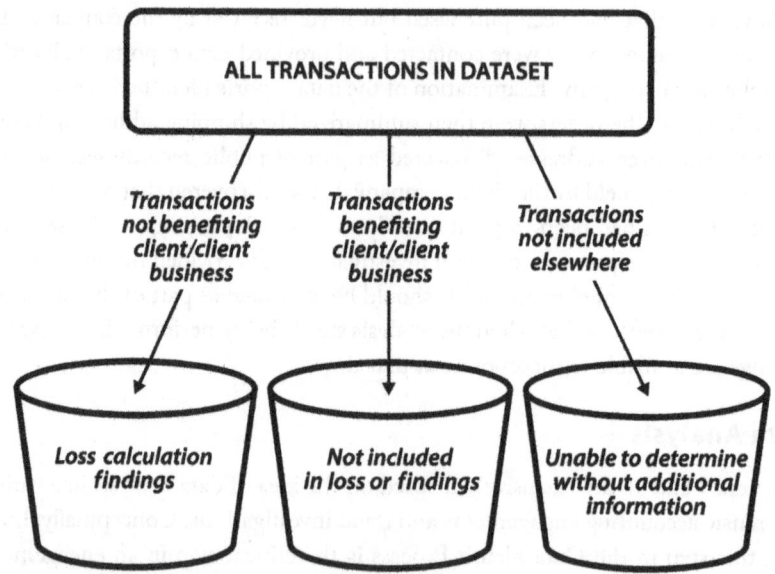

FIGURE 2.4   Illustration of data analysis findings buckets.

sources of information to make a bucket determination could include, but are not limited to:

- **Accounting software general ledger or transaction list reports.** If a subject controls the accounting software, reliance on the data to quantify a loss will be likely impossible due to missing information. However, using the transaction data to identify where the transactions were coded or any corresponding memos can be invaluable when needing to determine to which bucket the transactions should be assigned. For example, if a payment to a fancy clothing store is coded as an offset to an income account, and if there is a pattern of other transactions being coded similarly, it is likely that not only the original transaction being researched but also the other similar transactions in the general ledger account are not legitimate and did not benefit the client business.

- **Accounting software audit trail reports or user logs.** Identification of specific transactions in the accounting software audit trail or user log reports can be helpful in providing context as to whether the original transaction once existed and whether it was deleted. This type of report will also provide information on the user who performed the actions in the system – as long as individuals have their own logins and sharing passwords is not common practice. Once a pattern is established regarding transactions not benefiting the client business, the report can be used further to provide context to other transactions needing additional research.

■ **Confirmations from vendors.** Performing vendor confirmations usually involves contacting the vendor on the client's behalf and asking for copies of invoices originally sent to the client. This can identify whether payments made on the client's behalf were for legitimate business purposes.

■ **Invoices from customers.** If the allegations investigated include the siphoning of customer revenue from the business, it may be helpful to reach out to the client business's customers to obtain copies of the original invoices sent to the customer. This process is often more complicated than performing vendor confirmations as customers may not file or save their paid invoices in an easily accessible manner. Requesting lists of payments to the client business are usually easier to obtain and may prove helpful. When contacting customers, an investigator should obtain explicit approval from the client business as it may not be in the client business's best interest to alert customers to an issue of fraud, waste, or abuse until the investigation has progressed further.

■ **Subject emails.** Subject emails, when the contents specifically address a transaction that needs further research, can be helpful. At the same time, emails are what are known as "unstructured data" and can be messy and time consuming to review, so having the data organized in a format where search terms can be crafted to extract helpful information is key.

Subject Interviews

If the subject of an investigation is an employee of the client company, and if the company's policies permit, interviewing the subject using the findings gathered to date is a great last stop before finalizing the investigation. When interviewing a subject, it is recommended that someone on the interview team has experience in interviewing and that at least two investigators are present.

The goal of a subject interview is to take the transactions for which additional research is needed or for which a bucket could not yet be determined from the evidence obtained so far and to ask the subject about the specific items. Interviewing the subject at this stage, when the results of the research and analysis steps can be used to develop a much more targeted line of questioning, greatly increases the likelihood that the subject will share additional information. It is still possible that the subject will not provide anything new, but an investigator will never know if the subject is never interviewed.

Communication of Findings

An investigation may be perfectly executed, and all types of evidence may be obtained, but if the investigator cannot communicate the findings in a simple, concise, and clear manner to the client, attorneys, judge, jury, or other involved parties, the investigation will be ineffective. In communicating findings, an investigator should consider the following tips:

- For all findings, create tables, charts, or graphs summarizing the finding and listing the source information. Include them in the report or as attachments to the report.
- Simply state the facts resulting in each finding and explain why the finding is important.
- Do not provide opinions that accuse, or remotely accuse, the subject of fraud.
- Do not provide personal or professional opinions when the documented, substantiated facts will suffice.
- Group the facts discovered, or analysis results, by client concern, type of payment, or method by which the subject benefited from the transactions.

It may be surprising, but the steps of the Data Sleuth Process outlined in this chapter can be applied to virtually any forensic accounting or fraud investigation, whether a divorce, embezzlement, partnership dispute, or any of the other types of engagements discussed at the beginning of this chapter. By following this process consistently, the investigator ensures not only that their investigation is both thorough and efficient, but that their objectivity is maintained throughout, allowing them to uphold professional standards and most importantly, better serve their clients.

 NOTES

1. Arthur Conan Doyle, *A Scandal in Bohemia,* e-reader edition, Top Five Books, LLC, accessed August 28, 2021.
2. Association of Certified Fraud Examiners, *CFE Code of Professional Standards* (Association of Certified Fraud Examiners, 2020), 2, accessed August 28, 2021, https://www.acfe.com/uploadedFiles/ACFE_Website/Content/documents/rules/CFE%20Code%20of%20Professional%20Standards%20-%202020-11-01.pdf.
3. American Institute of CPAs, *Objectivity, Integrity and Disclosure* (American Institute of CPAs, 2021), accessed August 28, 2021, https://us.aicpa.org/interestareas/personalfinancialplanning/resources/practicecenter/professionalresponsibilities/objectivityintegritydisclosure.
4. American Institute of CPAs.
5. Doyle, *A Scandal in Bohemia.*

CHAPTER THREE

The Data Sleuth Necessity

LTHOUGH THE DEFINITION OF Data Sleuth to describe the work of our team did not originate until more recently, the Data Sleuth Process was developed out of a necessity for me starting a solo firm early in my career. The more I applied a data-focused strategy to cases, no matter the type of organization or scheme alleged, I gained confidence. I knew that if I could identify the best and most reliable sources of evidence determining the legitimacy of a client's allegations from the beginning of an engagement, I could then answer clients' questions early in the process instead of right before a deadline and would be found reputable as an investigator and testifying expert. What began as an effort to prove my legitimacy as an expert resulted in the creation of a professional team that has consistently provided answers to clients' questions in the most complex of cases using the Data Sleuth Process.

Forensic accounting engagements and fraud investigations are not detailed external financial statement audits. They are methodical, process driven, data-focused investigations targeted at answering the most popular client questions of "What happened?" and "How much money did I lose?" External financial statement audits, in general, remain an integral part of many organizations because they provide assurance as to the fairness of the representation of the information presented in financial statements. Additionally, external financial statement audits can contribute to an organization's fraud prevention strategies. However, they are not a replacement for proper internal controls or as a tool to detect fraud.

A widespread increase in the availability of financial data processing technology has provided opportunities to expand the application of forensic accounting procedures, to increase the efficiency of investigations, and to broaden the scope of an investigation beyond just the identified subject. As technology continues to be developed for purposes beyond our imaginations, data, and the information that can be derived and interpreted, may be endless. Although the Data Sleuth Process may have been developed out of necessity because I had nothing to rely upon except data, financial data, financial data analysis, and their uses in investigations are here to stay.

 ## FORENSIC ACCOUNTING ENGAGEMENTS VERSUS EXTERNAL FINANCIAL STATEMENT AUDITS

Frustrated by the number of years a fraud scheme continued while having external financial statement audits is all too common with our clients. In working with the management of organizations that have been victims of occupation fraud, or fraud perpetrated by an employee, we find that they commonly believe external financial statement audits should have detected the scheme. It is not until after their engagement with our firm that they truly realize the distinctions between a forensic accounting engagement and an external financial statement audit. Although the two may seem similar conceptually to someone not in the profession, they both serve distinctly different purposes.

In 2014, while working cases as a solo practitioner, I contracted on audit engagements to gain experience with external financial statement auditing procedures and using data analytics software. It was through these engagements that I began to appreciate the purpose of audits while recognizing stark differences between external financial statement audit procedures and forensic accounting procedures. Many of the procedures assigned to me were routine in testing internal controls and statutory compliance. Testing for internal controls involves an evaluation of the business procedures and corresponding duties assigned to personnel. The auditor evaluates whether there is accountability built into the procedure that would prevent or detect fraud should it occur in the process. Having solely worked investigations for eight years, I did not always understand the purpose of some of the procedures; therefore, I would often ask a supervisor or manager about the purpose of the procedure before beginning the assignment.

External audit procedures can be updated to address areas of concern, but sometimes, procedures are carried over year after year without considering their effectiveness or ongoing purpose. One such procedure was the comparison of a sample group of system exported check register entries and the corresponding paper check stubs. The paper check stubs were generated from the same system as the check register. Ultimately, I was comparing a data source to itself – which in some situations is valuable when testing for the accuracy of an exported report prior to performing data analysis. However, that was not the situation. From a Data Sleuth perspective, an improved procedure would be to compare the sample transactions from the system exported check register to the corresponding checks on the bank statement to ensure that the information in the system represents what actually cleared the bank.

If an organization is concerned about the fraud risk in an organization, an external financial statement audit will not likely detect it for several reasons, but ultimately, because a financial statement audit is not designed to detect fraud. It is simply the wrong tool for the job. The deadlines alone restrict the auditor's ability to examine in detail the individual transactions that make up the balances on the financial statements. The design of an audit includes mandated deadlines requiring an audit to be completed for some organizations in as few as 45 to 60 days. Even as the use of data analysis has improved the efficiency of audits and allowed for more strategic testing of transactions, there is still a constraint of time.

In providing an opinion on whether financial statements are fairly presented, financial statement fraud may be identified; however, the most common fraud schemes faced by businesses, not-for-profit organizations, governments, tribes, or schools are those of asset misappropriation, and many of the clients we serve do not have internal audit departments. Asset misappropriation refers to the theft of cash, inventory, equipment, or any other asset of value. Asset misappropriation schemes comprise multiple transactions that when combined over the life of the scheme may be material in total. However, over the course of a year, asset misappropriations in transaction value fall below most materiality thresholds established in an audit. Not to mention, many transactions representing the individual occurrences of theft are charged to profit and loss accounts whose balances are closed at the end of each year to retained earnings. Thus, the totality of the amount stolen over time is less obvious – especially in an organization with total revenue necessitating an annual external audit – such as a company that is publicly traded.

Although it may not be the specific intention of an external financial statement audit to detect fraud, it is possible. Additionally, an audit contributes to a fraud prevention program by decreased fraud risk in an organization to the extent that employees believe an auditor could detect their scheme. However, if an employee understands the audit procedures, he may be able to conceal the scheme, making it undetectable by the auditor. If an organization wants to prevent or detect fraud, or investigate fraud that has already happened, an external financial statement audit is not the most effective tool.

THE EVOLUTION OF FORENSIC ACCOUNTING

When I first started working in the private sector, I noticed several perceptions about forensic accounting engagements. The first perception about forensic accounting, from accountants and clients alike, was that forensic accounting engagements were essentially detailed audits with the involving procedures to examine any and all transactions within an organization – or at least in the area of the alleged occurrence of misappropriation of funds. Obviously, this approach created a perception with some clients that to request such an engagement would be cost prohibitive from the start. For other clients, the cost of the investigation itself did not feel justifiable as the client had already suffered a financial loss and knew that not much of the loss could be recovered. Then, there were others who, even though only a fractional part of the loss stolen may be realized, still believed the engagement would provide value because they could learn how the fraud occurred and receive consultation on how to prevent it in the future. The accountants' and clients' perceptions were not entirely wrong.

Familiar with the manual labor process of data entry, it was no surprise that cases in the private sector required the same manual labor process of gathering and entering data that I experienced when working with law enforcement. A significant difference between public and private sector investigations was a client's budget for the investigation. Although cases I worked on with law enforcement began with the manual data entry of all known bank statements, credit card statements, and the like, such work could be extremely cost prohibitive for private sector clients. Optical character recognition technology (OCR) was being used to search PDF documents but was not yet used to facilitate the importing of financial data into spreadsheets or accounting systems.

Because of the cost of digitizing financial information, private sector investigations seemed to begin by first identifying the scheme a client was alleging about a subject and then the investigator would try to find corresponding data/evidence to determine if the allegation was verifiable. Evidence of the scheme would be collected and documented, and a loss was quantified. This approach reduced the fees that would have been incurred from manual data entry; however, it greatly limited the scope of the investigation.

In order to perform the procedures beginning with an alleged scheme, case planning had to be based on understanding the characteristics of the alleged scheme and comparing the characteristics to the evidence available. An investigation could have several schemes for which this same process was followed. Although this method was successful with clients' cases, I personally did not enjoy the constant internal nagging and concerns. I worried that I might overlook something pertinent to the case, or that had I looked at other evidence, I would have drawn significantly different conclusions. The unsettled feelings led to constant reading, attending trainings, and inquiring of more experienced investigators so I could build up my mental database of schemes and corresponding characteristics. This approach also caused me to enter engagements already suspicious of the client's motives behind hiring a forensic accountant. Was a client singling out an employee because the allegations were true, or was the employer needing a way to fire an individual who was causing problems? This assumed requirement to trust that my clients' intentions were honorable was nearly impossible for me – no matter the client.

By the time I founded Workman Forensics, financial data processing technology was improving, but it was too expensive for my small firm. My desire to return to what I had learned at the Federal Bureau of Investigation (FBI) and to work cases once again from a data focus encouraged me to improve the process of digitizing data. I performed continuous research to find a more technologically advanced, but budget friendly, solution. Several years later, I discovered a technology solution while browsing the exhibition hall at the Association of Certified Fraud Examiners Conference. The improved automation of extracting financial information from PDF documents into a spreadsheet was a game changer for me and my firm.

As I was able to import data more efficiently, I could then switch the investigation starting point from a scheme identification approach to a data-driven approach and still work within a reasonable client budget. For example, rather than just looking into a known payroll scheme of one employee, we could look at the payroll data for all employees and identify outliers. The outliers discovered did not automatically indicate fraudulent payroll had been discovered, but it was an opportunity for further discussion with the client. Looking at an entire data set instead of something piecemealed or cherry-picked by a client gave me greater satisfaction that the investigation was objective. Finally, it reduced the need to trust a client's intentions; I could simply address their concerns and let the data-driven results speak for themselves.

 ## THE CASE OF THE CASH BACK PAYROLL SCHEME

Vince had been out at the ranch and missed a call from a number he did not recognize. Listening to the voice mail, he heard, "Hi Vince. This is Gina. I work for your company under Jane. I really need to talk to you." Vince immediately redialed Gina's number and set an appointment to talk with her the following day off site. Gina's hands were shaking as she carefully told Vince about a conspiracy in the home office. The conspiracy she described existed between Jane who was the chief executive officer (CEO), the chief financial officer (CFO), and other managers and supervisors. Vince was shocked, blindsided, really. He diligently reviewed his company's financial statements every month. The balance sheets and income statements were consistent, and the CFO had paid every shareholder distribution on time and without any discussion of cash flow issues. He knew Gina was well liked and part of the core team and would not risk that position to tell him something untrue, but he just could not believe it. Vince encouraged Gina to tell him all she had seen and heard so he could chart a course of action.

Jane had positioned herself to be responsible for payroll, even though it was outside the job description of a CEO. She would overpay the core team employees and then place envelopes on team members' desks with a handwritten amount on the front of the envelope. The team members knew that Jane expected them to return to her in the envelope the indicated amount of cash when their paycheck deposited. For example, if Jane overpaid an employee by $1,000, the envelope may have $500 written on the front. That employee was to return $500, and then he was able to keep $500 net of all the taxes that would be due on the extra $1,000.

Later that evening, Vince began to research Gina's allegations. Slowly but surely, he confirmed the worst – a team of trusted employees were stealing money. Vince interviewed the four employees from the list Gina prepared; they all immediately confessed. Then, Vince hired Workman Forensics to help him establish the amount of money missing. Although Gina advised about the employees involved in the scheme, and those interviewed confessed, I asked Vince if we could expand our scope to look at all home office employees – not just those known at the time. We had recently procured data analytics software to pair with our data processing system. I explained that if we ran our analysis on all home office employees at the same time, not only would he know who was involved based on data evidence, but it would be more efficient than generating a loss analysis every time he learned about another involved employee through the grapevine. Vince agreed to this method and provided us with the timesheet records and payroll reports from the provider for all home office employees.

Comparing the hours in the timesheet data to the hours paid in the payroll reports, we immediately identified 28 employees who had been paid for more hours than they worked. Most of the differences were between 150 hours and 300 hours, and the primary players in the scheme had been overpaid for between 4,000 to 5,000 hours over the five-year relevant period. The loss to the company and Vince was $208,000.

If our investigation focused only on those individuals Gina reported, Vince would have had a loss of $170,000. An additional loss of $38,000 was quantified that could be included by Vince in his recovery efforts moving forward. More significant than this, however, was that the analysis of looking at all home office employees identified that Gina had been overpaid during the period by 500 hours.

 ## START WITH THE EVIDENCE, NOT THE SCHEME

An FBI agent approached my cubical holding a banker's box to ask me if I would process the bank statements contained in the box for an investigation. As the student trainee working under a forensic accountant, entering bank statement information into a spreadsheet was my primary job and responsibility, and I had become extremely proficient in the first year of employment. I accepted the massive box of statements and got to work. As I entered each row of information, I became familiar with the repetitive activity within the accounts. When I saw the case agent the next week, I asked about the case. He obliged and explained the allegations and potential related charges. Within this discussion, I learned that the case involved a pump-and-dump stock scheme. The agent explained that a group of professionals were conspiring to promote penny stocks to victims; whenever the stock price would reach a certain price range, the professionals would sell their shares to make a lot of money. The people they had recruited to invest in the stock, the victims, would lose money. Knowing this information helped me identify patterns or indications in the bank statement data that might lead to recovering assets. My favorite types of transactions to look for while performing the data entry of bank statements were those that led to identifying assets and other related bank accounts for asset forfeiture purposes. Although I was not involved in the asset forfeiture process, I would leave a note for the analysts who were, and they would have a head start on their analysis. Such findings allow for possible forfeiture of the assets purchased with stolen money that, in turn, can be used to repay victims.

At the time, I did not know what kind of evidence was necessary to charge a pump-and-dump stock scheme, but as I continued to enter line after line of data, I kept the case story and charges in mind. One day, I entered a transaction in the amount of $450,000, identified as a wire transfer and the description on the statement included the word "Belize." I had not traveled much in my life by the time I was 20 years old, but my best friend in high school vacationed in Belize for her senior trip, so I at least knew the location was not in the United States. Pausing the data entry, I searched the Internet for the transaction description confirming that the transaction had occurred with a financial institution in Belize. Making note of this transaction in a memo to the agent, I completed the data entry assignment a few days later and moved on to other work.

One day while working on another assignment, I received a call from an attorney from a government agency in Washington, DC. He wanted to discuss the $450,000 transaction that I noted being wired to Belize. I wished I had more details for him, but there was no magic or pizzazz to the finding. I simply found it by entering the data into a spreadsheet and paying attention to the patterns and understanding the possible charges and goals of the investigation. We had a pleasant discussion, and he ended the conversation by letting me know they were going to work to seize the funds because of my finding. I focused on the evidence, I was curious, and I connected the data I was entering from the statements to the charges that had been explained to me.

 ## THE CASE OF THE GAMBLING EXECUTIVE DIRECTOR

During the week following April 15, 2010, when we were given a bonus vacation day to celebrate the end of a busy tax season, I began investigating a $3.5 million embezzlement by a loan officer at a local bank. As that case ended, preparation for the fall tax deadline began. This was the first time in my career that I experienced a panic attack although I did not know this was happening at this time. What I did know was I could not continue to prepare tax returns and work on forensic accounting engagements at the same time. After having given my manager ample notice, I started the job search process. I still remember the days following giving my notice as one of the lowest points of my life. Having left my dream job at age 21 felt as though my career life was all downhill, and I did not want to return to the FBI. Working with a headhunter, I explored several controller positions, but although the accounting job openings were a great step in an accountant's career, I felt lost. I did not want to be a great accountant; I wanted to be an investigator. One day, the headhunter suggested that I start my own business as a fraud examiner. This was the first option that did not feel terrible. I called my mentor from the FBI and my mom to see what they thought about the option. My mentor was surprised but encouraging, and Mom said, "If it doesn't work, what's the worst that will happen?" I responded, "I go get a job as a controller." A few weeks later, Workman Forensics officially opened – from my laptop on my dining room table.

My experience to this point was laser focused on tax strategy, forensic accounting engagements, and fraud investigations. I had never considered opening my own business, so I was facing an enormous learning curve – especially because I had no clients or even contacts in town. Starting in the fall of 2010, I worked odd jobs while I forced myself to meet with attorneys, bankers, and really anyone who would talk to me. Three months passed when the phone rang. On the other end was an attorney I had met a few months before. A local not-for-profit organization believed their executive director had stolen $1 million. He wanted to know if I wanted to work on it and if I would go meet with the interim executive director. I tried to sound as if I received these calls every day and made an appointment that was responsive but not too eager.

The interim executive director, Adam, was worked up to say the least and openly anxious of my arrival. Assuring him that I was just an accountant and not law enforcement, he began to tell me about his discovery. Before becoming the interim executive director, Adam had been the assistant executive director. Before the discovery, the former executive director, Ivan, was preparing for retirement and was training Adam to take his position. The organization did not use any kind of accounting software, or even Microsoft Excel, but still used green-bar ledger paper and a checkbook. Complaints around the organization were that Ivan was never there and that things were starting to fall apart. Ivan began teaching Adam about the financial preparations for board meetings when Adam noticed payments to a financial institution. Shortly after the training, Ivan would bring Adam credit card statements and represent to Adam that these statements were Ivan's personal credit cards. He would ask Adam to shred them. Recognizing that a couple of the statements were from the financial institution listed in the check register, Adam did not follow Ivan's orders and kept copies of the statements in his file drawer.

The next time Adam was asked to prepare financial information for the board, he took the credit card statements into Ivan's office while he was out and compared the payments listed on the credit card statements to the check register. The amounts matched. Adam was convinced Ivan was stealing from the organization.

The realization of the theft hit him, and in somewhat disbelief, Adam waited for Ivan to leave on several occasions to investigate other areas of potential theft including cash donations received. Records of the cash received were compared to cash deposited to the bank account. Having found no cash deposits over a period of time and knowing that Ivan was the person responsible for the deposits, Adam believed Ivan was stealing those funds as well.

Adam provided me with copies of all the credit card statements and showed me the matching check register entries. The credit card statements were several pages long and listed numerous transactions at local casinos within an hour from the organization. I was sent back to my home office with 11 extra-large banker's boxes full of paper documents including bank statements and green-bar check registers for 10 years. He also provided me with the records of cash donations and carbon copy deposit slips lacking cash or currency deposits. The attorney advised he was filing a civil lawsuit and was requesting a temporary injunction, so a sample of my findings proving the theft needed to be completed in 10 days and that I would be testifying.

The analysis goals for the 10-day deadline were:

- To determine if Adam's allegations were supported by available information and evidence, and
- To demonstrate payment of personal credit card charges and lack of cash deposits to the court so that Ivan's assets would be temporarily frozen.

Starting with the analysis goals in mind, I had to find the most efficient path from start to finish and be ready to testify with exhibits in less than two weeks. Additionally, at 26 years old, any testimony where I might have said, "based on my experience. . ." would not be seen as credible, especially if Ivan had hired a more experienced expert, so I knew my analysis had to be perfect. Out of necessity, I exclusively relied on financial data, specific transactions, and patterns that would substantiate my testimony and reputation – especially with my first case as Workman Forensics.

Ivan's credit card statements listing the gambling transactions and payments could not be subpoenaed and returned within 10 days, so I needed the next best type of evidence – the bank statements of the not-for-profit organization listing the payments on the credit cards. Returning to the data entry skills I learned at the FBI, I began entering banking transactions into an Excel spreadsheet for a relevant period of one year noting if any memo lines on checks referenced the credit card number associated with the payment and the signature authority on the check. I could have simply scheduled payments to the known credit card accounts for which Adam had saved statements; however, every time I had ever only processed select transactions instead of all the transactions listed on the statement to save time, I regretted it later and still ended up spending the time doing so.

This case was no exception; digitizing all the bank statement transactions and subsequent analysis identified two additional credit cards belonging to Ivan. These additional credit cards were paid using the organization's funds. To confirm that the credit card payments did not belong to the organization, a Dunn and Bradstreet report was obtained from a company specializing in background checks. The report confirmed that the organization did not have any credit card debt in the organization's name. Digitizing the bank statements also proved valuable because another area of loss to the organization was identified. Ivan had written multiple check payments for $1,000 each to himself in excess of his regular payroll. Tables listing the check payments to credit card companies and Ivan directly during the one-year period were prepared. I organized a binder for the hearing containing examples of the check payments made to credit card companies and Ivan's credit card statements retained by Adam.

The records of cash donations were compared to corresponding bank statement deposits that had been digitized to list cash and check totals. For the year under investigation, none of the cash donations had been deposited to the bank account. Tables were prepared summarizing the findings and were accompanied by examples of the paper donation records and carbon copy deposit slips.

More nervous than ever, I testified to my assignment, my findings, and the evidence upon which I relied. During cross-examination, the opposing counsel questioned me on the validity of my procedures and evidence relied upon, but despite his efforts, the judge granted the temporary injunction. Relying on specific transactions from third-party source documents proved reliable and accomplished the goals of the case: it verified the legitimacy of the allegations and demonstrated to the court that Ivan's assets should be frozen.

The origins of the Data Sleuth Process resulted from the necessity that I had to do what I could using the experience I had early in my career. The fundamental skills I had learned were to process data and to identify patterns within the data. This approach worked by addressing the concerns of the clients and the goals of investigations using data-driven results – instead of finding evidence to fit a scheme.

CHAPTER FOUR

Data Sleuth Considerations

W HEN ACCOUNTANTS DECIDE TO work in public accounting, they typically choose between the audit career path or the tax career path. Although people often think that audit would be most closely aligned with investigations, I did not choose the most obvious path. I chose to learn to prepare taxes. Although I learned an enormous amount about business, accounting, and tax, management knew I would jump at anything that afforded me an investigation opportunity and not be a long-term employee if my day consisted of only preparing taxes. Preparing taxes for this midsized local accounting firm ultimately evolved into the creation of a forensic accounting department including me and a Certified Fraud Examiner manager.

After three months of working for this firm, one of the partners received a call about a potential embezzlement in a doctor's office. The partners assigned the case to me. Feeling confident, the client provided her evidence in which she was certain I would discover that the office manager was stealing funds. This evidence, however, did not contain bank statements but rather only a general ledger exported from the accounting software. I asked the project manager to request the bank statements but began to feel extremely insecure about my investigative abilities when I was told I would not be receiving the statements.

Although my investigation skills were advanced at this point in my career, for my age and experience, I had never put my accounting education to use. What started as a feeling of confidence was now becoming a feeling of overwhelming stress because I did not know where to begin an investigation with only a general ledger. This was not best evidence, yet it was all I had to work from to ultimately communicate to the client whether embezzlement was happening in the practice. I asked a lot of questions and consulted with experienced investigators, but at the end of the day, I simply had to scroll through this client's general ledger and identify items that I thought seemed strange. Looking back, I have no idea how I defined what made a transaction strange, as I had no formal process or method other than simple logic.

After providing the client with a list of the seemingly strange transactions, the client ended the investigation. I later learned, from the client's account manager, that the client believed her husband was having an affair with the office manager and was hoping to find evidence that her husband was letting her take extra funds from the business. Having found none, the investigation ended. It was this investigation that brought a few things to my attention that I knew I had to understand for future case work:

- A subject's motivation to steal
- The client's goals and involvement in an investigation
- The evidence required for fraud allegations
- Verifying client allegations against a subject
- Possible loss recovery avenues for clients

 ## INVESTIGATIONS AFFECT REAL PEOPLE

Working with law enforcement as a support employee, never did I meet the victims of fraud cases and only rarely did I meet the subject of the investigation. When forensic accounting engagements began to call the public accounting firm on cases, interaction with the clients was unavoidable. Rather than an agent opening a case based on a complaint or tip received, or an initiative, the forensic engagement began with the client discovering a problem that required immediate response and constant communication. The first few meetings with the victim, or end-client, felt overwhelming. Previously, the investigation case details were filtered to only the information I needed when analyzing the financial transactions; but in the private sector, the information came firsthand through a client interview process and through a firehose. No one had refined and compartmentalized the facts from the drama-ridden narrative for me. However, this experience proved invaluable. Prior to meeting the victims, a career in financial investigations stemmed from a desire to have a fun job, but having met them, my motivation transitioned into empathy to help the victim.

Sitting across from and listening to a victim's story never fails to change my attitude and perspective on a case. It is easy to overlook the real people affected by an investigation or a subject's vulnerability in a perceived crisis. When an investigator sits outside of the situation and the daily commotion of a business, judgment of the victim owner's inaction or apparent negligence is tempting. However, when the victim shares his version of the story, the impact and importance of the investigation become more than just an interesting career; the realization that the results of the investigation decisions will affect a person's life is sobering.

To the business owner who has lost millions of dollars to an employee, the emotional loss tends to be greater than the financial loss. The business owner rarely sleeps with the normal workload, so the seemingly never-ending effects of the once-trusted employee's actions continue to be revealed, including:

- Identifying the tasks of the subject that must continue for the business to continue to operate
- Discovering tasks once believed to have been completed are outstanding
- Recruiting and training new talent to cover the duties of the subject
- Managing the other employee attitudes and perspectives when law enforcement action, or any type of criminal punishment, appears to be slow or lagging
- Continuous identification of other, usually smaller, schemes or methods of theft and disloyalty to the company
- The discovery of years of negative financial performance after years of believing the opposite
- Greater than any of these, the feelings of betrayal and loss of a trusted relationship

Interviewing a subject is not dissimilar. Judgment of a subject's actions and believing that *I would never do that* may tempt an investigator who is sitting outside of the situation. However, when listening carefully to a subject's retelling of the situation, when put into the situation with the same set of factors, who can really say he or she would not have made the same series of choices? Investigations directly affect the future of victims and subjects. Great care and consideration of the impact on real people's lives must be maintained throughout the engagement.

 ## THE CASE OF THE NONEXISTENT INVENTORY

Jeff's interview is one that I will never forget. It was not my first subject interview, but it changed my perspective of a subject. I had been analyzing the messiest data (to this day I have never seen worse) and compiling what I could determine as the loss. Before Jeff arrived at the interview, I coached myself on being direct, calling things as I saw them, and fighting for the victim client. But when Jeff arrived, he looked so human, humbled, relieved, and terrified. We introduced ourselves and barely finished establishing the purpose of the interview, having asked him to be truthful, when Jeff blurted, "Let me say this before we dive into everything. It's been a long, long time since I've had any kind of peace in my life. I've laid down most nights worried about getting caught. I'm at the point where I'm here to tell you the truth. I'm not going to cover anything up because I've covered up so much for so long that I'm really tired of it. I'm tired of stressing, having stomach cramps, and waking up in the middle of the night. I can't keep covering things up, hiding things, and lying about things. So, I'm just going to tell you the truth."

All my self-coaching about maintaining a tough exterior melted at his opener, and I all I could see was a person who made a mistake – a very costly and imprudent mistake – but still a person, nonetheless. Then he started telling his story, and although there were plenty of other alternatives to solving his financial problem than stealing money from his employer, his logic tracked – as much as I hated to admit it.

Jeff was an outside salesperson in industrial sales for 25 years for Industrial Distribution, LLC, and it was in his sales rounds that he met Trent. Trent was a manager for a company that would buy discontinued industrial products for pennies on the dollar, which Jeff's company could purchase from time to time for clients and earn a higher margin. When Trent lost his job with the supplier, Trent started his own discontinued industrial products company, Discount Supplies, LLC. Jeff arranged to continue purchasing products from Trent, only through Discount Supplies instead of Trent's previous employer.

After doing business with Trent for years, Jeff found himself in financial hardship with his three kids in college while paying their tuition and living expenses. Jeff knew that his managers at Industrial Distribution did not pay a lot of attention to him and his sales because he was one of the top producers for the company. Jeff approached Trent and told him he was going to start selling products on the side to make some extra money, but to do so, he wanted Trent to run the checks from customers through Trent's company, Discount Supplies, and then remit payment through Discount Supplies to Jeff. Trent agreed to do so because Jeff told him that he did not want Industrial Distribution to see the sales on the side to their customers as it was a conflict of interest.

Shortly after the scheme began, Industrial Distribution was acquired by a larger company, Acquiring Distribution, and Jeff became nervous that his scheme was going to be discovered when the acquisition team started their due diligence and counted inventory. However, the acquisition team did not perform due diligence related to the inventory of industrial supplies. Additionally, because of Jeff's trusted position in the company and his past success, he was the only outside salesperson at Industrial Distribution who had total access to the computer program with the ability to initiate purchase orders, receive products from the purchase orders, deliver products to customers, and prepare customer invoices.

When Acquiring Distribution purchased Industrial Distribution, even after the purchasing system was consolidated, Jeff retained his system access to the entire purchasing and sales processes. Jeff recognized his new employer was not paying any more attention to him than the previous employer, and his scheme continued, which involved the following steps:

- Initiating a purchase order to purchase products from Discount Supplies that did not actually exist
- Creating an invoice for the products that did not exist as if it was from Discount Supplies
- Acknowledging receipt of the nonexistent products
- Invoicing customers for the nonexistent products when asked about them; otherwise, they remained as unbilled in the employer's system
- Trent receiving the check at Discount Supplies and paying Jeff either by check or cash

Jeff had finally decided to resign, find a new job, and start over with the hope that his scheme would go unnoticed. But Jeff's decision was a few weeks too late. His employer discovered the fake vendor invoices when looking through purchases that had not been billed to customers. Jeff was cooperative throughout the entire engagement, including this interview, and when I would call him with questions about activity I discovered in the financial data analysis. The total loss exceeded $650,000. Jeff was fired, and in an effort to encourage the employer to not file criminal charges, Jeff offered to surrender his retirement account. The employer did not agree to not file charges in the matter, but when I followed up on making a referral, management advised that because of other acquisitions in progress, they did not want any potential negative publicity from the case.

Training event audiences dislike and feel uncomfortable when I share stories like Jeff's. Outrage is the typical response by audience members, as they believe that Jeff did not receive appropriate punishment for his actions. And maybe they're right. When I consider that if presented with the same set of circumstances as Jeff, I realize that I might have made the same decision to relieve the sense of pressure to provide for my children's college education. This is the truthful humility I realize every time I interview a fraud suspect – especially when the theft was a first-time occurrence. Acknowledging this human frailty reminds me to avoid the judgment and accusation trap and to stay in the objective lane of evidence, data, and piecing together from such what actually happened.

THE FRAUD FORMULA

In its most simplistic form, to prove fraud, one must provide evidence of the subject benefiting by deceitful intentions. If this concept was a formula:

$$FRAUD = INTENT + BENEFIT$$

When I worked my first case in the private sector, I originally believed that working cases without access to subpoena power was extremely frustrating, if not impossible. I worried that I would not be able to create value or answer client questions to help them take their next steps without access to this information. However, after working investigations from the private sector for over 12 years, I think private sector investigations possess great advantages that law enforcement investigations do not have the time to consider. Conversely, law enforcement investigations have great advantages in collecting information through subpoenas from financial custodians. When the two types of investigations work together, that is where I have experienced the greatest recovery for clients and client satisfaction.

Investigations beginning in the private sector, before being referred to law enforcement, create value by providing a greater foundation and context around the crime than that of a criminal investigation – if for no other reasons than being able to incorporate accounting expertise and more time to truly understand the situation. Starting with a criminal investigation may seem more efficient, linear, and cost effective considering the ability to subpoena bank statements and other financial information, and to avoid paying legal fees. However, several pieces of key evidence in financial investigations that law enforcement does not always have time to consider include a company's general ledger, accounting software reports, audit trail/user log reports, and payroll reports. These sources of information can provide a treasure trove of evidence supporting the intentions and motives within the scheme. The types of evidence and data key to private sector investigations are provided in greater detail in Chapter 8.

STAYING ON TASK WITH PURPOSE IN MIND

On my second day as a student trainee, the Federal Bureau of Investigation forensic accountant, and my supervisor, presented me with a stack of bank statements and an Excel spreadsheet. To this day, I do not remember the specific instructions, but I was thrilled to begin working on a real fraud case involving a check kiting scheme. A check kiting scheme involves a systematic process and cycle where the subject issues checks on accounts with insufficient funds that are then deposited into two or more bank accounts under the control of the same person held at different banks.[1]

I worked on this case for several days, only to discover several years later that my interpretation of the instructions had resulted in a chaotic, unusable Excel workbook. The resulting spreadsheet I so proudly sent to my mentor contained at least 50 different tabs with information I hand-entered from the bank statements.

I was eager to investigate, but I lacked practical skills. My supervisor graciously took the unusable spreadsheet, reworked the case on her own, and did not mention the reworking until years later. Starting that day, my supervisor began dissecting the investigation steps, beginning with the basics. She first taught me about the information that can be extracted from bank statements to build cases necessitating the tracing of money, quantifying losses, and mining complimentary evidence for even nonfinancial cases. From the guidance of my supervisor to entering transactions from thousands of bank statement pages into spreadsheets to listening intently to stories from agents and asking follow-up questions, little by little, evidence, statutes, and connections, and eventually, investigations began to make sense.

After a year, agents started recruiting me to help them organize evidence, financial and nonfinancial, for their grand jury testimonies, prepare interview questions from the bank statement analysis, and even testify before the grand jury about instances of fraud against the government by individuals during Hurricane Katrina. The understanding that I gained from this experience was twofold. First, I learned about the necessity and quality of evidence, where it came from, and its purpose. Second, I learned to identify the purpose of an investigation. For example, when criminal investigations are in progress, the purpose of the investigation is to provide the prosecutor with the story of "what happened" supported by evidence that will prove the "what happened" beyond a reasonable doubt. Additionally, evidence gathered is used by the prosecutor as a foundation to decide which, if any, crimes, as defined by statue, can be charged against the subject. I became familiar with the statutes for bank fraud, wire fraud, and mail fraud as they were the most commonly charged within the cases I worked. As I performed data entry and basic financial analysis tasks throughout the investigation, I tried to advise the case agent of transactions that may have assisted with the purpose of the investigation.

 THE INVESTIGATION DECISION TREE FOR A DATA SLEUTH

Working a case without a stated purpose can also result in opposing counsel accusing the investigator of having no guidelines and simply running in an open field going whichever direction the wind blows. On the other hand, if the investigator begins with a desired outcome in mind, she may be accused of bias, cherry-picking evidence to support a theory, or being an advocate.

The definition of investigate is "to observe or study by close examination and systematic inquiry" or "to make a systematic examination."[2] Perhaps the inclusion of "systematic inquiry," in the definition, references a process that justifies the connection of evidence discovered to the end purpose or statutes. However, the portion of the definition stating "to observe or study by close examination" creates the idea of separation between the observer and that being examined, which then appears to incorporate objectivity into the examination. Although interesting, this definition is more complicated when put into practice in the real world. Few are those who are given unlimited time and resources to explore without a specific destination and goal in mind. Such a state allows time for an investigator to follow rabbit trails.

How does a forensic accountant or fraud investigator navigate an investigation objectively, but also efficiently, which justifies the time spent observing and systematically inquiring to then articulate what happened in such a way that the client or prosecutor can take their next steps? One solution is presented in Figure 4.1 as an investigation decision tree.

Ensure the Allegations Fall Within the Investigator's Expertise

When a client or victim presents their allegations for investigation, the investigator should first ask herself, "Does the investigation necessary to examine the allegations fall within my area(s) of expertise?" If no, an investigator should either find experienced investigators to collaborate on the project or refer the project entirely. To make this determination, the investigator might consider whether she is able to or desires to gain the expertise needed for the investigation. If she does, collaboration with experienced investigators provides an excellent opportunity to do so. If she does not, she should make a referral to a well-respected professional. If she does not know of any, she should advise the client. For example, Workman Forensics receives calls inquiring about digital forensics services. Currently, none of the team members at Workman Forensics have digital forensics expertise or

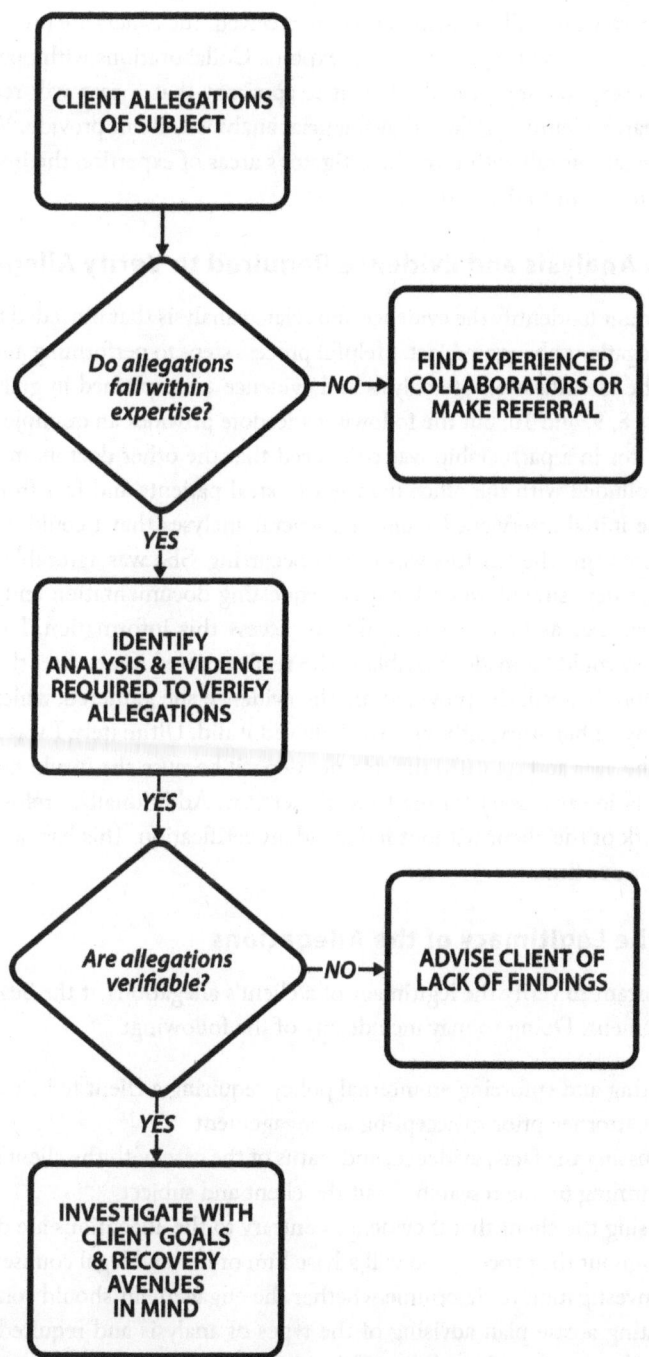

FIGURE 4.1   Illustration of an investigation decision tree.

experience, so when calls of such nature are received, the callers are provided with contact information of digital forensics experts. Collaborations with open-source intelligence experts are created when it is apparent that a case will require in-depth research identifying facts that financial analysis will not provide. When the client's allegations fall within the investigator's areas of expertise, the investigator may then move on to the next step.

Identify Analysis and Evidence Required to Verify Allegations

It is important to identify the evidence and related analysis that is needed to verify a client's allegations about a subject. Helpful process steps to performing and accomplishing the identification of analysis and evidence are explained in greater detail in chapters 8, 9, and 10, but the following anecdote provides an example scenario.

A doctor in a partnership was convinced that the other doctors in the practice had colluded with the office manager to steal patients and fees from her. As part of the initial interview, I identified several analyses that I could perform to help her confirm whether this was in fact occurring. She was agreeable and paid the retainer deposit, but when I started requesting documentation and data, she provided excuses as to why she could not access this information. I knew this information could be made available if she really wanted me to find the truth of her situation. Instead, she provided me the evidence she gathered, which did not confirm any of her story, although she believed it did. Ultimately, I was unable to work on the case and returned the retainer deposit because she would not provide the information necessary for me to work her case. Additionally, I refused to rely on the work of the client without independent verification. This has now become a policy for our firm.

Verify the Legitimacy of the Allegations

It is important to verify the legitimacy of a client's allegations at the beginning of an engagement. Doing so may include any of the following:

- Creating and enforcing an internal policy requiring a client to be represented by an attorney prior to accepting an engagement
- Discussing the facts, evidence, and status of the case with the client's attorney
- Performing online research about the client and subject
- Advising the client that if evidence contrary to the allegations are discovered throughout the process, you will advise him or her and legal counsel and stop the investigation to determine whether the engagement should continue.
- Creating a case plan advising of the types of analysis and required evidence needed to confirm the validity of the allegations

Verifying the legitimacy of the allegations creates value for the client and limits the investigator's exposure. The client should be advised as soon as possible if their allegations, or perceptions about what happened and how they were harmed, do not have sufficient evidence. Additionally, if the client's desired recovery avenues will not be available because of lack of evidence or otherwise, the client should be advised before he invests time and resources into fruitless efforts.

As for the investigator, communicating with the client continuously about lacking evidence or invalidity of the allegations can reduce the investigator's exposure for malpractice lawsuits. Reducing exposure does not mean that a client cannot file a lawsuit; however, contemporaneous documentation and communication with the client will provide great evidence should a complaint be filed.

Investigate with Client Goals and Possible Recovery Avenues in Mind

Investigating with the client's goals in mind helps the investigator stay on task and budget. In any investigation, there are plenty of rabbit trails that are tempting to explore, but time and resources are limited commodities, so connecting the goals with the analysis and necessary data is vital to avoid the areas that do not create value for the client. This approach also provides a process for an investigator who is also an expert witness to avoid being the "hired gun." A hired gun in the expert witness world tends to refer to those who consider only the evidence that supports their side's theories. Sometimes, the tactic of looking at only what the client provides comes from an attempt to save money or time, but if the opposing expert investigates with objectivity and communicates well, the shortcut incurs a great risk of failing. To balance the two, keep the client goals in mind to avoid the inefficient rabbit trails while allowing data to drive reliable investigation results. When the outcome of a financial investigation can be aligned with recovery avenues, the client not only benefits from the discovery of what happened and the quantification of the loss but may have an avenue to regain a portion of what was previously stolen.

 RECOVERY AVENUES

Clients of forensic accounting and fraud investigations often include individuals or companies who are missing money or are in a dispute about money. Each client envisions his or her own desired outcome; there is not a one-size-fits-all. The most common desired outcomes expressed by my clients in the past are detailed in the following sections; however, I have found that the clients who understand the reality of the potential outcomes, but focus their attention on recovery over revenge, are often the most successful and happiest clients after the investigation. The following outcomes can be pursued simultaneously and independently of the others, but not all avenues are beneficial or applicable to every client's situation. As Data Sleuths, we investigate every client matter as if it will be criminally prosecuted as the burden of proof is the greatest of all the outcomes.

When a client report is prepared considering a burden of proof beyond a reasonable doubt, it serves the other possible outcomes well. Additionally, it is never advisable to have multiple reports issued as an expert with multiple loss totals. Doing so will not only create confusion, but also provides the opposing counsel with an easy opportunity to discredit the investigation and create doubt. From the client's perspective, preparation in this way is also more efficient and cost effective when the issuance of one report can be used to pursue any, or all, of the desired outcomes.

Recovery Avenue: Criminal Prosecution

The most common desired outcome from investigations is criminal prosecution. Clients often believe that if the subjects face prison time, they will receive justice. Some of the distinctions and challenges within this outcome category include:

- There must be clear and convincing evidence that a prosecutor can use to prove beyond a reasonable doubt that the subject stole the financial resources contained in the allegations. The less convincing the evidence, the less likely law enforcement will pursue criminal charges. For example, if the loss to the victim involves a cash/currency-based scheme, the likelihood of prosecution diminishes because evidence is limited. Often, there is more than one person who handles the cash, which makes blaming one subject difficult when the standard is beyond a reasonable doubt.
- Loss calculations for the purposes of criminal prosecution should be based on specific item tracing and specific transaction identification. Quantifying specific transactions identifying how the trusted subject benefited at the victim's expense is a preferred method over estimating, or "backing into," a loss. Loss calculations are a primary driver in the subject's sentence, which is why it is important that it is as accurate as possible.
- Law enforcement has limited resources, including time and personnel to handle the crimes experienced by the public. Therefore, priorities must be assigned to the investigations pursued that may include whether it is a violent crime. Additionally, even within the context of white-collar crimes and fraud schemes, there are priorities given to the cases with a greater total loss

amount, the types of victims (i.e. the public or a community versus one individual), the number of subjects or conspirators, the repetitive nature of the scheme, the criminal history of the subject, etc. And all of these prioritizing factors are subject to the quality of evidence. Therefore, not all cases worked by an investigator in the private sector will be charged criminally.

- Detectives in law enforcement are required to be a jack-of-all-trades when investigating crimes – even when focusing on the area of financial crimes. Within one financial crime unit consisting of a few detectives, they at one point or another may need to work a credit card fraud case, an embezzlement, an elder financial abuse case, and a check fraud case. Although each of these investigations are financial in nature, the investigation approaches vary greatly. The more complicated the scheme, such as thousands of transactions moving in and out of numerous bank accounts or theft being hidden in the accounting of a company's records, the likelihood of charges being filed at the state and local level decreases – especially when combined with unclear evidence or lower priority cases explained previously.
- If financial crimes are not associated with a violent crime, drug rings, or organized crime, judges may be more lenient with the sentencing – especially when the subject has no prior criminal history. Many subjects of embezzlement investigations I have worked have few, if any, speeding tickets let alone a criminal record. When sentencing results do not feel severe enough to the victim, the victim is often left feeling helpless, as if he or she did not receive the desired justice and has been betrayed by yet another trusted system.
- It is possible for assets to be seized and restitution ordered to the subject in a criminal prosecution. However, it is important for the client to understand that criminal proceedings and law enforcement are not collection agencies.

To help your client successfully navigate the desired outcome of criminal prosecution, presenting findings to law enforcement will be further detailed in Chapter 11.

Recovery Avenue: Civil Proceedings

When a financial investigation involves an embezzlement, corporate fraud, or partnership dispute, civil proceedings are a recovery avenue for many reasons, but those that have been most helpful for clients in the past include the following:

- Filing a civil lawsuit provides the client with a way to subpoena financial accounts of the subject through the help of his attorney. Having this information streamlines the investigation for the forensic accountant or fraud investigator, which can often make the investigation more efficient from a cost standpoint for the client. It also helps the investigator prepare a report in which law enforcement can be more confident in the reliability and simplicity of the evidence to move forward with criminal charges.

- A civil lawsuit also provides opportunities to obtain a judgment to acquire assets purchased with stolen funds from the subject. If the client's attorney elects to do so, at the beginning of the lawsuit, a temporary injunction or restraining order can be obtained through this process to limit the disposal of assets by the subject while the investigation is ongoing. Preliminary investigation will likely be necessary to establish the existing assets and may require testimony at the hearing concerning the injunction by the investigator.
- The burden to prove fraud in a civil lawsuit is lower than that of criminal prosecution, which could be advantageous if the client's goal is to recover assets.
- If damages from a fraud claim are awarded to the victim, the judgment cannot be discharged through bankruptcy by the subject.
- A caveat to civil lawsuits involves the related fees from attorneys and experts. I recommend that before a client pursues this outcome, preliminary research and investigation be performed to identify if any of the stolen funds exist in the form of bank accounts, properties, related businesses, shell companies, or personal property providing a path of at least partial recovery for the client that is greater than the fees to be incurred. If this hurdle is overcome, then the remaining benefits of this avenue may benefit the client.

Recovery Avenue: Insurance Reimbursement

Submitting an insurance claim can be an advantageous recovery avenue when the case involves theft by an employee. Many general liability policies include coverage for employee theft, but the reimbursement amounts are limited to $10,000 or $25,000 with varying deductibles. This level of reimbursement, however, is advantageous in that although it does not cover the loss from the employee, it subsidizes legal and investigation fees. Greater coverage for employers can be achieved if they have fidelity bonds or employee dishonesty policies. The use of a forensic accountant or fraud investigator in the claims process creates value for the client establishing the validity of the claim for the insurance to review and provide funds in a timely manner.

THE CASE OF THE MAN CAVE

ABC Oil and Gas Exploration sold working interests to investors and managed the exploration and development process. Oil and gas prices were at a peak, and cash was flowing steadily until the chief financial officer retired and was replaced by a new CFO, Trent. As the new CFO was getting up to speed with the systems and procedures of his new employer, he discovered irregularities in the bank statements. It appeared that the previous CFO was behind in reconciling the operating account. Trent prioritized this project, and in doing so, he discovered images of checking withdrawal slips were included with the images of canceled checks. When he contacted the bank, they advised the withdrawal slips were accompanied by cashier checks.

Banks operate on a double entry accounting, which is important to understand as an investigator, because with every transaction or image listed on a monthly bank statement, a corresponding document exists for the other side of the transaction, as listed in Table 4.1.

Trent requested copies of the corresponding cashier checks to the checking withdrawal slips for the previous few months. When received, Trent was stunned when he immediately recognized the vendors to whom the checks were written. They were limited liability companies that he recognized because they belonged to his good friend and buddy, Bill Word. The same Bill Word who recruited him to work at ABC Oil and Gas Exploration.

Trent and Bill were friends from high school, and carried on through college as they earned accounting and finance degrees, respectively. They shared common interest in car racing events. After college, Bill began working for ABC Oil and Gas Exploration and began climbing the ranks. By the time he recruited Trent to replace the former ABC Oil and Gas Exploration CFO, Bill managed all operations and had recently become a partner in the company. Trent contacted the former CFO to ask him about the unreconciled issues to see if he was aware of these cashier checks payable to Bill's LLCs. The former CFO advised that he did not know what the withdrawal slips were for as, historically, they fell under Bill's operations. The former CFO said that he did not code the transactions to accounts, but rather, he would let Bill know about the unreconciled transactions

TABLE 4.1 Examples of bank statement transactions or images and corresponding financial institution items.

Bank Statement Item	Financial Institution Corresponding Item
Checking withdrawal slips	Cashier check or cash-out ticket
Deposit slip	Individual checks, cashier checks, or cash-in tickets deposited
Wire transaction	Wire details identifying beneficiary name, account, and financial institution
ACH payment	ACH payment report listing recipient and recipient bank account

each month, and Bill would code them to the appropriate job or general ledger account. Trent made sure to not let the former CFO sense his suspicions and continued to perform the reconciliations.

After completing several months' worth of reconciliations, Trent could not deny his findings. Bill was paying personally owned LLCs affiliated with car racing events with ABC Oil and Gas Exploration's money. Trent prepared a memo of his findings for the owners whose reactions vacillated from disbelief to outrage. The chief executive officer contacted the company's attorney and private investigator. The private investigator convinced the company to refrain from letting Bill know about their discovery so that a forensic accountant could examine the evidence, prepare sample findings, and then the private investigator could interview Bill possibly to obtain a confession. The attorney supported this plan, and the company agreed to give the forensic accountant a week because they feared they would respond out of emotion if they had to wait to confront Bill much longer.

The forensic accountant began with a relevant period of one year and identified multiple LLCs owned by Bill that received payments from ABC Oil and Gas Exploration. Similar transactions were also extracted that did not appear to be for the benefit of the company. The findings memo was provided to the private investigator who used it to confront Bill. After an hour-long interview, Bill confessed to the theft. The private investigator not only obtained a confession, but Bill also advised how the money was used, bank accounts holding some of the funds, and where assets purchased with the company's money were stored. The private investigator recruited the help of the local sheriff's deputies to travel with Bill to the site storing personal property and physical assets to seize:

- One-of-a-kind, collector, and military-grade firearms
- Sixteen to 18 race cars and parts to work on the cars
- Four-wheelers
- Vehicles
- Trailers
- Tractor

The private investigator learned through the interview that Bill enjoyed purchasing items for his buddies to enjoy, and because of the size and volume of the personal property purchased, he needed a place to store all of it. That is when he used his employer's money to build a metal building on his property, separate from his house, that cost $100,000.

A civil lawsuit was filed by the company and its attorney, which was used primarily to obtain a judgment for the assets collected by the sheriff's office. Once accomplished, the company was able to auction and sell the assets – including the property on which the metal building was built.

When the loss calculation and financial investigation was completed, the theft loss totaled over $3 million. The report of findings was provided to federal law enforcement at the request of the client. The investigative agency was the Criminal Investigation Division (CID) of the Internal Revenue Service, as Bill never paid taxes on the $3 million he stole from his employer.

Using the forensic accountant's investigation, the client was able to recover approximately one third of their loss through the civil lawsuit and sale of the property sold through auction. At the same time, IRS CID agents completed their investigation, and within a year, Bill was sentenced to three years in prison.

This case illustrates the success of an investigation when an investigator considers a client's goals, verifies the allegations, and identifies potential loss recovery avenues in a financial investigation.

 NOTES

1. Janetta Maxwell, "Check Kiting and Ponzi Schemes," *The Investigation Game Podcast*, Tulsa, OK, accessed June 26, 2019, https://www.workmanforensics.com/podcast-episodes/episode-5-check-kiting-and-ponzi-schemes?rq=check%2Ukit.
2. Merriam-Webster, "Investigate," accessed October 4, 2021, https://www.merriam-webster.com/dictionary/investigate.

CHAPTER FIVE

Client Communication and Involvement

M ANAGING CLIENT COMMUNICATION AND involvement while performing analyses is a complicated juggling act for any investigator that can be improved by implementing a client onboarding process using scheduling software. The client onboarding process can become even more strategic in capturing high-quality leads of clients who can be helped by a forensic accountant or investigator.

Client education regarding the value that a forensic accountant and investigator can provide to a case begins at least from the initial client interaction with the firm – if not the client's interaction with the firm's website. Time should be allotted to address any misconceptions about the roles of forensic accountants, investigators, law enforcement, and the client's attorney to consistently reinforce realistic expectations.

The quality of the analysis in a Data Sleuth engagement is ultimately dependent on the quality of the communication and involvement of the client in the investigation. The better the communication between the case manager or investigator and the client, the better the data and information the client will provide throughout the entire investigation. Client involvement also reduces the risk of over- or understating losses and mistakes in the analysis because of the investigator overlooking significant events or findings specific to the client's business, marital estate, or trust.

Many forensic accounting engagements and fraud investigations originate from a negative event of some kind – often resulting in extreme skepticism of everything and everyone where there once was absolute trust. As an investigator, it may feel more comfortable to request information and have a "just trust me," hands-off approach with a client. In my experience, however, this only creates problems in the future and may result in client dissatisfaction. Although private sector investigations are to be objective, the investigators are still serving clientele who are paying for a service and promoting a positive client experience in the middle of a traumatic situation contributes to favorable client satisfaction.

 THE CASE OF THE INITIAL CLIENT MEETING

Knowing the lifestyle, assets, and business run by her husband, Susan would not settle for her soon-to-be-ex-husband's property settlement offer in their divorce. She searched the web for a "forensic accountant" to find an investigator. Susan called the investigator and explained her situation during a one-hour phone call. To wrap up the call, the investigator suggested they schedule a meeting where she could bring the case documents for the investigator to review. At her scheduled appointment time, she hauled six banker's boxes up two flights of stairs to the investigator's office. She began the meeting by pulling out piece after piece of paper theorizing about how her ex-husband was omitting assets from the marital balance sheet to give her an unfair property settlement. The investigator listened for a couple of hours to Susan jumping from one theoretical explanation to another, suppositions of girlfriends, and anything else she could imagine her husband doing to ensure she was not adequately compensated at the end of the divorce. Susan left the investigator's office. Exhausted by the lengthy stories of the day and knowing the remaining case work piled on her desk to complete, the investigator settled in for a long evening.

The next day, Susan called with more stories and theories. Susan's personality, when she was not upset about the divorce, was fun, upbeat, and positive. However, each phone call would result in the investigator offering some sort of advice or consoling Susan about the divorce itself. Over the next few weeks, the investigator started cringing when the phone rang – not because she did not want to help Susan but rather, that when the investigator was on the phone for an hour at a time, she was not making progress on the actual tasks at hand – finding the hidden assets. These long phone calls would derail concentration on the investigation and cause the investigator to work even more unexpectedly long days that began frustrating the investigator's spouse, family, and friends.

The internal conflict felt by the investigator involved the necessity of client feedback to learn more about Susan's ex-husband's business to help her find important evidence of hidden assets, but the valuable information was woven into the emotional expression of the drama Susan felt, which was inefficient and draining to the investigator. The investigator decided to allow client communication to continue its course with Susan but determined that with the next client, she would try a new approach.

Client Inquiry and Initial Meetings

The client inquiry and intake process should complement the personality of the investigator or investigative team. The process currently used by the Workman Forensics team results from numerous reiterations, and it will likely continue to change as team roles shift and change or other members are added. The current process was created out of necessity like most processes within this book. Client inquiry calls refers to individuals interested in explaining the problem they are facing and inquiring to see if our services might help in their situations and generally includes a discussion about our process and fees. Initial meetings refers to the individuals who are closer in the decision-making process to hiring us to work on their case, and these are in person or virtual video meetings where the clients, their attorneys, and our team can establish if working together makes sense.

When I was a sole proprietor, I handled all client inquiry calls and initial meetings. At first, the time on the phone with an inquiry or in a meeting with a potential client and their attorney was valuable, but as my schedule filled, fielding general inquiry calls was no longer feasible – especially when the caller realized that an expert was on the other end. By personally answering the calls, the caller whose original intention was to learn more about our services and fees would then shift the conversation into a consultation that resulted in a much longer conversation, putting a strain on the remainder of the day's schedule. I originally worked to improve the efficiency of my day by using a shared assistant to address the general inquiry questions, and if the client was interested, she would schedule an appointment on my calendar for a consultation call. This process worked wonderfully for several years until even this process was no longer feasible. I decided to collaborate with the team to incorporate the entire client inquiry and initial meeting steps into the Data Sleuth Process by implementing procedures that would filter the general callers out of the process before reaching the initial meeting stage. The external goal was to provide the best service for all individuals who called no matter where they were in the decision-making process in hiring a forensic accountant and investigator. The internal goal was to schedule initial client meetings only with clients who were highly likely to hire us. We were able to do so by first creating client-friendly content on our website in various media forms to explain what forensic accountants can do for clients in hopes to begin educating clients from their initial interaction with our website. Then we began incorporating the following client inquiry process:

- **Client inquiry.** Using a scheduling widget on our website or by calling the office, clients are able to schedule a free consultation call with a case manager.
- **Client Concerns Questionnaire.** After scheduling the consultation call, prospective clients receive a Client Concerns Questionnaire with questions guiding them to provide details about their case prior to the consultation call. This allows the prospective client an opportunity to gather his thoughts and consider the purpose behind hiring our team. Sometimes, this step alone helps the client determine that he does not need a forensic accountant, and no consultation call occurs. The completion of the questionnaire also allows the case manager to prepare for the consultation call by preparing clarifying questions for the prospective client and asking the team for input regarding the prospective client's concerns.
- **Consultation call.** The consultation call between the prospective client and the case manager is guided by the responses from the Client Concerns Questionnaire. The case manager advises of the areas in which we can help the client and those we cannot. The case manager provides a high-level overview of the Data Sleuth Process and the associated fees. This step is imperative in educating the client and forming expectations.
- **Follow-up to consultation call.** If the prospective client advises that he would like to hire our team, the case manager sends a welcome packet and engagement letter. If the prospective client is unsure or does not believe hiring would be helpful in his situation, we still provide an information packet and then follow up later to see if he would like to move forward. With either packet of information, the goal is to reinforce client education forming expectations as previously explained in the consultation call.

The initial response from prospective clients to the client inquiry changes was that of frustration and prospective clients insisting they speak with me. However, my team graciously explained that our process ensured they would be served well and that my involvement would occur later in the process. We also became proactive in publishing content by other team members on the website and hosting them as guests on the podcast, which promoted their expertise and professionalism to build trust with prospective clients prior to inquiry calls. After a few months of diligently, and at times uncomfortably, following the process, the resistance decreased, and now most of our client inquiries do not even ask to speak with me.

Initial Client Meetings

The client onboarding portion of the Data Sleuth Process has greatly reduced the number of long prospective client meetings prior to being hired. Sometimes, even after a prospective client has been through each of the process steps, he will still want to meet in person, or virtually, with his attorney or other members of his team in attendance before making a decision, and this is when I am happy to oblige and begin my involvement in the case.

Whether an initial client meeting is before or after hiring our team, we consistently prioritize communicating realistic expectations with the client.

CLIENT EXPECTATIONS

- Online content is where we begin educating prospective clients through client-targeted podcast episodes, blog posts, and YouTube videos. Most of our end-clients (i.e. nonattorneys) have never worked with a forensic accountant or investigator before, so their perspective of an investigation is shaped by what they have seen on the news, documentaries, or fictional investigation television shows – and many of those outlets do not address financial investigations. Some common misconceptions from clients include:

- **Financial databases can be used to uncover hidden bank accounts.** Financial databases are rumored to exist in uncovering bank accounts belonging to subjects or spouses by using their names, dates of birth, and social security numbers. Financial information is supposed to be protected; even law enforcement is required to obtain bank records through a grand jury subpoena. So if financial information exists in a database, the information is possibly obtained through an unethical method that would make the information inadmissible in court. It is our policy that we do not use financial databases like these.

- **When fraud is uncovered, law enforcement will arrest the subject immediately, and the subject will serve time in prison.** Because most financial investigations are nonviolent, when a police report is filed, an arrest rarely happens immediately – if at all. Regarding sentencing and prison time, many clients do not feel the punishment for the fraud against them is equitable and is too light. Most of our cases with losses between $500,000 and $3 million that were prosecuted on the federal level received sentencing within a range of house arrest for six months to three years in prison followed by several years of probation.

- **The subject has stashed the stolen funds in a hidden bank account or under her mattress.** Many clients believe that it would be impossible for subjects to spend the large sums of money that are stolen from their businesses. In all of the cases of embezzlement and corporate fraud I have worked to date, the largest amount of money identified in a subject's bank account was $80,000, and the total loss in the case exceeded $5 million. In another case, the subject stole money and invested it in real estate rentals. These are the exceptions and not the rule. Although anything may be possible, most white-collar criminals steal to gamble, shop, purchase drugs, or to fund some other habit. It is highly unlikely that a subject has stolen money to save the money.

- **Complete recovery of stolen funds, legal fees, and expert fees is possible.** If criminal charges are filed and result in restitution ordered to be paid to the client, the client may recover some of the loss. However, the subject is allowed to pay restitution based on their earnings, and because they have lost their job due to fraud, they may be limited in their future employment and thus be required to pay only $100 per month on a multimillion-dollar loss. Clients need to understand that law enforcement is not a collection agency. Even through a civil lawsuit and insurance reimbursement as possible recovery avenues, it is unlikely the client will recover all of the funds stolen. It is advantageous to investigate the situation, quantify the loss, and take reasonable steps within the recovery avenues. But the best form of recovery for a client is to implement fraud prevention and detection procedures and get back to work to earn a profit without an employee stealing it.

- **A financial investigation will be resolved in a few weeks.** Using the Data Sleuth Process, if complete information is received by the client in a timely fashion, most of our large investigations are completed within three to six months. The Data Sleuth Process does not begin on a client's case until substantively all requested information has been provided by the client. We advise clients that they affect the turnaround of the case by the timeliness, quality, and completeness of the information they provide for our analysis. The quickest resolution in which our work was followed by a criminal investigation involving a $3 million embezzlement was approximately 18 months from the initial client meeting to the subject's sentencing by a federal judge.

- **Spouses or business partners will go to prison for embezzlement.** In my experience, criminal fraud charges are not filed against spouses or business partners who have stolen from the other spouse or business owner(s) as they themselves are the owners of the assets. Embezzlement charges are filed against individuals who were entrusted with assets they did not own when they stole them.

- **All fraudulent acts are investigated by law enforcement and prosecuted.** It is helpful if clients understand that if they believe someone is intentionally defrauding them, but there is little to no evidence of the person benefiting, or there is no quantifiable loss, and it will likely not be prosecuted by law enforcement.

DATA PROCUREMENT

A financial investigation is only as good as the data and evidence available; therefore, communicating with a client to procure the best data is essential. After the case plan has been prepared, the case manager provides the copy of the case plan to the client for their approval. Accompanying the case plan is a document and information request list. The most common types of information requested for cases involving a business or not-for-profit organization include:

- Operating agreement
- Closing document
- Bank statements
- Credit card statement
- Tax returns
- Schedule K-1s
- Annual financial statements
- Loan history statements
- Accounting software backup or access to accounting software
- Accounting software password to login
- Payroll records
- Inventory records

The most common types of information requested for cases involving an individual dispute includes:

- Bank statements
- Credit card statements
- Brokerage account statements
- Retirement account statements
- Tax returns
- Personal financial statements
- Loan history statements

- Prenuptial agreements
- Pay stubs
- Life insurance policies
- Trust documents

When requesting information, we advise clients of the best formats to provide the information to improve efficiency and timeliness of data processing. We recommend formats including PDF statements downloaded directly from the bank or financial institution are preferred to paper scanned copies and, when obtaining reports from a payroll provider, to request they provide in the information in a tabular format instead of PDF reports.

If there are complications in procuring data from clients, it is in the area of payroll reports. Payroll reports are commonly provided in a PDF format that is easy to print and record in the accounting software; however, data analysis requires a tabular format to a printer-friendly report. Some payroll providers have advised in the past that a tabular export of the payroll information is not available. Printer-friendly reports can be imported by some software, but it can be time consuming, so we try to exhaust all possible options in obtaining tabular data. One successful method, when we were advised that tabular data was unavailable, was to provide the payroll provider with a spreadsheet template listing the data we needed in columns. The template was the key to obtaining the information we needed, avoiding the costly process of converting PDF payroll reports to a table.

 ## CLIENT INVOLVEMENT DURING AN INVESTIGATION

There are different theories and perspectives from forensic accountants on a client's involvement in an investigation. Some professionals believe the client involvement taints an investigation. On the other hand, some forensic accountants rely solely on the loss determined by clients, and then they will testify on their behalf. My current perspective on client involvement in an investigation is somewhere in between the two.

Having worked with law enforcement, I began my private sector investigation career from the perspective that after I obtained all the information a client wanted to provide, I would sort through it, conduct my investigation, determine a loss, issue a report, and close the case file – unless testimony was required later. The problem I continued to face with some – not all – clients was a sense of disappointment with the loss that I had calculated if certain components or nuances of their business was not factored into the resulting loss. Even though this was not the client response in every case, it still bothered me.

I began to realize that although I could use data to investigate allegations and quantify a loss, I could never fully learn, in the span of an initial interview and even follow up questions, what the client knew about his business (or marriage). Additionally, it was impossible for me to fully understand the details within every type of industry a client represented. This is when I decided to try involving the client in at least one segment of the investigation – the part of the investigation for which knowledge of a business or marriage was most valuable – feedback on analysis results.

Client Feedback

After an analysis is performed, the client's feedback is requested, if possible. The client feedback step is incorporated into the Data Sleuth Process after the completion of the Interesting Data Findings (IDF) explained in Chapter 10. Transactions may be flagged due to either the high-risk nature of the transaction or the anomalous nature of the transactions. There are Interesting Data Findings that, although they are strange from a data perspective, may be normal to the client's business, marriage, or family situation. By requesting client feedback on findings, which we generated independent of their influence and as objective professionals, then the result is a healthy balance of both approaches. If the client is able, obtaining their feedback on the data anomalies can be extremely helpful to narrow down the transactions requiring further inquiry, research, or investigation.

A great case example of the value of client feedback on analysis results was a case in which there was a jewelry purchase totaling $90,000. Based on the data analyzed, this purchase appeared suspicious compared to the other transactions. When I sat down with our client and asked her about all of the findings, and the jewelry purchase in particular, she advised it was a purchase made by her husband for her, and showed me the $90,000 ring as she was wearing it during our meeting. This example illustrates how something can appear to be an anomaly, and if I had not incorporated client feedback, I may have mistakenly included it in the loss calculation. Of course, in my early process, the client may have advised after I issued the report, but involving the client in the investigation process prior to the issuance of a report is much simpler and cleaner moving forward.

When clients provide us with feedback on the IDF, we ask them to specify if the transactions fall into one of three basic categories:

- Did the transaction, or group of transactions, benefit the business, the marital estate, or trust?
- For all of the transactions that are marked as not benefiting the business, marital estate, or trust, then we work with them to locate supporting documentation, or additional evidence, to confirm it did not benefit the client.

- For some transactions, the client is unable to advise as to whether it benefited the client, and these transactions are marked as unknown. Additionally, if the client believes a transaction did not benefit the organization, but he does not have supporting documentation, we mark the transaction as unknown. If transactions are marked as unknown by the client, or our team, additional research, interviews, or other additional investigative methods are used to obtain evidence to determine who benefited.

Upon receiving feedback on the IDF, we then will review the Source and Use Summary again for any additional transactions, or groups of transactions, necessitating client review and perform the same process of the client feedback that we did for the IDF. Many of our clients want to be involved in the investigation, and this feedback allows them to do so. Sometimes, they can even employ staff members to review emails and archived documentation while we continue with our process to expedite the turnaround of the investigation results.

Although not the most common, in some cases, the client is too far removed from the matter to provide valuable feedback. When this occurs, we still make sure to communicate findings to them, but the additional research, investigation, and analysis are performed by our team.

The Case of the Overlooked Loss

Investors in a start-up discovered two years into the project that the general manager was using investor funds for trips, meals, and other extraordinary expenses that benefited her personally. The investors hired an investigator and provided him with all of the information they believed was pertinent to the case. The investigator began reviewing all of the debit card, credit card, and check expenditures and categorized each one based on how they should have been categorized on the financial statements. If a transaction appeared to be completely personal, it was assigned to the loss category. The updated categories were totaled and compared to the profit and loss statement provided by the general manager to the investors.

The investigator presented the findings in report form to the client, and the client was outraged because they believed the loss to be grossly understated. The investigator began asking the client to specifically identify what they believed the loss did not include. The clients were particularly concerned about the expenses that had been treated as legitimate travel expenses instead of a component of the loss. Even though the expenditures were travel related, the nature of the travel was not business related and needed to be reclassified. Additionally, they advised that the investigator's loss did not uncover the excess payroll the general manager had paid himself. The loss related to payroll resulted from the comparison of checks paid directly to the general manager as a contractor versus the contractor agreement. However, the client advised that he was also paying himself through regular employee payroll at the same time.

Categorization approaches to data analysis and making decisions about the benefit of a transaction without client involvement require that the analyst make judgment calls that are dependent upon situations that occurred in which the analyst was not present. The risk associated with this type of analysis is that an investigator may overstate or understate a loss.

ONGOING CLIENT COMMUNICATION

We have found that providing clients with direct access to the case manager, from the initiation of a client engagement, works best for our team. All client communication from requesting information initially and throughout the engagement is submitted to the case manager and then the case manager contacts the client. The case manager's schedule is designed to allow for interaction and communication with the client, and it allows the analysts and other investigators to focus on their specific tasks without also needing to respond to client questions throughout the project. The case manager is assigned a routine task to follow up with each client to advise as of the status – especially if there has not been much recent communication.

When the analysis findings are compiled in a Findings Summary (further explained in Chapter 11), the case manager reviews the findings to ensure that all of the client's concerns and investigation priorities have been addressed. The case manager then schedules a meeting to review the findings with the client. This final client involvement step provides one more opportunity to address any and all outstanding items with the client before issuing a final report. In this way, when the client receives the final report, there are no surprises.

CHAPTER SIX

The Data Sleuth Case Plan

A N ATTORNEY ASKED TO meet over lunch to discuss our firm's services, and before we had even placed our order he said, "I've hired forensic accountants before who took months to look at my client's information only to report that they found nothing. They offered no consultation or recommendations for how their review would add value to my work for the client. What do you do that they don't?"

This is not the only attorney who has asked me questions similar to this one. My explanation of our services always includes advising of our case planning process that considers the client's concerns, the attorney's legal theory, and a prioritization of investigation priorities. In doing so, we avoid chasing down every rabbit trail to try to identify all of the things someone did incorrectly. Instead, this process allows us to use data to find answers that advise whether the theory of the case can be supported based on the information reviewed. In the story of the attorney lunch, the next day, we received a referral from his office to do just that.

 ## THE DATA SLEUTH PROCESS

The challenge in forensic accounting and fraud investigation engagements is that the client story, business, and data sources are always different. At first glance, these types of engagements appear to have little continuity and to require a custom approach. However, almost all financial transactions are reported on some type of account statement: a bank statement, a credit card statement, a brokerage statement, and so forth. By combining these third-party statements with business records – and personal financial records, in divorce or estate cases – most engagements can follow a structured process that will provide reliable results to the client.

The Data Sleuth Process was created to focus on the client's concerns, efficiency and accuracy in data analysis, the best evidence available, and clear communication. With these process goals in mind, the specific steps are then dependent on the types of data sources available and the analyses that can be performed using the data. Figure 6.1 illustrates the Data Sleuth Process case planning steps to be covered in this chapter.

Within this chapter, practical applications and implementation of the Data Sleuth Process case planning process will be explained and demonstrated using

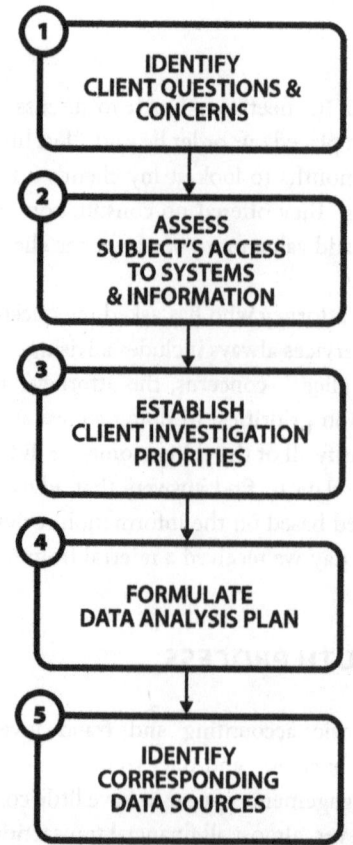

FIGURE 6.1   Data Sleuth Process case planning steps flowchart.

the following case example. Although this case involves duplicate payroll, the same process goals and implementation steps can be applied and adapted to most common forensic accounting and fraud investigation engagements.

The Case of the Duplicate Payroll

Stacey ensured she was the first person to arrive at the office daily. She started the coffee, rummaged through the previous day's mail, and familiarized herself with the boss's schedule. When her boss, George, strolled in later in the morning, he could simply start his calls with a fresh cup of coffee and get to work. With George happily busy, Stacey dutifully began her bookkeeping tasks – paying bills, running payroll, filing taxes, and tracking everything in the accounting system.

Several years of this routine passed when Stacey's mom, her best friend and long-time roommate, passed away. Even after the time off for bereavement, Stacey's grief was unbearable. She struggled to arrive at work on time, let alone early, and when she was at work, she took care of the bare minimum and passed the time by buying oddities and knickknacks online. She eventually became reactive and performed tasks only at the deadline when George yelled at her; the majority of her time at work was spent online shopping. Stacey began ignoring the negative balance and overdraft charges in her checking account. Shopping was the only thing that numbed the pain of the grief.

On one such occasion, when George was yelling at her to process payroll as it was nearly the end of payday, he told her to learn how to pay an out-of-state employee through direct deposit instead of the usual mailing of a paper check so he could receive his pay on the same day as the local employees. Stacey set up the direct deposit as requested, and while she was at it, set up her own direct deposit profile in the system as well. She considered removing her paper check from the stack for George to sign that day but, thinking of her negative bank account balance, decided against it—it would only be this one time.

Stacey's "one-time" duplicate payroll turned into four years. George was working countless hours on client projects but was unable to hire additional help because the business was not making money. He had even stopped paying himself two years prior. Stacey was on vacation when payroll needed to be issued. As if he needed another task to complete, George logged into the accounting software to print checks and submit the out-of-state employee's payroll in Stacey's absence. It was then that he noticed Stacey's name on both a check to be printed and a direct deposit profile. The amounts to be paid on both payment types were identical, and suddenly, it all made sense. Outraged, he called Stacey and told her not to return to work after vacation.

THE CLIENT'S INVESTIGATION PRIORITIES

When money goes missing, one apparently obvious way for an investigator to begin is by interviewing the client and reviewing the paper documentation the client believes is important. However, as explained in greater detail in Chapter 3, this manual approach has several issues, including potential bias and an incomplete loss calculation.

When investigating cases like George and Stacey's story, the first step in the Data Sleuth Process is to understand the client's concerns and to identify the investigation priorities. These priorities are created by listening to the client's communication of the events that transpired and the issues they observed. As they are sharing their stories, area(s) of concern can be recognized. These areas of concern can then be translated into investigation priorities. For example, the top investigation priorities detected in the initial consultation with George were to:

- Quantify the amount of money overpaid to Stacey through payroll
- Identify any other areas where Stacey may have stolen money and quantify accordingly

EVALUATE THE SUBJECT'S ACCESS THROUGH RISK-BASED ANALYSIS

When a client has just discovered fraud and emotions are running high, it is easy to see how the areas of client concern – and the time and budget required to address them – can quickly multiply. This is where the investigator's understanding of fraud risk can improve the efficiency of the investigation. For each investigation priority, an evaluation of the subject's access to the client's financial systems and information must be performed. If the subject does not have access that would give her the opportunity to steal funds, the likelihood that the client's allegation will be substantiated with further analysis is greatly reduced.

In the initial client consultation, as George explained the circumstances surrounding his discovery, he was overwhelmed with the seemingly infinite number of ways Stacey could have stolen from him. One such example was his concern that she could have diverted customer payments to her personal bank account. As part of the consultation, George was asked about the client billing and payment receipt process. He advised that:

- Stacey prepared the client invoices, but George reviewed, approved, and submitted the invoices to the clients for payment.

- Due to the nature of the business, client invoices were charged against a client-approved project budget.
- The clients served by George's business paid invoices via ACH directly to the business bank account.
- George received email confirmations of the payments, which he then forwarded to Stacey to mark the client invoice as paid in the accounting system.

Although the diversion of customer payments was a concern, talking with George about his business process in relation to Stacey's access allowed him to realize the risk of theft in this area was low. It was then determined that the area of customer payments was not going to be an investigation priority – unless evidence uncovered later in the process suggested otherwise.

However, if the subject did have access to the systems and information that provided the opportunity to steal funds, understanding the subject's level of access to the systems and information is necessary to prepare an investigative plan. With this understanding, the preferred data sources and resulting data analysis procedures will be identified based on the subject's access.

Stacey had the following access to the client's business systems and information:

- Administrative access to the accounting system, including the reconciliation of bank and credit card statements
- Administrative access to prepare, submit, and release payroll funds
- Direct access to the client's business online banking including the abilities to use bill pay and initiate interbank transfers
- Direct access to use the business credit card, obtain credit card statements, and release funds to pay the monthly credit card bill

With this information, the investigation priorities could be more specifically defined as follows:

- Quantify the amount overpaid to Stacey through payroll.
- Identify any other areas Stacey may have stolen money and quantify accordingly:
  - Payments from the business bank account benefiting Stacey.
  - Charges to the business credit card benefiting Stacey.

Business processes vary from business to business, and investigators who may not be as familiar with accounting processes may find the Data Sleuth Fraud

Detection Worksheet to be a valuable tool when it comes to evaluating a subject's access and narrowing down the investigation priorities. This worksheet will be explained in greater detail in Chapter 7. Download a copy of the Data Sleuth Fraud Detection Worksheet at www.datasleuthbook.com.

DATA SLEUTH ANALYSIS FRAMEWORK

Before preparing the Data Analysis Plan, it is important to understand the Data Sleuth Analysis Framework. Data analysis in other disciplines often involves large data sets or "big data" for which much of the analysis is statistical in nature. In a traditional audit engagement, statistical sampling is used to identify transactions to test with the goal of providing an opinion as to whether a company's financial statements are without material misstatement. An audit does not look at every transaction within the company; therefore, because of materiality thresholds, an audit is not designed to uncover fraud.

In forensic accounting and fraud investigation engagements, the investigation and resulting findings must be performed and prepared in anticipation of civil litigation or criminal prosecution, whether actualized or not. For the investigation findings to be effective in these venues, the total loss amount must be supported by specific, itemized transactions in order to contribute to the plaintiff attorney's or prosecutor's case in meeting their relative burdens of proof. In order for a prosecutor to file embezzlement charges against a business's former employee totaling $100,000, every transaction comprising the $100,000 must be specifically identified. A loss estimate based on statistical sampling that identifies a few instances of theft and uses these to represent the entire population of transactions will not assist a plaintiff's attorney or prosecutor.

Most data analysis in forensic accounting and fraud investigation engagements involves the comparison of at least two data or information sources. This framework is illustrated simply through the use of a Venn diagram (see Figure 6.2).

When a data or information source that supports the events that happened are compared to the data or information source that supports the events that should have happened, at the intersection of the two, transactions or events that occur in both data sources are identified. These are generally considered verified and need no further investigation. The transactions or events that remain outside of the intersection are those that should be investigated further or, depending on the data sets being compared, may represent the loss.

USE DATA SUPPORTING

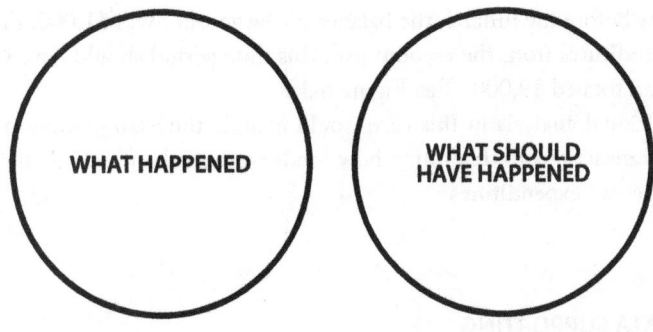

TO PERFORM A COMPARATIVE ANALYSIS

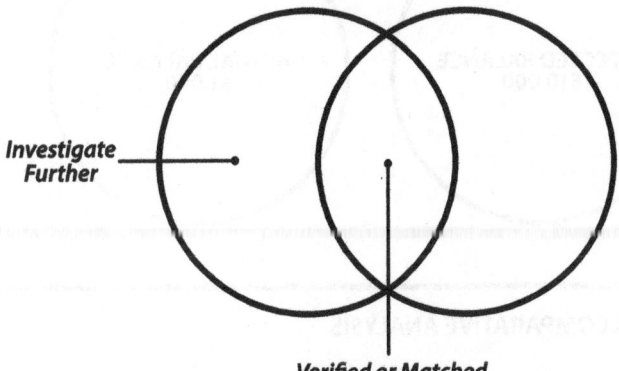

FIGURE 6.2 Illustration of using conceptual Venn diagram in engagements.

Data Sleuth Analysis Framework Applications

Analysis of the data sources comparing what happened to what should have happened can be applied to almost every type of dispute over missing money. The following case examples illustrate the application of comparative analysis to different types of common forensic accounting and fraud investigation engagements.

Case Example: Estate Dispute

A family claims the balance of their father's bank account should have totaled $10,000 as of the date of his death, as it was to be used to pay his funeral expenses.

Instead, the ending bank account balance totals $1,000. The balance of the father's bank account as of the date of death was confirmed as totaling $10,000; however, on the day before the funeral, the balance of the account was $1,000. Put another way, expenditures from the account over this time period should have totaled $0, but instead totaled $9,000. (See Figure 6.3.)

Additional analysis in this case would include the examination of the bank account transactions to determine how funds were used and who benefited from the unexpected expenditures.

USE DATA SUPPORTING

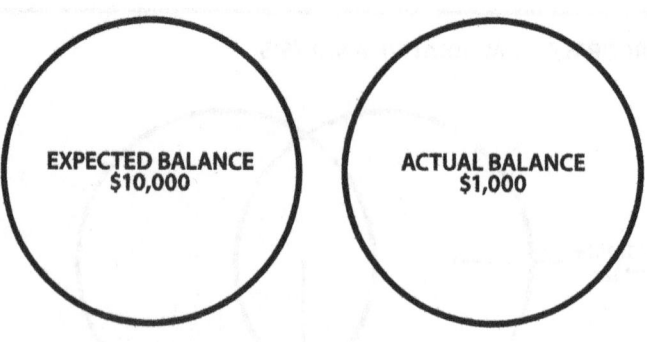

TO PERFORM A COMPARATIVE ANALYSIS

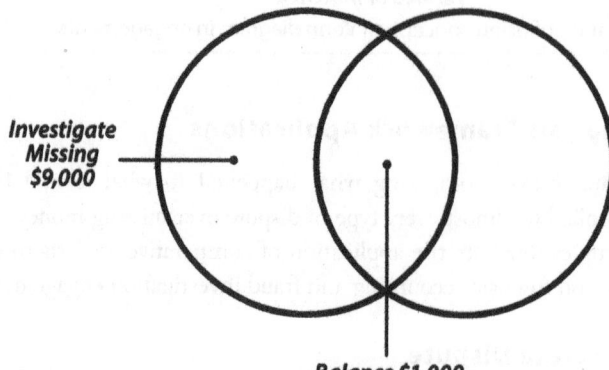

FIGURE 6.3 Venn diagram illustration comparing expected balance to actual balance.

Case Example: Embezzlement

A business owner has an employment contract in which an employee agreed to be paid on commission as the employee sold products based on the product type code. The employee discovered a malfunctioning module in the inventory system that allowed him to override the product type code without affecting the item code or description, which would have resulted in inventory count issues. When the employee would sell a product, he would change the product type code to that which paid a higher commission.

The overpayment of commission to the employee is determined by comparing the commission paid with the incorrect product type codes to the commission that should have been paid with the correct product type codes. The resulting difference will quantify the overpayment of commission and the loss to the business. (See Figure 6.4.)

USE DATA SUPPORTING

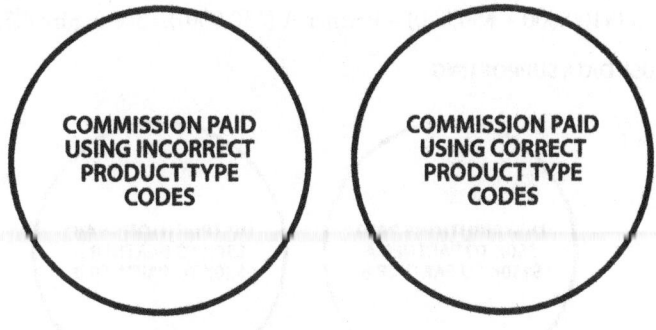

TO PERFORM A COMPARATIVE ANALYSIS

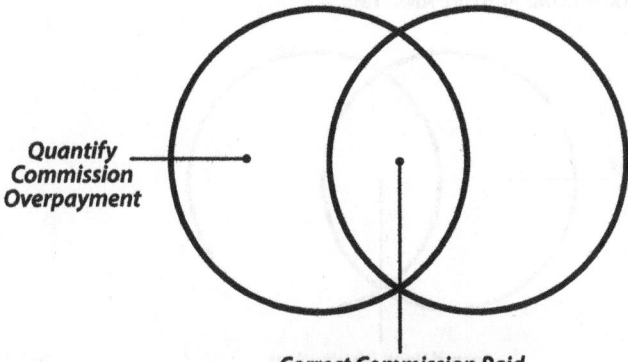

FIGURE 6.4 Venn diagram illustration comparing commission paid under incorrect and correct product type codes.

Additional data analysis that would be helpful in this case would be to examine audit logs, if they exist, providing evidence as to the employee's actions in changing the correct product type code to the incorrect product type code resulting in higher commission payments. This analysis would assist in providing evidence demonstrating the "intent" component of the fraud.

Case Example: Partnership Dispute

Business Partner A accused Business Partner B, who managed the business's finances, of paying himself an additional $100,000 from company funds beyond their total agreed-upon distributions to date of $50,000. Using the parameters defined in the operating agreement regarding the timing and amounts of distributions to partners in conjunction with a list of payments to all partners derived from the business bank statements, the expected payments, based on the operating agreement, were compared to all payments paid to all partners. Excess distributions were calculated based on this comparison, and the money missing from the business totaled $100,000 (Partner B ($100,000 + $50,000) – Partner A ($50,000)). (See Figure 6.5.)

USE DATA SUPPORTING

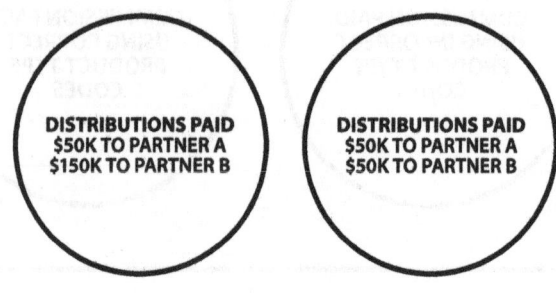

TO PERFORM A COMPARATIVE ANALYSIS

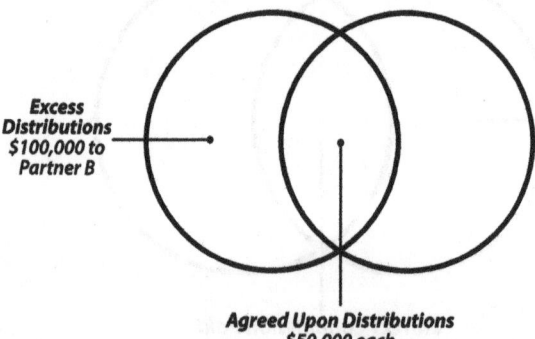

FIGURE 6.5   Venn diagram illustration of excess distributions to Partner B.

Case Example: Divorce

Before filing for divorce, a husband claimed he earned a gross salary of $20,000 per month. However, after filing for divorce, the husband advised he earned $10,000 per month. The wife discovered that their joint bank account supported this claim as only $8,000 per month was being deposited to the account, after taxes and other benefits deductions. Although it was reasonable that a portion of the gross salary would not be deposited to the checking account due to deductions for taxes and benefits, the direct deposit of less than half of the salary claimed prior to filing indicated money was missing. By comparing the wages listed on the couple's tax returns to the prior year deposits to the joint account and to the deposits after filing, it was determined that, at most, $12,000 per month was missing ($20,000 – $8,000). An adjustment was then needed to account for tax and benefits deductions to calculate a more precise total of missing money. (See Figure 6.6.)

USE DATA SUPPORTING

TO PERFORM A COMPARATIVE ANALYSIS

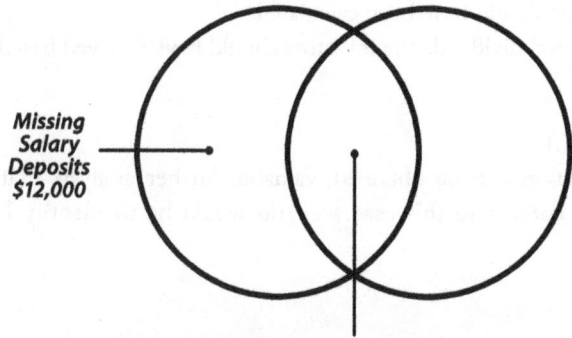

Known Salary Deposits $8,000

FIGURE 6.6   Venn diagram illustration of missing salary in joint bank account.

Additional data sources helpful in cases such as this include copies of the husband's paystubs for the relevant period. A common way funds are diverted in divorce when the spouse is employed, or receives regular payroll, is by directing the deposits to be split into multiple bank accounts. The paystubs requested should list the amounts deposited to each account. A paystub is another example of third-party "best evidence" in that the subject of the investigation did not control the reporting of this information.

Case Example: Economic Damages

A closely held company told its investors they would receive a percentage of the net profits on a quarterly basis from a subsidiary. There was an agreement between the subsidiary and the parent company that required the subsidiary to pay management fees totaling 10% of the subsidiary's gross revenues. The investors did not receive the quarterly dividends as promised, so evidence was obtained through discovery in a lawsuit to recalculate the intercompany management fee. The management fee paid from the subsidiary to the parent company was 15% of the subsidiary's gross revenues instead of the 10% stated in the agreement. This increase caused the subsidiary to operate at a loss, and the investors did not receive the quarterly dividends originally promised.

The overpayment of management fees to the parent company and resulting loss to the investors were calculated as follows:

- Recalculate the subsidiary's quarterly net income using management fee percentage as stated in the agreement (in other words, identify what the net income "should have been").
- Compare the resulting quarterly net income from the recalculation to the net income reported with the overstated management fee. Assuming all other factors remain the same, the difference between the two for all quarters quantifies the total overpayment of management fees and the lost net income on which dividends should have been calculated.
- Calculate the total dividends the investors should have received based on the agreement.

(See Figure 6.7.)

If the information can be obtained, valuable further analysis that would provide additional context to this case scenario would be to identify how the

USE DATA SUPPORTING

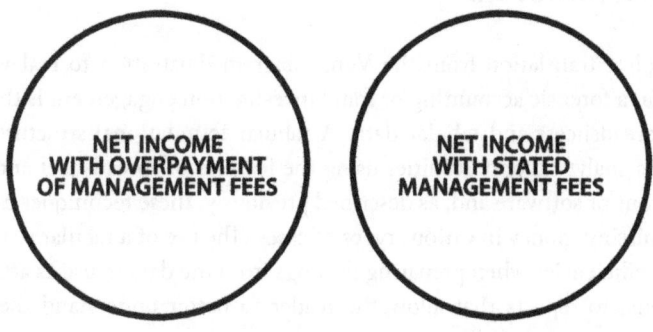

TO PERFORM A COMPARATIVE ANALYSIS

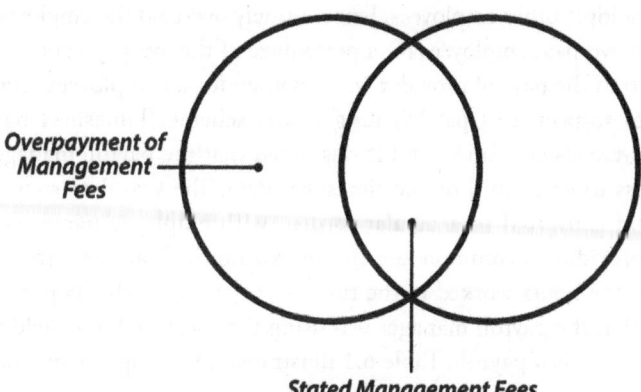

FIGURE 6.7 Venn diagram illustration comparison of net income with inflated management fee to net income with stated management fee.

overpayment of management fees were used by the parent company (e.g. executive bonuses). Any evidence that can be obtained where the accounting staff members were instructed to charge this overstated management fee could be helpful evidence of management's intentions (e.g. emails).

FROM CONCEPTUAL VENN DIAGRAM TO COMPARATIVE DATA ANALYSIS

The simplest translation from the Venn diagram illustration to real-world data analysis in a forensic accounting or fraud investigation engagement is through the use of spreadsheets and tabular data. A tabular foundational structure provides numerous analytical opportunities using the features of spreadsheet and database applications or software and, as described previously, these techniques can be used to find missing money in various types of cases. The use of a tabular structure also provides efficiencies when preparing findings from the data to use as attachments, or exhibits, to reports that allow the reader to better understand the resulting conclusions.

A great example illustrating the multiple benefits of tabular comparative data analysis is "The Case of the Cash Back Payroll Scheme" from Chapter 3 in which Vince discovered money was being stolen from his company by his chief executive officer, Jane, and multiple other employees. Jane routinely overpaid the employees and then asked the overpaid employees for a percentage of the overpayment.

Payroll data from the payroll provider was obtained for all employees – not just the employees suspected of participating in the scheme. Timesheet data for all employees were also obtained, and it was noted that the payroll manager did not have access to or control of the timesheet data. The two data sources were processed and converted to a tabular format, with employee names and pay period dates providing a common key. By comparing the hours reported in the payroll data to the hours worked in the timesheet data for each pay period, it was discovered that the payroll manager was using the vacation hours field to inflate the other employees' payroll. Table 6.1 illustrates this comparative tabular analysis.

Because the data were in a tabular format in which calculation formulas could be applied to the entire data set, not only were the inflated hours and resulting overpayments quantified, but it was also discovered that there were more employees participating in the scheme than originally believed. Performing data investigations in this way allows the investigator to evaluate all employees efficiently instead of focusing on just the known employees under investigation. This approach will often uncover additional discrepancies throughout the organization, as it did in this example, and it is helpful should the subject employee accuse management of bias.

TABLE 6.1   Comparative analysis of payroll data and timesheet data.

Comparison of Payroll Reports to Timesheets For the Relevant Period						
Payroll Reports			*Timesheets*			
Pay Date	Employee	Gross Hours	Pay Date	Employee	Hours Worked	Difference
01/07/16	Employee A	262.00	01/07/16	Employee A	161.00	101.00
01/07/16	Employee B	251.00	01/07/16	Employee B	173.00	78.00
01/07/16	Employee C	231.50	01/07/16	Employee C	154.50	77.00
01/07/16	Employee D	264.50	01/07/16	Employee D	174.50	90.00
01/07/16	Employee E	257.50	01/07/16	Employee E	179.50	78.00
01/07/16	Employee F	234.50	01/07/16	Employee F	167.50	67.00
01/07/16	Employee G	257.00	01/07/16	Employee G	171.00	86.00
01/07/16	Payroll Mgr	355.00	01/07/16	Payroll Mgr	170.00	185.00
01/15/16	Employee A	220.50	01/15/16	Employee A	152.50	68.00
01/15/16	Employee B	243.00	01/15/16	Employee B	204.50	38.50
01/15/16	Employee C	219.50	01/15/16	Employee C	147.00	72.50
01/15/16	Employee D	192.50	01/15/16	Employee D	163.50	29.00
01/15/16	Employee E	245.00	01/15/16	Employee E	104.50	140.50
01/15/16	Employee F	226.00	01/15/16	Employee F	175.00	51.00
01/15/16	Employee G	227.00	01/15/16	Employee G	172.00	55.00
01/15/16	Payroll Mgr	241.00	01/15/16	Payroll Mgr	173.00	68.00
TOTALS		3,927.50			2,643.00	**1,284.50**

As also shown in Table 6.1, the tabular structure makes the creation of tables, attachments, or exhibits to the findings report simple, and it clearly depicts specific, itemized transactions. This allows the business owner, attorney, or prosecutor to take their next steps with clear, concise, and simplified information. Comparative analysis is only one of several standard Data Sleuth analyses that will be explained further in chapters 9 and 10.

 THE DATA ANALYSIS PLAN

After connecting the understanding of a subject's access to systems and information to the data available, a data analysis plan can be created. The data analysis plan should address the investigation priorities considering the data that should be available based on the examination of the subject's access.

Investigation Priority Number 1

To quantify the amount overpaid to Stacey through payroll, the data analysis plan would likely include the following:

- Compare the payroll reports to the bank statements to ensure the total amount paid on the payroll report reconciles to the amount debited from the bank account.
- If the payroll reports do not reconcile to the bank statements, examine the audit log to see if any of the payroll entries from the accounting software were deleted or altered. If so, identify the details of the original item deleted or altered. If possible and reliable, note the username associated with the deletion or change.
- Compare the total amount paid to Stacey (perhaps requiring a recalculation if step number two is necessary) to the employment agreement and documentation of bonuses and/or raises.
- Make inquiries regarding any differences, if needed. Often this difference, net of any responses to inquiries, will result in the amount of overpayment and loss to the client or business.

Investigation Priority Number 2

To examine payments from the business bank account and to identify potential payments benefiting the subject instead of the business, the data analysis plan would likely include the following at a minimum. More details regarding how to perform each analysis listed here will be explained in chapters 9 and 10.

1. Identify whether or not the bank account has been reconciled within the accounting software. If it has not, it is likely that any transactions benefiting the subject were never recorded. If it has been reconciled, special attention should be paid to step number five in this list.
2. Using the most reliable data source, which in this example is the bank statement data instead of the accounting system data, summarize transactions by payee to identify potential payments benefiting Stacey instead of the business.
3. Analyze individual bank transactions for irregularities including, but not limited to, even dollar payments, payments to unknown vendors/entities, and total number of payments by payee.

4. Compare the irregular transactions identified in steps two and three to their categorization on the general ledger.
   - This step allows the investigator to evaluate whether or not the categorization of the transaction is reasonable. For example, if Stacey wrote a check to herself and categorized the transaction as rent in the general ledger, and if she does not own the property being leased by the business, further research regarding this transaction should be performed. This step in the analysis process may provide evidence of the subject's intention to hide the transaction from the owner or management in addition to potentially flagging additional irregular transactions for investigation.
5. Search the audit log for any transactions that are not identified on the general ledger or check register that may have been changed or deleted.
   - The transactions listed on the bank statement are the most reliable source to determine how the business's funds were spent. However, reviewing items in the audit log to identify deleted and/or changed transactions may be used to provide evidence indicating the intention of the subject to hide the actual transaction from the owner or management.

Investigation Priority Number 3

To examine payments from the credit card account to identify potential charges benefiting the subject instead of the business, the data analysis plan would include steps similar to that from priority number 2. One distinctive step related to credit card transaction analysis includes:

- Reconcile credit card payments listed on the business bank statement to the known credit card statements. This step will identify if business funds were used to pay the balance for an unknown credit card account. Inquiry into the additional payments could uncover an additional business credit card (for which the same analysis steps should be performed), or the additional payments could identify a personal credit card of the subject, or another employee, being paid with business funds.

 ## DATA AND INFORMATION GATHERING

During case planning, a relevant period is defined. The investigator and client should have an agreement as to the period of time for which the data should be analyzed. This is extremely important when a client is being charged by the consultant, because fees for financial investigations will strongly correlate with the number of years of data to be analyzed. Additionally, defining the relevant period is necessary when gathering data to ensure the data obtained is as complete as possible for the entire period before beginning the analysis. This prevents the need to continue to return to the client for additional information once the analysis step has begun and greatly improves the efficiency of the investigation.

Having determined a relevant period and using the subject's access and the investigation priorities as the foundation, a list of data sources and related information should be requested. The list of information requested from George included the following:

- **A backup copy of the client's accounting system.** A backup copy allows the investigator to import the data into her copy of the accounting system and export the appropriate and preferred reports for analysis. When the investigator does not have a copy of the accounting software, specific reports and/ or exports should be requested. It is recommended to obtain both PDF and CSV or Microsoft Excel versions of each report, when possible, to ensure that the tabular data reconciles to the printed or PDF version of the report in the system.

  In the example of George and Stacey, the reports and exports necessary for further analysis included the following organized by investigation priority:
  - Priority No. 1: Detailed payroll reports
  - Priority No. 1: Audit log reports
  - Priority No. 2: General ledger reports
  - Priority No. 2: Check register reports for bank account transactions and credit card transactions (if recorded using detailed transactions by Stacey)
- **Bank account statement copies, including check images.** Bank account statement copies will assist with the analysis related to investigation priority numbers 1 and 2 as they are the most reliable data source in identifying how the business's funds were actually used. It's important to note that in many cases, accounting records do not constitute "best evidence" and are not a substitute for the account statements themselves.
- **Credit card account statement copies.** Credit card account statement copies will assist with the investigation priority number 2 as they are the most reliable data pertaining to how the credit card was used to ultimately determine whether the charges benefited Stacey personally or benefited the business.
- **Employment agreement and documentation concerning bonuses or pay increases.** As explained in greater detail in Chapter 9, many data-focused

financial investigations require a comparison of at least two of these sources of information:

1. **Always required.** A data source that was least likely to be controlled or altered by the subject. This is the most reliable source, or the baseline for the comparison. This source often provides evidence showing what transactions occurred. The most common example of this type of data source is a bank statement.
2. **Comparative source option.** A data source that was controlled by the subject that often shows what the subject wants the client to believe happened. The most common example of this type of data source is the accounting system and/or exported reports.
3. **Comparative source option.** A data source that identifies what should have happened if the subject had not stolen funds. A common example of this type of data source is an employment agreement.

In this case example, an employment agreement would state the terms of employment for Stacey including whether or not she was to receive a salary or hourly pay. Documentation of bonuses and pay increases, in addition to the employment agreement, provides the baseline for the total pay Stacey should have received, which can then be compared to the amount she actually received. Any difference between the two would either indicate additional investigation is needed or would provide results to quantify the overpayment of payroll.

COMMUNICATION OF THE CASE PLAN

A case plan should be developed in every engagement and provided to the client for review. This ensures that the priorities the investigator developed from the initial client consultation accurately reflect the priorities of the client before the actual work begins. Table 6.2 illustrates a case plan for all investigation priorities in George's case.

The case plan also provides a list to the client of the most important data sources necessary to perform the analyses listed in the Data Analysis Plan column of Table 6.2. It is not uncommon that the client does not have the information or lacks access to the data requested. Collaboration and communication with the client is vital in this step as the client may need assistance in troubleshooting access issues. Sometimes the Data Analysis Plan may need to be adjusted to create an analysis that will have meaningful results despite the missing information. Upon the client's acceptance of the case plan, the investigation begins.

TABLE 6.2 Case plan prepared for George's example case.

Priority No.	Investigation Priority Description	Data Sources	Data Analysis Plan
1	Quantify the amount overpaid to subject through payroll.	*Detailed payroll reports *Audit log reports *Bank statements *Employment agreement *Documentation of raises and bonuses	1. Payroll reports versus bank statement payroll debits 2. Compare total amount paid to subject to employment agreements and other documentation.
2	Identify any other areas subject may have stolen money and quantify accordingly.		
2a	Examine payments from the business bank account to identify potential payments benefiting subject instead of the business.	*General ledger reports *Check register reports *Bank statements/check images	1. Determine whether or not the bank accounts are reconciled in the accounting system. 2. Summarize and analyze bank transactions to identify potential payments benefiting the subject. 3. Identify irregularities in general ledger categorization and in the audit log.
2b	Examine charges to the business credit card to identify potential payments benefiting subject instead of the business.	*General ledger reports *Check register reports *Credit card statements	1. Summarize and analyze credit card transactions to identify potential charges that did not benefit the business. 2. Identify irregularities in the general ledger categorization and in the audit log.

 THE CASE OF THE DUPLICATE PAYROLL – CONCLUSION

The analysis of payments to Stacey through payroll identified that not only had she duplicated her payroll over the four years, but she also paid herself outside of the payroll cycle, including payments issued on weekends, using the direct deposit profile she created. Check payments and direct deposit payments were plotted on

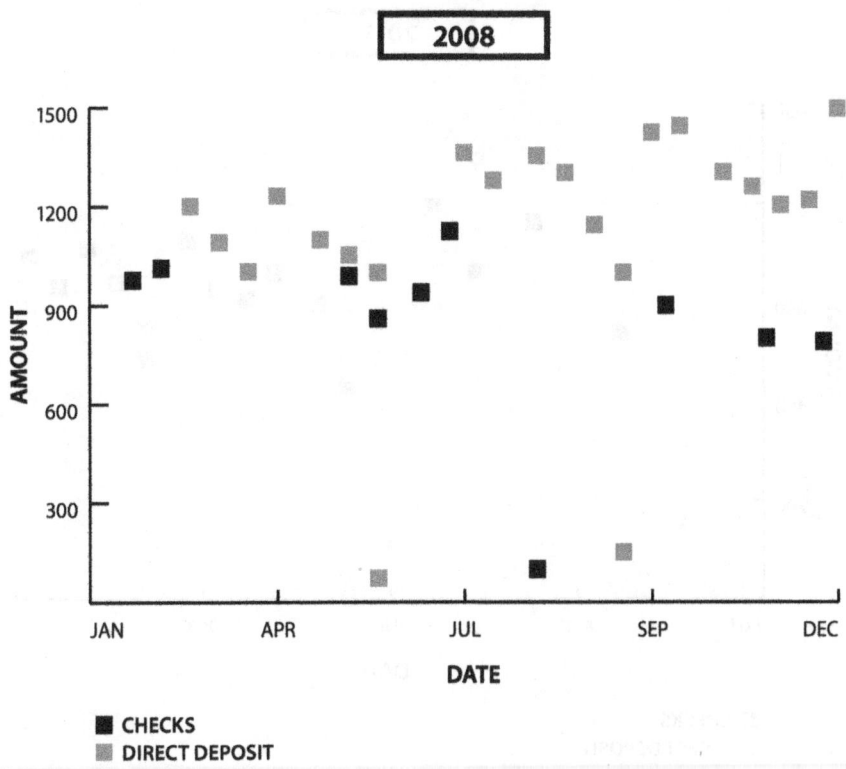

FIGURE 6.8   Check and direct deposit payments to Stacey during 2008.

a graph by year for the relevant period. As shown in Figures 6.8 and 6.9, the number of extra payments to Stacey from 2008 to 2011 increased greatly in frequency. The additional payments over the four-year relevant period totaled approximately $101,000. Audit log entries provided evidence of Stacey's intention to hide the additional payments from George as she deleted many of them from the accounting software.

Stacey did not regularly reconcile the business bank account. However, examination of the bank account statements, and credit card statements, did not uncover any additional payments benefiting Stacey during the relevant period. She simply overpaid herself through payroll.

Stacey was charged federally with wire fraud because the direct deposit payments were initiated at the business's local bank and were transferred to Stacey's bank, whose headquarters were outside of the state. Stacey pleaded guilty and was sentenced to 6 months in prison followed by 36 months of probation and was ordered to pay restitution.

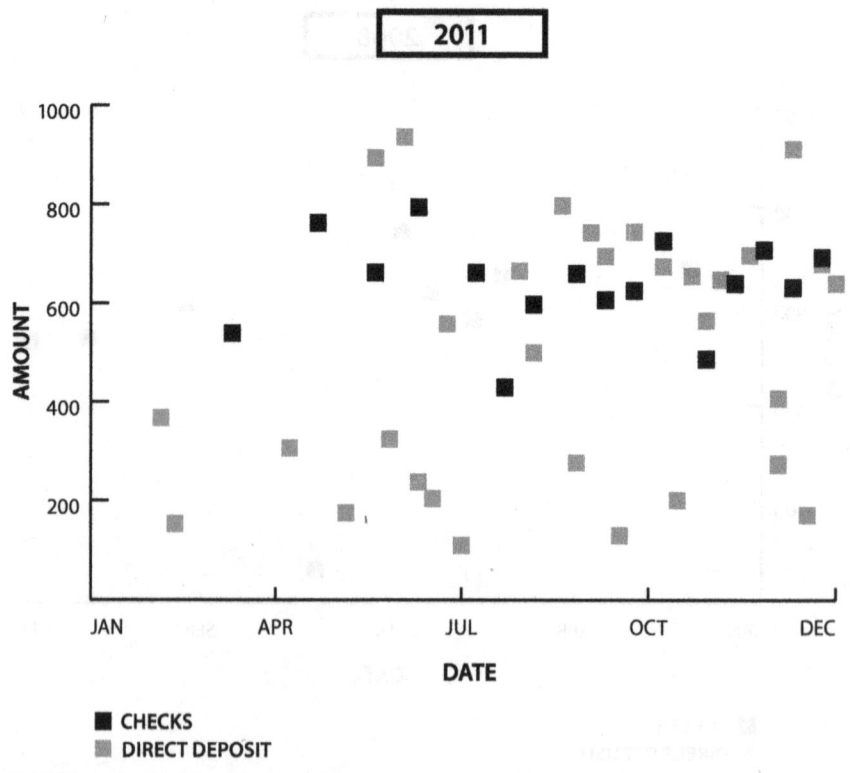

FIGURE 6.9 Check and direct deposit payments to Stacey during 2011.

CHAPTER SEVEN

Risk-Based Analysis

B EFORE PREPARING A CASE plan, evaluating the most vulnerable areas of fraud, hidden assets, understated income, or any other client concern is important in a forensic accounting engagement or fraud investigation. This evaluation is especially important when a client does not know where the issues originate within the organization. A risk-based analysis helps an investigator prioritize the areas to examine, addressing the client's concerns while making the best use of their time and financial resources. It also serves as a guide for the investigator and prevents them from jumping to conclusions and making claims not supported by evidence. A similar analysis is performed in engagements involving individuals, such as divorce or estate and trust disputes, as discussed at the end of this chapter.

Such an analysis should begin by focusing on the sources and uses of cash as further described in Chapter 9 and the procedures associated with the collection and distributions of cash. It can be tempting to start with accounting records and journal entries, but these are not the primary data sources that will identify missing money, though they can be useful as a secondary source to understand how an event occurred and provide evidence of the context or intent behind the potential diversion of funds.

With cash sources and uses as the primary focus, the investigator should next consider the internal controls surrounding how funds are received into the organization and how they are disbursed. Understanding these internal controls will allow the investigator to identify the areas of highest risk and prioritize these within the investigation.

The Data Sleuth Fraud Detection Worksheet provides a framework for identifying key questions and observations to facilitate this understanding. Later in this chapter, further demonstration will be provided regarding how the worksheet can be used to identify the risks associated with cash flows into and out of an organization.

 ## THE CASE OF THE PUZZLING ENTRIES

Randy owned several businesses in the healthcare sector that involved billing Medicare, the US Department of Veterans Affairs (VA), and health insurance companies. Randy was very successful with the marketing and sales side of the business, and he reviewed the company's financials on a regular basis. After several months had passed in which he found himself repeatedly thinking, "Something is wrong with cash. We should have more cash than this," Randy reached out to an investigator. The investigator began the engagement by learning about the irregularities Randy had noticed, which included the following:

- The company's costs had remained the same, and patient count was steady, but the business was now operating at a net loss.
- When asked about the losses, the CFO gave Randy a variety of reasons but ultimately explained it away as a "timing difference."
- Randy knew that there were quite a few bank accounts handling the cash for the business's various locations, but he did not know how many bank accounts existed. The CFO and Randy both had signature authority on the bank accounts.
- The CFO had requested that Randy contribute several hundred thousand dollars over the last couple of years to help the business's cash flow shortages.

With this information, there were several approaches the investigator could take. Because Randy did not know where the cash issue was originating, the investigator's next step was to ask questions that would help them identify areas of highest risk and design the case plan accordingly.

Focus on Cash

The primary reason a forensic accountant or fraud investigator is hired is to find missing money, and in turn, the investigator's job is to identify how the money went missing, if unknown, and to quantify the amount missing. Because these tasks comprise the investigator's primary responsibility in an investigation, he should focus on areas involving cash. The term "cash" in this context does not exclusively refer to green paper money or currency but rather any liquid resource or method of funds transfer that increases someone's purchasing power. These resources include cash, currency, credit card receipts and payments, PayPal, Venmo, and so forth.

It is a common error for those with a professional background in auditing and accounting to want to begin by reviewing the financial statements and journal entries and the internal controls surrounding them. However, journal entries do not allow someone a lot of playing time at the casino. In other words, someone who is committing fraud (with the exception of financial statement fraud, which is for the most part outside the scope of this book) is doing so to fund expenditures such as shopping, gambling, drugs, or medical bills, and these require cash. Later in the chapter, the concepts regarding how and when accounting records are useful in an investigation will be detailed, but they are not the starting point. The most efficient, effective investigators begin by understanding the internal controls surrounding the sources and uses of cash within an organization. Figure 7.1 is an example illustration of how cash sources and uses, internal controls, and accounting records fit together in the investigator's initial conceptualization of a case plan.

Tools like the Data Sleuth Fraud Detection Worksheet (available for download at www.datasleuthbook.com) can be used to facilitate the identification of cash sources and uses and the level of risk associated with the internal controls (or lack thereof) relating to each. The following sections will demonstrate how the Data Sleuth Fraud Detection Worksheet can be applied to the investigation of Randy's healthcare businesses.

Money In

Cash comes into an organization primarily through sales and/or donations. There may be some other income from investments or scrap sales, such as in manufacturing, but most cash generated in a business is through sales of goods or services and in a not-for-profit organization through donations. For this example, the Fraud Detection Worksheet will focus on a business issue – that of Randy's healthcare businesses. The Fraud Detection Worksheet is divided into two sections: "Money In" and "Money Out." Table 7.1 shows the "Money In" section with columns completed for "The Case of the Puzzling Entries" based on Randy's initial consultation with the investigator. Note that although all sources of funds are essentially sales revenue, they have been distinguished based on the specific source and/or method of payment, as different sources or methods may have different internal controls and be associated with different risks.

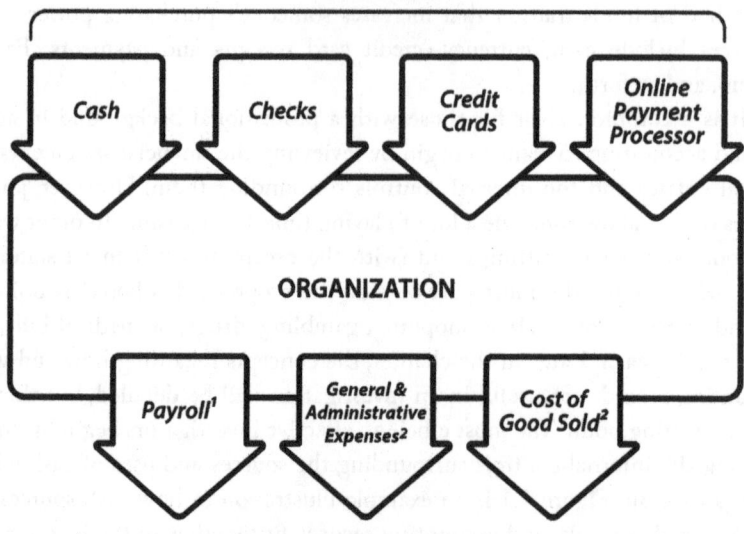

CASH SOURCES/MONEY IN

Sales Revenue

Cash Checks Credit Cards Online Payment Processor

ORGANIZATION

Payroll[1] General & Administrative Expenses[2] Cost of Good Sold[2]

CASH USES/MONEY OUT

Use understanding of internal controls to identify areas of highest risk; focus investigation here

Consider where accounting records and journal entries can be used to provide context, demonstrate how funds were diverted and detection avoided, and ultimately show intent

[1]Third-Party Processor
[2]Operating Account

FIGURE 7.1 Illustration of interconnectivity of cash, internal controls, and accounting records.

Having completed the worksheet based on Randy's responses, the investigator identified the highest fraud risk areas in the cash collection process to include those under the control and responsibility of the CFO. It was possible under the existing controls that the CFO could:

■ Divert check payments to a bank account with a similar name to that of the business;
■ Divert credit card payments to an account controlled by the CFO; or
■ Change direct deposit instructions with Medicare, the VA, and insurance companies to an account controlled by the CFO.

TABLE 7.1 "Money In" section of the Data Sleuth Fraud Detection Worksheet for "The Case of the Puzzling Entries."

Data Sleuth Fraud Detection Worksheet
MONEY IN

Payments from Medicare and Veterans Affairs via Direct Deposit

People who touch the payment from the origination to bank deposit	When and where do these people touch the payment?	If this person stole funds, where could it happen?	If funds were stolen, how would you know?
No one – direct deposit	N/A	CFO could change the bank accounts associated with direct deposits; however, it would not be a simple process with Medicare.	Compare expected Medicare payments to those deposited to the known bank account(s).

Payments from Insurance Companies via Check, Direct Deposit, or ACH

People who touch the payment from the origination to bank deposit	When and where do these people touch the payment?	If this person stole funds, where could it happen?	If funds were stolen, how would you know?
Corporate headquarters office manager	*Checks:* At corporate headquarters, retrieve checks from mail; prepare a deposit slip; provide deposit to CFO to post to patient accounts; run checks through check reader to deposit to bank. *Direct Deposit:* N/A	Divert check payments to a bank account with a similar name to the business.	If payments were posted to patient accounts: The bank reconciliation would show a discrepancy and would be noticed by the CFO who performed the reconciliations. If payments were not posted to patient accounts: Patient account aging would be high, and patients may report the statement balance is incorrect or that payments were sent and were not applied correctly.

(continued)

TABLE 7.1 (Continued)

People who touch the payment from the origination to bank deposit	When and where do these people touch the payment?	If this person stole funds, where could it happen?	If funds were stolen, how would you know?
CFO	*Checks and Direct Deposit:* Apply payment to patient balance and make the deposit through a check reader to the bank.	Divert check payments (private party or insurance checks) to a bank account with a similar name to the business. Change the bank account associated with direct deposits, but would not be a simple process with the insurance company.	Total checks returned to office manager would not match the deposit slip originally prepared by the office manager. If payments were posted to patient accounts: The bank reconciliation would show a discrepancy. If payments were not posted to patient accounts: Patient account aging would be high, and patients may report the statement balance is incorrect or that payments were sent and were not applied correctly.
Payments from Private Party/Copayments via Check or Credit Card			
People who touch the payment from the origination to bank deposit	When and where do these people touch the payment?	If this person stole funds, where could it happen?	If funds were stolen, how would you know?
Receptionist at each location	*Checks and Cash:* Prepare deposit and run report of payments from system; return deposit and report to corporate headquarters.	Take cash from the deposit. Divert check payments to a bank account with a similar name to the business.	Deposit report would not tie to the total deposit received by the CFO. Patient account aging would be too high. Patients may report inaccurate statements and account balances.
CFO	Performs reconciliation monthly.	Divert credit card payments to bank account controlled by CFO.	Compare expected credit card payments to credit card deposits in known bank accounts.

Identifying these fraud risks within the business' sources of funds, the investigator included the following analyses to address investigation priorities within the case plan:

- Patient payments that were on installments were reviewed for months that appeared no payment had been made. Patients, with the approval of Randy, were then contacted to request copies of canceled checks to confirm whether the deposit had been made to the business bank account.
  - *Finding:* All checks tested had been deposited to known business bank accounts.
- The credit card processing company records were requested. Total credit card payments applied to patient accounts in the system were compared to the credit card processing records, which were then compared to the credit card deposits to business bank accounts.
  - *Finding:* All credit card payments applied to patient accounts reconciled to the credit card processing reports, which also reconciled to the business bank accounts.
- Randy contacted Medicare, the VA, and insurance companies to determine if any changes to bank accounts receiving deposits had been made during the period under investigation.
  - *Finding:* All the bank accounts on record with the payors belonged to the business.

Money Out

The uses of funds within an organization vary depending on the purpose of the organization. The pie charts in Figure 7.2 list common, possible uses of cash in an organization by expenditure category comparing financial information for when there is no occupational fraud versus a situation of occupational fraud. The uses of cash and corresponding percentages are for illustration purposes only and include:

- Cost of goods sold
- General and administrative expenses
- Payroll
- Equipment
- Investments, securities
- Taxes
- Owner salaries, distributions, or dividends.

The first pie chart illustrates a reasonable representation of the categories as a percentage of total expenditures when occupational fraud is not occurring in an organization. In Figure 7.2, the portion of the example expenditures that is most

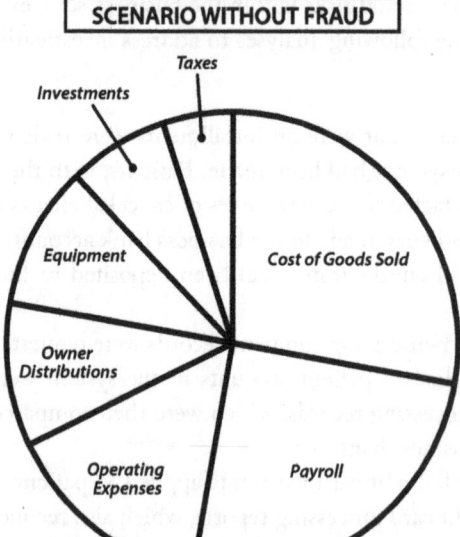

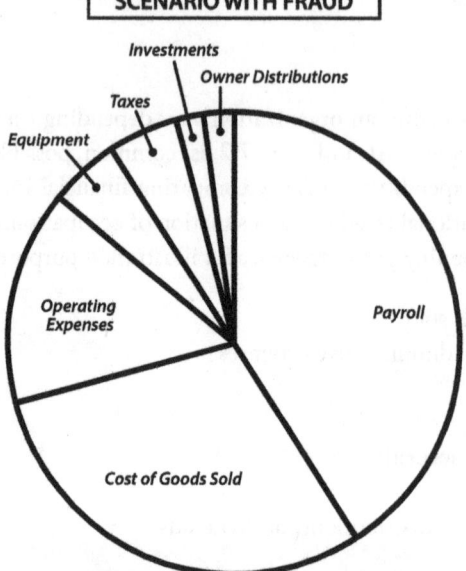

FIGURE 7.2 Pie chart of possible cash uses with an organization.

vulnerable to fraud or theft are the funds that remain after all of the required payments are made.

The second pie chart represents the same example organization if occupational fraud is occurring. Total expenditures between scenarios do not change. The difference is in the apportionment of the expenditures.

When an organization does not have fraud, there is cash available to reinvest in the organization through purchasing equipment, to invest in opportunities outside of the organization, to pay taxes, and to pay the owner distributions or dividends. However, when fraud is being committed, the opportunities for investment, owner distributions, and ability to pay taxes are usually the areas most affected.

The portion of the chart in Figure 7.2 that is most vulnerable to fraud or theft are the funds that remain after all of the required payments are made. For example, a business will struggle to operate if the basic expenses are not paid such as employee payroll, vendors, and rent. But when funds are not strictly accounted for or reserved for the vital expenses, they become more vulnerable to theft. The most vulnerable group of funds from an expenditure point of view, is the leftover – the funds available for profit, reinvestment, owner's salary, distributions, and dividends. Without theft, the leftover funds allow for adequate cash flow and reinvestment; however, these funds also allow the subject to steal without stakeholders realizing it – until there is a cash flow issue.

The Fraud Detection Worksheet section "Money Out," as provided in the spreadsheet download, is represented in Table 7.2 with columns completed for "The Case of the Puzzling Entries" based on the Randy's initial consultation with the investigator. Note that some uses of funds appear over several lines, as each step with a different individual responsible for authorization is assessed separately for associated risks.

Having completed the worksheet based on Randy's responses, the investigator identified the highest fraud risk areas in the cash disbursement process to include those under the control and responsibility of the CFO. It was possible under the existing controls that the CFO could:

- Use company funds to pay personal expenditures such as utilities, credit card bills, charitable contributions, or taxes;
- Transfer or wire funds to bank accounts under the control of the CFO; or
- Inflate CFO's payroll, expense reimbursements, and benefits to more than stated in the employee agreement.

TABLE 7.2 "Money Out" section of the Data Sleuth Fraud Detection Worksheet for "The Case of the Puzzling Entries."

©2020, Workman Forensics, LLC.

Data Sleuth Fraud Detection Worksheet
MONEY OUT

General, Administrative, and Equipment Expenses Paid via Check, Transfer, or Wire

People who authorize the expenditures	Who releases the funds to pay the expenditure?	If this person stole funds, where could it happen?	If funds were stolen, how would you know?
Purchase requests: location manager	N/A	Request items that once delivered are taken for personal use.	Personal/unnecessary items could be questioned by headquarters office manager and CFO.
Makes purchases: headquarters office manager	N/A	Purchase items that once delivered are taken for personal use.	Personal/unnecessary items could be questioned by CFO.
Authorizes funds to pay expenditures: CFO	CFO	Pay for personal expenditures.	Review bank account canceled check images to see vendor payees; review transfers and wires leaving the account.

Payroll Paid via Direct Deposit or ACH to Employee Bank Accounts or Taxing Authorities

People who authorize the expenditures	Who releases the funds to pay the expenditure?	If this person stole funds, where could it happen?	If funds were stolen, how would you know?
Approves timesheets: location manager	N/A	Inflate timesheet hours, benefits, etc.	Review payroll variances between expected payroll by location versus actual payroll by location; Compare payroll between similar locations.
Enters timesheet information into payroll system: headquarters office manager	N/A	Inflate timesheet hours, benefits, etc.	Review payroll variances between expected payroll by location versus actual payroll by location; compare payroll between similar locations.
Final approval and disbursement of funds to pay payroll, taxes, benefits, etc.: CFO	CFO	Inflate timesheet hours, benefits, etc.	Review payroll variances between expected payroll by location versus actual payroll by location; compare payroll between similar locations.

Identifying these fraud risks within the business's cash disbursements, the investigator included the following analyses to address investigation priorities within the case plan:

- Review all expenditures paid from business bank accounts with special attention paid to the number of monthly payments to utility companies, purchases not benefiting the business, payment of personal income taxes, and personal credit card payments.
  - *Finding:* No expenditures were identified from the bank accounts as not benefiting the business or being personal in nature.
- Trace transfers from business bank accounts to the corresponding destination accounts. Review supporting documentation identifying the beneficiaries of wire payments from the business bank accounts.
  - *Finding:* No transfers were made to accounts not owned by the business. All wire transfers benefited the business and were not personal in nature.
- Payroll for the entire company was reviewed, including the CFO, and variances were researched with the help of Randy.
  - *Finding:* No overpayments of payroll or unsupported expense reimbursements or benefit payments were identified.

Accounting Records and Interviews

Whether or not a thorough review of an organization's sources and uses of cash identifies missing money, questions may remain:

- If missing funds are quantified, it is often still valuable to the client to identify the methods used to divert the funds and/or avoid detection in order to improve internal controls and prevent future losses, as well as to show the subject's intent if a legal case alleging fraud is to be made.
- If no funds have been diverted to the subject's benefit, there may still be financial or accounting issues within the organization that justify additional investigation. Note that even in these cases, although the findings may seem disappointing to the client, using a cash-focused, risk-based analysis framework has already provided an often overlooked but important benefit in preventing the investigator from seeing fraud where there is none.

In these cases, the next step is to use accounting records and interviews to provide context to the cash-related findings.

In "The Case of the Puzzling Entries," it was this next step that ultimately identified the issue and gave the case its name. Despite the negative findings from the investigator, although relieved that theft had not been discovered, Randy remained convinced that something was wrong with his cash balance and asked the investigator if there was anything else she could think of to solve this problem. It was at this point that the investigator incorporated a thorough review of the general ledger into the case plan to look for accounting errors and irregularities. Beginning with a review of the revenue accounts, it was discovered that backdated quarterly adjustments had been made to several of the accounts reducing the balances by an annual total of over $1 million. Questioning this approach, the investigator decided to examine the expense accounts for bad debts as the company used the accrual basis of accounting; oddly, the investigator did not just find an absence of bad debt entries but did not find a general ledger account for bad debt expense at all on the chart of accounts. Returning to the strange revenue account entries, the CFO's backdated quarterly entries were as follows:

Debit	Revenue
Credit	Retained Earnings

Knowing that the CFO was an experienced CPA and that he should know this was improper treatment of uncollectible revenue, the investigator began to wonder if there was a motivation behind the apparent nondisclosure, and perhaps hiding, of the writing off of bad debts. The investigator narrowed her procedures to the revenue accounts by type: Medicare, VA, and insurance billings. By revenue type, she compared the total gross revenue in the accounting system to the billing software and discovered that the gross revenue in the billing software was consistently greater than that in the accounting software and ultimately the profit and loss statement provided monthly to Randy. The investigator reached out to numerous accountants explaining the discovery and performing further research to understand why someone might be using these types of entries when missing cash was yet to be identified. Lacking an affirmative answer, and with the client anxiously waiting for the investigator to solve the cash balance anomaly, the investigator requested to interview the CFO. Randy agreed to this idea, and an interview was scheduled.

The interview got off to a rough start. The CFO was initially angry that Randy suspected that he was stealing money and had hired an investigator. Randy smoothed things over by explaining to him that the longer his concerns were ignored and dismissed by the CFO, Randy's suspicions grew. Shrugging, the CFO complied and told the investigator he would answer her questions.

When presented with questions about the odd accounting entries, the CFO admitted that he had been writing off bad debts by debiting revenue and crediting retained earnings instead of using a direct write-off method. The direct write-off method involves writing off specific customer accounts when they are determined uncollectible. The accounting entry for this method is:

Debit	Bad Debt Expense
Credit	Accounts Receivable

When the investigator questioned him further on why he was performing these entries instead of listing them as bad debt expense on the profit and loss statements, the CFO advised that he knew if he booked the entries in this manner, Randy would call the corresponding location and ask them about the write-offs, and the location managers would not be able to explain them.

In healthcare-related industries it is not uncommon for Medicare, VA, and insurance claims to be denied for various reasons. It is the responsibility of the business to follow up on all claims that are denied ensuring that they received everything they were due on that claim. The CFO admitted that he was the employee who was not following up on claims and pursuing collections – not the location managers. By hiding the uncollected claims he was able to neglect collections in the revenue accounts, and cover up the shirking of his responsibilities. Because most of the revenue within this business was derived from Medicare, VA, and insurance, the lack of follow-up on collections landed the business in a cash flow crisis.

The Benefits of Risk-Based Analysis

Using a fraud risk-based analysis approach with a client's internal control environment as the foundation helps investigators avoid jumping to conclusions about an individual's guilt or innocence. The Data Sleuth Fraud Detection Worksheet uncovered multiple avenues for the CFO to have committed fraud, but after performing the analyses that should have uncovered evidence supporting any fraud allegations, the investigator discovered that the CFO did not take advantage of the opportunities he had to steal money. Having investigated the areas at highest risk for theft of funds by the CFO, the investigator could then move on to identifying nontheft activities that were affecting the business's cash flow – that of the negligence of the CFO to follow up on collections and aging accounts.

The Case of the Puzzling Entries – Conclusion

The CFO resigned after the interview, and a new CFO was immediately brought on board with the instructions to hire a collections clerk and to proactively collect from payors and overdue patient accounts. Randy called the investigator several months later to tell her that their cash flow was better than it had been in years thanks to the new CFO doing his job.

RISK FOCUS IN AUDITS VERSUS RISK FOCUS IN INVESTIGATIONS

An earlier section of this chapter contrasted the fraud investigator's focus on cash with an auditor's interest in accounting records and journal entries. Another contrast can be made in the approach taken to understanding internal controls in these two contexts. In both a financial statement audit engagement and a forensic accounting engagement or fraud investigation, an understanding of an organization's internal controls is a primary input into the risk-based analysis and preparation of an engagement plan. The difference between the two lies in the focus and purpose of the internal control understanding and evaluation.

In a financial statement audit, learning about the control environment guides the auditors to look more closely into those areas within an organization where the financial statements are at a higher risk of material misstatement.

Forensic accounting engagements or fraud investigations, however, are typically not focused on the fairness of financial statement presentation but rather on concerns about missing money. Therefore, the focus of the investigation is to locate the evidence of specific transactions and ultimate disposition of the money. This level of detail often falls below a financial statement audit's materiality limit, and thus a different perspective and approach is necessary when considering an organization's control environment. Although the approaches are different, they are not necessarily contradictory; in fact, sometimes a case arises where the two approaches prove to be complementary.

THE CASE OF THE MOM OF THE YEAR

Employee Credit Union (ECU) was a small employee-owned credit union. The credit union would collect member deposits and loan payments either by members visiting the physical office or by mail. Because of the small size of the credit union, ECU would collect cash and check deposits and loan payments from the members, apply the deposits and payments to their member accounts in ECU's system, and then prepare and deposit the funds to an account at a larger banking institution to actually process the items. The member cash and check deposits and payments were prepared for deposit much like a business prepares a daily deposit.

The employee responsible for these payments was ECU's internal accountant, Emily. Each day, the tellers would provide her with the members' payments and deposits. Emily would compare the funds provided to her from the tellers to the members' accounts; prepare a deposit slip; and on her way home each day, take the deposit to the bank for processing. At the end of each month, Emily would reconcile ECU's general ledger identifying all of the members' balances and transactions to the bank statement.

Because ECU was a financial institution, routine agreed-upon procedures were completed each year by an auditor from a public accounting firm. As part of the procedures, the external auditor would vouch the amount listed on the year-end bank reconciliation as "deposits in transit" to the following month's bank statement. To vouch a transaction, the auditor would identify a deposit in transit on the bank reconciliation and locate where it had cleared the bank on the following month's bank statement. As illustrated in Figure 7.3, if items on the bank reconciliation were marked "deposit in transit," the auditor should have been able to identify their clearing of the bank account in the following month's statement. However, as illustrated, the deposits did not clear in the first week of the following month but rather the last week of the month.

For several years in a row, ECU's report from the auditor for the agreed-upon procedures included a finding that the amounts listed as "deposits in transit" on the year-end bank reconciliation took too long to clear the bank. Each year the president of ECU noted this finding, spoke to Emily about making the change to her process, and business continued as usual.

One of Emily's children was battling health issues, which caused her to miss several weeks of work. One week while Emily was out of the office, a teller performed the monthly reconciliations. After multiple attempts, the teller could not get the reconciliation to balance between the member accounts and the balance at the processing bank. When Emily returned, management brought the issue to her attention. Avoiding the questions completely, she abruptly blamed management for overworking and underpaying her and subsequently submitted her resignation.

It was at this point that an investigator was called to identify the problem. Management did not want to believe that funds had been stolen or were missing; instead, he stated repeatedly that Emily would never steal and that it was probably "just an accounting issue." During the initial interview with the investigator, the manager advised of the external auditor's finding and tried to explain it away as Emily's incompetence at her job.

Consideration of Risk in Fraud Investigations

In this case study, management did not want to believe money was missing, which is contrary to owner in "The Case of the Puzzling Entries"; however, the same approach in prioritizing the examination of sources and uses of cash with respect to the internal control environment in case planning was still used to begin the investigation. This is once again a situation in which a client has not yet identified where the problem initiated. To effectively investigate "The Case of the Mom of the Year," understanding Emily's access to cash and the organization's controls was imperative.

Bank Reconciliation as of 12/31/XX

Balance Per Books	$380,009.04
Additions	$324.87
Deductions	-$8,092.61
Adjusted Total	$372,241.30

Bank Balance per Statement	$507,072.92
Deductions	-$151,845.30
Additions	
Deposit in Transit	$7,168.28
Deposit in Transit	$9,845.38
Wrong check amount cleared	$0.02
Adjusted Total	$372,241.30
Difference	$0.00

Bank Statement as of 1/31/XX

Beginning Balance	$507,072.92
+ Deposits	$157,978.56
- Checks & Withdrawals	$(145,368.25)
- Service Fees	$(15.00)
= Ending Balance	$519,668.23

DEPOSITS	
01/05 DEPOSIT	50,641.71
01/05 DEPOSIT	16,438.68
01/13 DEPOSIT	8,702.00
OTHER DAILY DEPOSITS	
01/29 DEPOSIT	7,168.28
01/29 DEPOSIT	9,845.38

Deposits in Transit should be identified as clearing within the first week of following month's bank statement.

FIGURE 7.3 Illustration of vouching procedure for deposits in transit on a bank reconciliation.

Money In

As part of Emily's job responsibilities, she was responsible for the following tasks as funds received from members by ECU.

- Received the daily cash and check deposits and loan payments from the tellers,
- Prepared the deposit slips,
- Delivered the deposit to the bank,
- Reconciled the bank statements to the general ledger, and
- Worked directly with the external auditor.

Money Out

As part of Emily's job responsibilities, she was responsible for the following tasks related to paying the expenditures of ECU.

- Received approved vendor invoices from management,
- Recorded the vendor invoices in the accounting software, and
- Issued checks weekly to pay outstanding invoices.

Management would receive the expense checks, compare the checks to the invoices, sign the checks, and then provide the signed checks to his assistant to mail to the vendors. Emily was not responsible for any of ECU's payroll process. Because of Emily's limited access to funds through the expenditure process, the investigator advised management of procedures that could be performed in this area but recommended that they be given a lower priority than the procedures related to deposit collection.

Knowing that Emily controlled the entire deposit and reconciliation process from start to finish, the investigator was intentional in the planning process to consider the risks of theft, fraud, and misrepresentation in this area.

Case Findings 1

The ECU accounting and member account systems had not yet been upgraded and were thus extremely limited in the data reports to provide to the investigator. In fact, the investigator was told that no historical reports could be exported digitally, but that she would have to work from file cabinets storing the paper reports from the end of each day. Determined to find the data source that would provide evidence of what caused the discrepancy, the investigator prioritized verifying information Emily prepared as part of her monthly tasks. The first procedure performed by the investigator was the reperformance of several months' worth of reconciliations, as that is what led to the discovery of the original discrepancy by the other ECU employee. As the investigator recreated the reconciliations and compared them to those previously prepared by Emily, the investigator's reconciliations did not match those Emily prepared. The primary discrepancy was identified in the "Bank Statement – Additions" section of the reconciliation. It appeared Emily had simply forced the reconciliation by "plugging" amounts and then labeling them as "Deposits in Transit."

The secondary, and most detailed, data sources available for the analysis were the printed daily member deposit reports, the carbon copies of the daily deposit slips prepared by Emily, and the deposit slip images accompanying the bank statements. The daily member deposit reports were compared to the carbon-copied deposit slips that listed the member names, which were then compared to the deposit slip images that accompanied the bank statement. The following were identified from the comparisons of daily information:

- Cash listed on the carbon-copy deposit slips was marked out and was not deposited to the processing bank.
- Cash deposits were posted to members' accounts, yet the corresponding processing bank deposit did not contain the same total amount of cash for the day that had been collected from members.
- When cash deposits did not match the amount of cash that was collected on a given day, a check (or multiple checks) from Emily would be deposited, equaling the difference.
- Check deposits were posted to members' accounts, but the same check items were not found in that day's corresponding processing bank deposit items.
- As the scheme continued, the carbon-copy deposit slips and processing bank deposit slip images no longer contained an itemized list by member of check deposits but instead had the words "Checks" or "List" written on the deposit slip.

Altered Bank Statements

As the investigator consulted the printed bank statements accompanying Emily's reconciliations in ECU's files, she noticed that a couple months' worth of statements did not look or feel like the rest. The bank statements for the processing bank normally were delivered with three-hole punches, but the copies in the folder had not been three-hole punched. Additionally, the bank used a very specific color of red, and the statements in the folder showed a more muted color of red. The investigator then compared the statements in the folder to statements for the same months obtained directly from the bank and in doing so discovered that transaction line items on the folder statement had been altered and then printed.

Further examination revealed that for the first month of the altered bank statements, Emily forced the reconciliation to balance. Instead of plugging the difference with checks she was holding, she falsified two months of bank statements. The reconciliation balanced in that first month by adding, deleting, or changing transaction amounts on the bank statements. In the following month, she was able to make a few more adjustments to the statement as she then only either used checks from future deposits or her own account to make up the difference. Understanding Emily's access and the lack of internal controls surrounding her tasks allowed the investigator to be critical of the bank statements provided by management. Because Emily controlled the entire deposit process, without any accountability or oversight – other than that of the external auditor once a year – she was able to remove cash from deposits and use multiple methods to cover up the missing funds. Additionally, identifying the falsified bank statements provided key evidence as to intent by Emily and the cover-up of her scheme.

Case Findings 2

It became apparent that although member deposits or loan payments included cash, that cash was not being deposited to the processing bank. In comparing the date on which check deposits were collected by ECU tellers to the carbon copy deposit slip listing the corresponding check deposits and to the processing bank deposit slip image, it was discovered that some check deposits were deposited to the processing bank several days after being posted to the members' accounts instead of the same day or next day.

Table 7.3 demonstrates in table form several of the findings from the detailed reconciliation analysis. As noted, although members deposited a total of $2,230.00 during the period listed in the table, none of the cash was deposited to the bank. All of the deposits that cleared the bank consisted of check deposits. Additionally, from January 2, 2013, through January 7, 2013, member deposits totaled $66,790.07, but only $55,941.01 was deposited to the processing bank – a difference of $10,849.06. By January 10, 2013, total deposits for the month to date differed by only $0.09. Patterns similar to this were noted throughout the entire life of the scheme.

The detailed comparison of the daily member deposit reports to the daily carbon copy deposit slips uncovered the method Emily was using to steal from ECU. By removing the cash from the daily deposit, the processing bank account would be short at the end of the month by at least the total amount of cash taken. To ensure the monthly reconciliation did not show a difference, Emily would cover the missing cash through reconciling items labeled "Deposits in Transit" to force the reconciliation to balance. Emily would delay the end of month check deposits

TABLE 7.3 Sample daily data sources comparisons.

	Daily Member Deposit Report Totals			Carbon Copy	Processing Bank Deposit Image		
Date	Cash Amt	Check Amt	Total Deposit	Deposit Slip Date	Cleared Date	Total	Cumulative Difference
01/02/13	1,000.00	6,858.26	7,858.26				7,858.26
01/03/13	700.00	23,628.90	24,328.90				32,187.16
01/04/13		11,442.30	11,442.30				43,629.46
01/07/13		23,160.61	23,160.61	01/07/13	01/09/13	55,941.01	10,849.06
01/08/13	390.00	23,306.17	23,696.17				34,545.23
01/09/13	140.00	8,944.32	9,084.32	01/09/13	01/09/13	43,629.46	0.09
01/10/13		71,003.08	71,003.08	01/10/13	01/10/13	71,003.08	0.09
TOTAL	2,230.00	168,343.64	170,573.64				

*Note: None of the deposit slips listed amounts for cash.

until she could create a deposit from check deposits held that would closely match that of the deposits in transit. Then, she would make a deposit of the members' check payments. This delay was noticed by the external auditor, which resulted in the repeated finding that in turn uncovered Emily's scheme.

Emily's scheme was fundamentally similar to an account lapping scheme, or "robbing Peter to pay Paul." By stealing the cash, she had to rob from future deposits to cover what was missing that same day. Her scheme also relied on a delay in the processing of funds to avoid detection – a delay that in part she controlled. A loss associated with one of these schemes is easiest to identify when the subject is no longer in control to keep lapping. By performing the reconciliation for the month after Emily had resigned, the investigator knew the loss was approximately $85,000. Were this an investigation involving a business or non-profit organization, it is possible the client would have been satisfied with the findings at this point.

However, because the organization involved was a federally insured financial institution, the case was going to be worked by law enforcement whether management wanted them to or not. To prepare the case for both civil and criminal charges, quantifying the lump sum loss at the end is not normally as useful as identifying the specific transactions that make up the loss. Because of the inefficiencies of ECU's systems and evidence that Emily was repaying ECU throughout the period when she would write a check for reconciliation differences, a hybrid approach was performed. Specific item comparisons, similar to that in Table 7.3 were performed for a several months over the relevant period connecting the identification of cash missing from deposits to the month-end reconciliation. This calculation was used by law enforcement in making a determination of the loss for the related federal charges.

By understanding the risks within Emily's access and responsibilities, the investigator was able to discover additional clues and evidence that money was missing and confirm that the reconciliation issues the employee discovered in covering responsibilities during Emily's absence was not just an accounting mistake. Often, management will want to initially believe that irregularities in financial information are simply accounting mistakes and will say, "It's just a timing difference." These beliefs and statements should not deter an investigator or interfere with following the investigation process – especially when reconciling between an accounting system and third-party source documents such as bank statements. These two sources of financial transactions should always reconcile, with an allowance for reconciling items that are substantiated. Reconciling items usually include checks or deposits that have not yet cleared the bank or bank fees, charges, or errors that have not yet been recorded in the general ledger. If a reconciliation is reviewed and recalculated by the investigator, and a difference exists and/or supporting documentation is unavailable or does not exist for the reconciling items, the likelihood that money is missing is high.

The Case of the Mom of the Year – Conclusion

Even after the specific transactions identifying missing cash had been reported to management, the manager could not believe that Emily had stolen the money. He insisted there had to be another explanation. The investigator suggested that she and another investigator attempt to interview Emily. Management agreed, and the team set out to Emily's house for an interview. When the two arrived, they drove up a long driveway to a beautiful, large two-story home on acreage. The investigator knocked on the door. Emily was home and opened the door enough for the investigator to advise of the nature of the visit. Emily led the investigators inside while she called her attorney. Sitting in the dining room, the investigators noticed that every corner of Emily's house was decorated from floor to ceiling. On the front of a refrigerator was a family calendar completely filled with kids' activities, sporting events, and doctor appointments. When Emily returned, she advised that on the advice of counsel, she was not to answer their questions. The investigators and Emily chatted briefly about the weather and her children's activities and health, and then the investigators left. Even though Emily did not answer the interview questions, the visit told the investigators what so many had been curious about – there was no money stashed away in a bank account somewhere. She stole the money for her kids.

 ## EVALUATING RISK IN DIVORCE CASES AND ESTATE AND TRUST DISPUTES

When the end-client is not an organization but instead an individual, a risk-based analysis should still be performed. The basis of that risk analysis is just slightly different when an organization is not involved.

Divorce Cases

The most common reason our Data Sleuth team is engaged in divorce matters is to identify hidden or undisclosed assets and understated income for the purposes of a property settlement. As part of a divorce matter, property settlements involve the division of the marital assets of the couple getting a divorce. Our role as investigators is most often to assist the spouse who controlled few, if any, financial assets ("out-spouse") during the marriage. A risk-based analysis in a divorce matter shifts from the areas of vulnerability due to fraud in business systems to the risk areas of undisclosed assets or understated income.

As part of the property settlement negotiations, it is imperative that the list of marital assets, or the marital balance sheet, is complete because only those items on the marital balance sheet will be divided. If there are assets existing that do not make it onto the list to divide during property settlement negotiations, then without legal action in the future, the spouse who omitted the disclosure of the asset will likely own the asset going forward. Understated income becomes a contention when it is being used as a basis for alimony, spousal support, or child support. If income reported by either party is not accurately represented, then one side may not receive the support they need.

To perform the risk analysis, identification of what is known by the out-spouse about the financial situation is helpful in creating a place to start:

- **Identify all known sources of income.** By listing all known sources of income, then a corresponding analysis and information request can be created as part of the case planning step.

   For example, if the spouse who controlled the finances during the marriage ("in-spouse") was employed and received a W-2 each year, the risk is that the in-spouse deposited only a portion of net payroll to marital bank account(s) and the remainder was deposited to another bank account that may not have been disclosed. As part of case planning, an analysis addressing this risk would be described and the corresponding data request would be sure to include copies of the in-spouse's W-2 and paystubs. The analysis would address both a potential risk of an undisclosed asset and understated income.

   In another example, if the in-spouse owns a business, then all known sources of income would be evaluated starting from the revenue sources of the business to ensure all income received was recorded by the business. Although the business of the asset would likely need to be valued by a business valuation expert, the risk of underreporting income at the business level exists and should be evaluated as part of the risk-based analysis step prior to case planning.

- **Identify all known financial accounts.** Through the identification of known financial accounts, personal and business related if applicable, analysis can be determined in the case planning step to analyze bank accounts, credit card accounts, investment accounts, cryptocurrency wallets, etc. to address the risk of undisclosed assets and understated income.

- **Identify all known real property.** Reviewing tax returns and property records may uncover additional assets not previously disclosed. Incorporating this review into the case plan will address this risk is advised.

Estate and Trust Disputes

Financial investigations for estate and trust disputes typically involve misappropriation of assets or embezzlement – although not always a criminal offense. The greatest difference between misappropriation in an estate or trust dispute is that normally the theft, or financial abuse, is from an individual instead of an organization. For instance, a son is managing the finances of his elderly, incapacitated father and uses funds from his father's bank accounts to buy a new car leaving insufficient available funds to pay for his living accommodations and care. Another example is that of a trustee distributing assets of a trust to himself instead of the designated beneficiaries.

To perform a risk-based analysis prior to preparing a case plan two things should be considered:

- Similar to that of a financial investigation in a business, the subject's access to funds must be evaluated to address the vulnerabilities of theft from the individual, estate, or trust.
- Much like in a divorce matter, the identification of known assets, financial accounts, and properties must be considered.

Understanding the subject's access to the known assets, financial accounts, and properties establishes the risks associated with the client's concerns that can be used in creating investigation priorities.

Further analyses and data sources recommended for divorce matters are beyond the scope of this book; however, by using the starting points described here, an investigator can follow the Data Sleuth Case Plan process to identify appropriate analyses to address the risks in divorce matters.

CHAPTER EIGHT

Data Sources and Data Processing Techniques

D ATA SHOULD NOT BE a formidable term as forensic accountants and fraud investigators have been looking at data throughout the entire evolution of the field. Data just looked different, as historically, they were stored on paper instead of in databases. Nevertheless, it is important to explain the data terms that will be used throughout the remaining chapters in the explanation of the Data Sleuth Process.

Because of the types and quantities of information that may be collected over the life of an engagement, systematic, thorough organization is required, and although time consuming on the front end will allow for simplified administrative, wrap-up processes at the end of the engagement.

Data Sleuth projects are entirely reliant on the quality of data relied upon and the manner by which those data are processed. This chapter contains detailed explanations of the Data Sleuth data processing steps and simple spreadsheet-based tools that have proven helpful on Data Sleuth engagements.

DATA SOURCES EXPLAINED

A data source is the origination of the data being used in the investigation. For example, if transactions that cleared a bank account are to be analyzed in an investigation, the data source for the transactions is the collection of bank account statements. Data sources, however, are not limited to just statements from financial institutions; they can also include things such as a collection of invoices from a vendor, payroll reports from a payroll provider, timesheets submitted by employees, or accounting software.

A data set is created from the extracted transactions provided by the data source. The transactions are typically arranged in a tabular format where each variable is grouped under columns representing the unique characteristic of the variable. For example, checks listed on a bank statement are identified by the date the check cleared the bank, the check number, and the amount of the check. To convert this information into a data set, each check would be represented on one row of a table with the check date in one column, the check number in one column, and the check amount in one column. An example of a data set created from a bank statement is illustrated in Table 8.1.

Data points are the individual variables, or transactions, that create a data set.

TABLE 8.1 Illustration of a data set created from a bank statement data source.

Transactions Data Set from Bank Statement				
Line No	Date	Check No	Payee	Check Amount
1	07/02/12	4325	ABC PAYEE	56.32
2	07/03/12	4327	MR. BROWN	250.00
3	07/03/12	4398	DRY CLEANING	195.25
4	07/03/12	4350	BUSINESS LLC	506.52

 ## QUANTITATIVE AND QUALITATIVE DATA SOURCES

Data sources used in Data Sleuth investigations are categorized as quantitative and qualitative data sources. The first category of data sources provides necessary quantitative evidence to calculate the client's loss or the benefit to the subject at the client's expense. The second category of data sources provides qualitative evidence lending to the understanding of the subject's intention behind the actions that caused the loss or the correlation between the subject and the loss.

 ## DATA SOURCES FOR QUANTITATIVE EVIDENCE

Financial statement fraud investigations have been less common in my career than those involving misappropriation of assets or hidden assets. In financial investigations of missing or hidden money, knowing where to look – or which data sources to use to find evidence uncovering what happened and where the money went – is paramount. Data sources of this nature can be categorized into two groups: standard and nonstandard.

Standard Data Sources

Standard data sources are those for which the presentation of the contents, or data, may vary, but the data contained in the information is standard.

Standard Data Source: Bank Statements

Bank, or credit union, statements always contain the following data points if they occurred in the account:

- Statement date
- Account number
- Deposits/credits to the account
  - Dates of deposits/credits and corresponding amounts
  - Dates, source, and amounts of electronic deposits/credits
- Checks/debits to the account
  - Dates, check numbers, and corresponding amounts of checks that have cleared the account
  - Dates, payee, and amounts of electronic payments/debits
  - Dates, payee, and amounts of wire transfers
  - Dates and amounts of internal transfers

Additional information supporting each transaction can be requested from the financial institution if it is not provided with the statement itself.

Standard Data Source: Credit Card Statements

Credit card statements always contain the following data points if they occurred in the account:

- Statement closing date
- Account number
- Transaction date, posted date, payee, and corresponding amount for each transaction
- Transaction date, posted date, transaction description, and corresponding amount for each fee or interest charge
- Transaction date, posted date, transaction description, and corresponding amount for each payment and/or credit applied

Standard Data Source: Payroll Reports

Payroll reports vary the most in presentation out of the three standard data sources; however, payroll reports contain consistent data from provider to provider as the information presented will be provided to the Internal Revenue Service at the end of each year for tax purposes. Some of those standard data points include:

- Gross pay
- Employee and employer taxes
- Net pay
- Employee and employer contributions to retirement plans
- Other benefits
- Reimbursements
- Employee's Tax Identification Number

Because all the standard data sources have predictable types of data points, the information from the statements or reports can be entered into a tabular format for further analysis. Each data point is entered into one field per row within a spreadsheet in the corresponding data source type column.

Nonstandard Data Sources

Nonstandard data sources are those for which the information available is not consistent from custodian to custodian or provider to provider. The use of accounting systems, in general, varies from company to company and even user to user. The data input into these systems also varies. Information gathered by one company or user often differs from that gathered by another company – even if the source of the data is the same. For example, if an invoice from Company A is sent to two clients X and Y, client X may include Company A's name, address, federal employer identification number, and contact information in the setup of the vendor. However, Client Y may include only Company A's name and contact information. If the master vendor report is exported from both clients' systems, the information exported would differ.

Standard data sources are used frequently in investigations because they are simple to understand and analyze because of the predictable characteristics of the data points. However, nonstandard data sources are used when standard data sources are not sufficient to calculating a loss or if additional qualitative information is needed, as further explained in the next section. Nonstandard data sources are typically less reliable than standard data sources as they are commonly prepared by parties involved and/or they are derived from data entry with the risk of human error in the input.

Nonstandard Data Source: System Exports

An example of a nonstandard data source are system exports. In "The Case of the Nonexistent Inventory" in Chapter 4, Acquiring Distribution system exports provided information from vendor invoices including invoice number, invoice date, item number, item descriptions, unit price, quantity purchased, and total amount by item. The information derived from the vendor invoices were listed in a tabular format with one line for each item invoiced. System exports were also provided for purchase order details and customer billing. As part of the loss calculation for Acquiring Distribution, Jeff's actions of creating purchase orders in the system and then immediately creating corresponding customer invoices was verified with the system exports. Using the system exports, the dates on which purchase orders were created were compared to the dates on which invoices were issued. Through this analysis, it was discovered that the only customers with this pattern in the data were those who Jeff admitted were charged for the products that did not exist. Identifying the purchase order to invoice date pattern for the known customers allowed me to also look for the same pattern with customers who were unknown. To further clean up the mess Jeff had made with his scheme, and to keep the customer relationship, Acquiring Distribution needed to know all of the customers who were affected by Jeff's actions – not just the ones Jeff identified.

Another example of the use of a nonstandard data source is within "The Case of the Man Cave." When Bill would register LLCs with the Secretary of State, he would list the LLC as the Registered Agent. This setup made it more difficult to establish all of the entities owned by Bill when searching by Bill's name. Concerned that I had not identified all of Bill's LLCs, I noticed that the checks payable to Bill's LLCs identified were missing address information. Most of the company's vendor records contained name and address information that would print onto the checks, so the financing department could mail the payments. An export of the master vendor file was requested and filtered for those records without an address. Using the list of vendors without addresses in the system, the LLC names were searched using the Secretary of State website. This process identified multiple LLCs that were registered to the LLC but listed Bill's home address as the registered address. After the LLCs were identified, then the standard data source of bank statements could be searched for payments to the LLC and added to the loss calculation.

Examples of other nonstandard data source of system exports from previous cases include:

- Audit/user logs
- General ledgers
- Employee information

Nonstandard Data Source: Paper Conversion

Another nonstandard data source involves converting any type of record, report, or list that was written on paper. As discussed in further detail in Chapter 9, loss calculations in financial investigations can require a comparison. Sometimes, one side of the comparison is a standard data source, such as a bank statement, and the other side is a nonstandard data source. For example, in the "The Case of the Gambling Executive Director," standard data from bank and credit card statements were used, but in addition to the standard data, nonstandard data including information from cash donation records were also digitized and analyzed and compared to the bank deposits. By converting the paper nonstandard data source into a tabular format, like a spreadsheet, the comparison can be made with results able to be organized for communicating findings to clients and creating attachments for reports and related testimony.

Examples of nonstandard data source paper conversion from previous cases include:

- Paper point of sale receipts
- Cash receipt books
- Paper calendar entries
- Daily cash drawer logs
- Inventory count sheets

 DATA SOURCES FOR QUALITATIVE EVIDENCE

Fraud investigators who love digging for evidence more than data analysis tend to enjoy the qualitative data sources the most. For those who love data analysis, the quantitative evidence gathering and related analysis is their favorite way to investigate a case. The best cases, and the ability to prove a case beyond a reasonable doubt, are those in which both qualitative and quantitative data sources exist and there is time to use both.

The primary example of a qualitative data source are emails. When an employee has stolen money from her employer, and the employer stores the employee's email for future reference, this evidence is the favorite among many fraud investigators. Qualitative data sources are where many feel the story and drama are uncovered. Examples of qualitative data sources include:

- Memos and notes within a company's general ledger and/or journal entries
  - One co-conspirator was responsible for the accounting entries to hide the stolen funds from the company's owners. He would leave notes in

the memo field of journal entries stating things such as, "Reclass to [co-conspirator's] job." These journal entry notes confirmed employee interviews and other evidence that the conspirators were stealing money and hiding the missing funds in a fake job in an inventory/asset account.

- Spreadsheets
  - Employees were instructed by the owner to enter only checks into Quick-Books and manage inventory and the rest of the business on separate spreadsheets that did not tie to each other. However, financial statements had been prepared and provided to a bank to obtain a loan that was in default. Copies of the spreadsheets were collected and provided great evidence of multiple schemes in which not only was the bank defrauded but also the company's customers.
- Receipts in desks
  - An employee paid funds from a corporate holding account to an inheritance scam. In the books of the company, the employee recorded the payments to the scammers as a distribution to the company's owner. The owner, however, was not aware and did not receive the distributions. To confirm the recipient of the funds was not the owner, a receipt listing one of the bank accounts was discovered in the employee's office.
- Documents in file cabinets
  - The investigation involved verifying the assets of a company who defaulted on a loan. The company eventually was closed, but the investigation continued. As the company records were being packed up and taken off site for storage, paper bank statements with the account name, "Owner Name – Special Account" were discovered. Payments that should have been used to pay down the loan at the bank and to purchase supplies for customer orders were being paid on expensive cars and Ivy League college tuition.

USING QUANTITATIVE AND QUALITATIVE DATA SOURCES

A Data Sleuth begins with the quantitative data analysis. It is the qualitative data sources that compliment and complete the data analysis. Qualitative data sources could be used to investigate financial crimes or in forensic accounting engagements; however, it can be tedious, laborious, and inefficient.

Quantitative data sources should be analyzed first to confirm or deny the allegations made by the victim, or client, followed by the identification of patterns and data indicators that can be used to uncover any other schemes or losses incurred by the victim. Qualitative data source investigators are limited to known schemes and related losses. Without analyzing all activity during the relevant period, other schemes and losses may not be uncovered. In "The Case of the Gambling Executive Director," if I had focused on only quantifying the losses Adam had discovered, I would have missed the use of organization funds to pay additional personal credit card payments, of which Adam was unaware.

At the same time, quantitative data source investigators should remember that qualitative data sources are extremely valuable in providing the client, attorney, or prosecutor with evidence of intent and connecting the missing funds to the subject. However, when using quantitative data sources and related analyses, locating qualitative data for each item can be unnecessary and redundant. The amount of qualitative data obtained can simply represent a category of the findings instead of every transaction comprising the loss.

 ## DATA PROCESSING TECHNIQUES

Within each of the following sections, important terms will be defined and helpful data processing steps will be provided as a guide to setting up the detailed data sets for the standard Data Sleuth analyses explained in Chapters 9 and 10. Successful, thorough, and accurate data processing creates a much smoother analysis step reducing the need to update and revisit underlying data to correct mistakes. The adage "Garbage in, garbage out" holds true in the Data Sleuth Process starting with data processing. When processing data, it is a good rule of thumb to process everything an analyst or investigator believes they may need whether they use it all or not. Selecting data points instead of processing entire statements usually results in revisiting this step – and the worst part of the process to revisit data processing is when a report is being written just before a deadline.

 ## RELEVANT PERIOD

As part of the case planning process, a relevant period should be defined prior to any work beginning. A relevant period is the period of time under investigation and drives the data and information requests throughout the case. The most efficient investigations are those for which data processing and analysis do not begin until complete information is received for the agreed-upon relevant period.

The client and/or attorney typically decide on the relevant period. However, in general, the relevant period is often determined based on several factors or a combination thereof. A few examples regarding common forensic accounting engagements and fraud investigations include:

- **Embezzlement.** The time period for which an individual, or group of individuals, was employed by an organization.
- **Partnership dispute.** The period of time for which partners were in business together.
- **Divorce property settlement.** The length of time in which a couple was married.
- **Elder financial abuse.** The period of time in which a personal representative, trustee, caregiver, or individual with power of attorney acted on behalf of, or cared for, the individual.
- **Loan fraud.** The term of a loan or financing agreement.

For the cases in which subjects were associated with the clients in some business, marital, or fiduciary capacity for long periods of time, limitations do exist that impact the relevant period.

- **Financial institution records.** Most financial institutions only maintain copies of records (i.e. bank statements) for five to seven years. Unless the client has maintained records exceeding that which can be obtained from the financial institution, the primary limiting factor on a relevant period will be the number of years for which information can be obtained from a financial institution.[1]
- **Statute of limitations.** A statute of limitations is the time limit established by law or statute in which someone is able to initiate civil or criminal proceedings in a matter. In the state of Oklahoma, the statute of limitations for civil fraud is two years from the date of discovery. When filing civil complaints or criminal charges, attorneys or law enforcement must consider the relevant statutes of limitations as a first consideration to determine whether legal proceedings or criminal charges can be filed at all based on the discovery of the act or when the act occurred. Second, if someone's actions occurred over a long period of time in which some of the actions are outside and inside the statute of limitation, the relevant period will be limited to those actions or occurrences within the statute of limitations.
- **Employee versus ownership responsibility.** When an employee has been entrusted with financial responsibilities by a company and uses the trust and

responsibility of the position for her financial gain over that of the organization, criminal charges of embezzlement, wire fraud, bank fraud, etc. can be charged. However, if at any point the employee becomes a partner of the business, criminal charges are much more difficult to file because the employee is no longer entrusted with the property of the owner but has become an owner. In the Northern District of Oklahoma, unless there are other crimes committed against perhaps a bank or government, criminal charges are not filed for partnership disputes. In the event an employee becomes a part owner in the client's business, the relevant period will likely be limited for criminal charges, and thus, splitting the period to delineate between the subject's position and responsibilities is important to assist the client with their next steps in pursuing the matter – both in civil and criminal proceedings.

▪ **Admissibility and practicality.** In my experience of locating hidden assets or performing forensic accounting procedures for divorce matters, the relevant period has frequently been limited by the number of years a judge will allow for consideration should the matter go to trial. If the case requires a business valuation, the business valuation expert typically considers three years of financial information prior to the date of the divorce filing. Occasionally, the attorney for our client has requested that we examine five years' worth of financial information. The primary objective in a divorce matter for a forensic accounting expert is to help identify and locate all assets to complete the marital balance sheet that will be used for the property settlement or division of marital assets. At some point, reviewing old financial information may have diminishing returns; however, old records may prove helpful in tracing the source of certain assets – such as retirement accounts or in disputes about the use of inheritance funds.

▪ **Budget.** Much of a client's budget in a case is used for data processing – or putting the information into the format in which it can be analyzed. The number of years being examined affects the budget of a case. A strategic approach to working within a client's budget is to limit the relevant period by choosing a period for which the greatest value would be provided to the client. For example, a loss trend in embezzlement cases is that the subject starts his scheme by stealing a small amount, and as the scheme goes undetected, the loss increases exponentially over time. If a client is unsure whether embezzlement is happening, it may be beneficial to limit the relevant period to the most recent year or two. Such a strategy may confirm the client's suspicion and help the client decide whether to expand the scope of the investigation.

GETTING ORGANIZED BEFORE BEGINNING DATA PROCESSING

Prior to processing data, a relevant period should be defined, and information should have been requested. Although the Data Sleuth Process emphasizes that information be strategically and specifically requested and initiated by the investigation team rather than the client providing the information, they believe to be important, information gathering can be a messy process. The disorganization in receiving information necessitates the continuous organization on the side of the Data Sleuth team. Incorporating the tedious administrative step of document inventory is required throughout the life of an investigation. The Data Sleuth Process uses three primary organization tools and has incorporated the automation of tasks to ensure that every time information is saved to the client's folder, the information is added to the inventory:

- **Client documents folder.** To preserve the original files provided by a client, it is a fundamental step in the information gathering process that the files are saved in their original format in a folder designated as "Client Documents." Copies of the information needed for analysis are copied and saved to the analysis working files to maintain a preserved copy. They are further organized by the date the documents were received from the client. When preparing a final report in which testimony is likely, a list of information relied upon is normally provided with the final report. Organization of client information in this manner tracks the receipt of information in a contemporaneous manner and is documented in the document inventory resulting in a simple conversion of the inventory in preparing the list of information for the final report.
- **Document inventory.** The Data Sleuth document inventory is prepared in a tabular format using a spreadsheet software and includes the fields shown in Table 8.2 at a minimum to support future searching of client files.
    - **Date received.** Date on which information was located by the investigator or provided by client or other data providers, such as statements from a financial institution.
    - **Doc year.** The year, or range of years, for the documents to be described as part of the list, if applicable.
    - **Doc date range.** The date of the first transaction included in the document through the date of the last transaction, if applicable.

TABLE 8.2 Example Data Sleuth document inventory.

Example Document Inventory

Re: *<Case Ref.>*

Date Rcvd	Doc Year	Doc Date Range	Document Type	Document Description	File Name	Folder Name	Bates Stamp
08/05/15	2015–2018	01/01/15–05/31/18	Bank Statements	ABC1234 Bank Statements	Rec'd 2019–0201	Bank Statements	SMITH_0001–SMITH_2505
08/05/15	2015–2018	01/01/15–05/31/18	Credit Card Statements	EFG5678 Credit Card Statements	Rec'd 2019–0201	Credit Card Statements	SMITH_2506–SMITH_3001
08/05/15	2015–2018	01/01/15–05/31/18	Loan History Statement	BANK9876 Loan History Statement	Rec'd 2019–0205	Loans	SMITH_3002–SMITH3005
08/05/15	2015–2018		Tax Return	Personal 1040 Tax Return	Rec'd 2019–0205	Tax Returns	SMITH_3006–SMITH6517

- **Document type.** This field simplifies future searching of client information by identifying the type of information provided such as bank statement, credit card statement, loan statement, tax return, or paystub.
- **Document description:** This field includes a description of what the document contains or represents so that the Data Sleuth team can recognize the contents without having to look at the document itself.
- **File name:** The file name of the document saved to the Client Documents folder.
- **Folder name:** The folder name for which the document is filed in, such as the date of receipt.
- **Bates stamp:** When information is provided through an attorney, some documents will show a stamp in the lower right-hand corner of a document that usually lists the parties' last name, or case reference, and a number. The Bates stamp is unique to the page on which it is stamped and is contiguous, like a page number, for all information received or exchanged throughout the process. Inclusion of this number in the document inventory helps in communicating specific information with the attorney and for referencing specific pieces of evidence in a final report as well as the resulting list of information relied on in the analysis.
- **Account Index.** The Account Index is a reorganization of the just the financial account information summarized on the Document Inventory to create dashboard detailing specific information regarding all financial accounts provided to date. The Account Index requires updating every time new financial account information is received. As shown in Table 8.3, it is organized into four sections: Bank Accounts, Credit Card and Loan Accounts, Other Accounts, and Unknown Accounts.
  - **Account Name/Loan Name/Other Account Name.** This field contains the complete name(s) of the account holder(s) as listed on the corresponding statement.
  - **Bank Name, Credit Card Company, Investment Company.** This field contains the name of the financial institution where the account is held. It is recommended to use the most recent name available as sometimes the financial institution name will change over the relevant period.
  - **Account Number (Account No.).** This field contains the full account number identified on the statement, usually located on the first page of a statement.
  - **Account Reference (Acct Ref.).** This field is used to identify a shortened reference for the account using an abbreviation for the bank name and the last four digits of the account number. For example: the account reference for an account at ABC Bank with account number 1234567 would be listed as "ABC4567."

TABLE 8.3 Example Data Sleuth Account Index.

Account Index
Re: <Case Ref.>
Relevant Period: 01/01/17–12/31/18

BANK ACCOUNTS

Account Name	Bank Name	Account No.	Acct Ref	INVENTORY		Beg Bal	End Bal	MISSING		Check Images	Deposit Items
				From	To			From	To		
CLIENT LLC OPERATING ACCOUNT	STATE BANK	11223344	SB334	01/05/17	12/31/18	12,852.00	5,849.00	03/05/17	04/31/17	YES	NO
								08/05/17	10/04/17		

LOAN AND CREDIT CARD ACCOUNTS

Loan Name	Bank Name	Account No.	Acct Ref	INVENTORY		Beg Bal	End Bal	MISSING		Loan History Statements	Loan Docs
				From	To			From	To		
CLIENT LLC	CITIBANK	0555-5555-5555-5555	CITI5555	01/10/17	01/09/18	273.45	1,789.50			N/A	N/A

OTHER ACCOUNTS (INVESTMENTS, ETC.)

Other Account Name	Bank Name	Account No.	Acct Ref	INVENTORY		Beg Bal	End Bal	MISSING		Check Images	Deposit Items
				From	To			From	To		
CLIENT INVESTMENT ACCOUNT	INVESTMENT CO	12345678	IC5678	01/01/17	12/31/18	250,000.00	0.00			N/A	N/A

- **Inventory From/To.** This field contains the first date on the first statement and the last date on the last statement in inventory for the account even if some months are missing. If months of statements are missing, identify and list those months in the "Missing From/To" columns.
- **Beginning Balance (Begin Balance).** This field lists the balance of the account on the first date of the first statement. This information is usually located on the first page of the statement and is labeled as the beginning balance.
- **Ending Balance (End Balance).** This field lists the balance of the account on the last day of the last statement. This information is usually located on the first page of the statement and is labeled as the ending balance.
- **Missing From/To.** Gaps in the months/dates within the information provided can be tracked in this field by listing the first date that is missing and the last date that is missing.
- **Check Images.** Most bank statements include small images of the checks that cleared the bank account. This field is used to identify if check images were provided.
- **Loan Activity/History Statements.** Helpful supporting documents for loans to request from a financial institution are the loan activity/history statements. These statements list advances on the loan and principal and interest payments.
- **Deposit Items.** Deposit slips are the summary of deposits made to the bank that are not electronic in nature such as the depositing of cash, currency, checks, money orders, or cashier's checks. These deposits can be made at the bank location through a counter deposit or through mobile or ATM deposits. Deposit slip copies normally accompany and precede the small check images when included with a bank statement. "Deposit items" is the term used to reference the items that were deposited, such as the checks or cash in tickets, accompanying the deposit slips. To obtain the detail behind the deposit slips, a special request must be made of the financial institution; the financial institution will then provide copies of each item deposited to the account. *Note: Some financial institutions provide online access to the deposit slip and deposit items that can be downloaded directly; however, sometimes access to the information is less than that required by the relevant period.*
- **Loan Documents.** In some cases, requesting loan supporting documentation is helpful to understanding the original purpose and intention of the loan. These documents typically contain information regarding the type of loan, the interest rate, the term, collateral, and other conditions.

CONSIDERATIONS BEFORE PROCESSING DATA

It is recommended that several decisions be made up front before processing data for a case, including:

- **Start and end dates for each data source.** Keeping the relevant period in mind, each data source to be processed should be reviewed to determine the start and end dates within the data source that should be processed. In this way, the team member processing the data processes only what is intended to be used.
- **Checks.** If bank account information is to be processed, much of the information on a statement can be converted into an account schedule using software; however, a determination should be made as to what information should be included from check images as they currently require manual data entry. If check information is to be digitized, helpful fields to include, as applicable to the case, include the dates checks were written (in addition the date the check cleared the account), payees, name of the signer of the check, any notes recorded on the memo line, and endorsements on the back of the check. *Note: The backs of checks normally must be obtained through an additional request of the bank as they are not provided with the monthly bank statement.*
- **Deposit items.** A determination should be made as to whether digitizing the individual deposit items for each deposit is pertinent and useful in addressing client concerns and investigation priorities.
- **Information to process from each data source.** Each data source should be reviewed to determine what other potentially valuable information might need to be digitized for further analysis. For example, when processing credit card account information, it may be relevant to the case to digitize the location of transactions, the transaction dates, and merchant categories.
- **Combination of data sources.** If data sources will be combined for future analysis, knowing this in the data processing step will improve the efficiency and allow for normalizing payees across the data sources at one time.
- **Budgets and deadlines.** Most forensic accounting engagements or fraud investigations involve some sort of data processing on the front end of the project. As such, if there are budget or time restraints, these should be considered in this step to limit the time processing information that is unnecessary or will not be used later in order to maximize the efficiency of the client's budget and to meet the deadline.

ACCOUNT SCHEDULING STEPS

An account schedule is the foundation of most Data Sleuth analyses. It is simply the conversion of account statement data from paper or PDF statements into a tabular spreadsheet. Account schedules can involve the conversion of any account statement, but the most common, and the ones specifically in this chapter, are for bank accounts and credit card accounts. Account statement conversions from PDFs can be assisted using various bank statement and credit card statement processing software. Although not perfect, PDF processing software is much more efficient than entering data manually. Some accounts are able to be downloaded to a spreadsheet using online access; however, some online information is only available for a period shorter than that of the relevant period.

An Account Schedule includes all transactions listed on account statements. As a secondary step to processing account schedules, currently we have not identified a cost-effective automated solution to scheduling check and/or deposit item information, and thus, information from those sources must be manually entered. One account schedule is created for each account to be analyzed. An example of an account schedule template is provided in Table 8.4.

Key items to note from the example bank account schedule are:

- **Account reference.** The account reference listed on an account schedule should match that listed on the Account Index.
- **Date.** Enter the date of the transaction as shown on the statement. This is the date the transaction cleared the bank. If both cleared dates and check dates (i.e. the date the check was written) are needed, another column can be added to manually enter the dates, as shown on the check images.
- **Check number (CHK NO).** If the transaction is a check, the check number of the check is listed in this field. This field can also be used to identify ATM withdrawals and cash withdrawals by entering "ATM" or "CASH" without quotes in the field, respectively. For all other transactions, this field remains blank.
- **Name.** This field is used to identify the general type of transaction, payee, or payor based on the information available. The information to include in this field is determined by the most descriptive source of information. If the transaction is a deposit, a general category such as "DEPOSIT" might be used if deposit items are not to be scheduled. If deposit items are to be scheduled, the payor name should be listed. If the transaction is an expenditure, a general category might include "TRANSFER," and a specific payee might include "WALMART."

TABLE 8.4 Example bank account schedule and credit card account schedule.

Example Bank Account Schedule

Bank Name: XYZ Bank
Account Reference: Bank Name Abbreviation + Last Four Digits of Account Number (XYZ5675)

DATE	CHK NO	NAME	ACCT REF	DEPOSITS	EXPENDITURES	BALANCE	MEMO
02/02/15	4519	AUCTION			152.04	32,715.36	
02/02/15	4516	BOOKSTORE			615.00	32,100.36	
02/02/15	4517	WALMART			37.67	32,062.69	
02/04/15	4522	EQUIPMENT RENTAL			1,724.21	30,338.48	
02/04/15	4521	TIRE			602.36	29,736.12	
02/05/15	4523	EQUIPMENT COMPANY			4,312.26	25,423.86	
02/09/15	4529	BUSINESS CARD			9,095.48	16,328.38	
02/09/15	4526	PAINTING			2,765.00	13,563.38	
02/09/15	4525	THIRD PARTY LLC			5,833.67	7,729.71	
02/09/15	4527	THIRD PARTY LLC			1,278.85	6,450.86	
02/09/15	4528	EQUIPMENT RENTAL 2			1,024.82	5,426.04	
02/12/15		EQUIPMENT COMPANY			365,000.00	(359,573.96)	
02/12/15		TRANSFER	1234		846.84	(360,420.80)	
02/12/15		TRANSFER	1234	365,000.00		4,579.20	TRANSFER FOR NEW EQUIPMENT
02/12/15		TRANSFER	1234	100,000.00		104,579.20	
02/12/15		DEPOSIT		7,000.00		111,579.20	

Example Credit Card Account Schedule

Bank Name: CHASE
Account Ref: Credit Card Name Abbreviation + Last Four Digits of Account Number (CHASE9876)

TRANSACTION DATE	POSTED DATE	NAME	PAYMENTS	CHARGES	BALANCE	LOCATION	MERCHANT CATEGORY
06/10/17		SECURITY SYSTEM		20.00	1,814.64	ILLINOIS	SUBSCRIPTION
06/16/17		TUITION PAYMENT		2,700.00	4,514.64	TULSA, OK	EDUCATION
06/17/17		RESTAURANT 1		1,986.86	6,501.50	TULSA, OK	RESTAURANT
06/18/17		RESTAURANT 2		250.57	6,752.07	TULSA, OK	RESTAURANT
06/19/17		DONATION		1,000.00	7,752.07	TULSA, OK	RESTAURANT
06/22/17		CLOTHING RETAILER		273.00	8,025.07	OKLAHOMA CITY, OK	RETAIL
06/23/17		RESTAURANT 3		1,242.53	9,267.60	OKLAHOMA CITY, OK	RESTAURANT
06/23/17		CABLE COMPANY		255.18	9,522.78	ILLINOIS	SUBSCRIPTION
06/29/17		GROCERY STORE		25.75	9,548.53	TULSA, OK	GROCERY
06/29/17		PAYMENT	9,548.53		-		PAYMENT

- **Account Reference (ACCT REF).** If the transaction is a transfer, the reference of the corresponding bank account from/to which the funds were received or sent should be listed if known using the appropriate account reference (e.g. ABC4567). For other transactions, this field remains blank. If the transaction is a transfer, but the corresponding account is unknown, use this column to list "UNKNOWN" as a data point for future analysis and information requests. It is also recommended that unknown accounts be listed on the Account Index if or until the information is received.
- **Deposits.** If the transaction is a deposit to a bank account, this field lists the amount of the deposit as a positive amount. If the transaction is an expenditure or debit from the account, this field remains blank as payments and expenditure amounts are listed in the adjoining column.
- **Expenditures.** If the transaction is an expenditure or payment from a bank account, this field is used to list the amount of the expenditure as a positive amount. If the transaction is a deposit or credit to the account, this field remains blank.
- **Balance.** The balance column should begin using the beginning balance of the account located on the first page of the first month's statement, and a formula should be used that will automatically calculate a running account balance as transactions are entered. The running balance should reconcile to the ending balance of each statement and should be used to ensure all transactions were entered accurately. The formula to use on each row is:

BEGINNING BALANCE FOR ACCOUNT (or from the previous transaction)
+DEPOSIT AMOUNT
– EXPENDITURE AMOUNT
_____
= BALANCE AFTER TRANSACTION ENTERED

- **Memo.** If the transaction is a check, digitizing any information from the Memo line may be helpful. We also recommend using this field to record any additional descriptions from the statements for transactions that are not checks.

Credit card account schedules are similar to that of bank account schedules with a few differences. Key items to note from the example credit card account schedule are:

- **Transaction date and posted date.** Credit card statements contain information for both the date of the transaction and the date the transaction was charged to the credit card account. Capturing transaction dates can assist with future analysis if the days of the week on which the transactions occurred are relevant to the client's concerns and investigation priorities. Creating columns listing both dates may be important to the data processing step.

- **Payments and charges.** Payments on credit cards reduce the balance of an account while credit card charges increase the balance of the account. Columns are created to differentiate between the two and allow corresponding amounts to be recorded as positive values.
- **Balance.** The balance column should begin using the beginning balance of the account located on the first page of the first month's statement, and a formula should be used that will automatically calculate a running account balance as transactions are entered. The running balance should reconcile to the ending balance of each statement and should be used to ensure all transactions were entered accurately. The formula to use on each row is slightly different from that of a bank account balance formula:

BEGINNING BALANCE FOR ACCOUNT (or from the previous transaction)
+CHARGE AMOUNT
–PAYMENT AMOUNT
= BALANCE AFTER TRANSACTION ENTERED

- **Location.** If the location information is pertinent to the case, the information can be extracted from the automated conversion of the PDF statement or the downloaded spreadsheet or manually entered into this field.
- **Merchant category.** If the merchant category listed on the account statement is pertinent to the case analysis, the information can be extracted from the automated conversion of the PDF statement, or downloaded spreadsheet, or manually entered into this field.

FORMATTING ACCOUNT SCHEDULES AND NORMALIZING PAYEES

Account schedules create efficiency for the data analysis step through consistency in the data processing. General formatting recommendations include:

- Use ALL CAPS for all fields including payees, memos, locations, and merchant categories.

- Avoid using punctuation, with the exception of the ampersand (&). For example: Wal-Mart should be entered as WALMART, and Ben & Jerry's should be entered as BEN & JERRYS
- Consistency is pertinent when entering payee names, locations, and merchant categories. The goal is to list only one unique name for each payee across all account schedules – especially if multiple accounts will be combined in the data analysis step. For example: If checks have been written to John Smith and John S. Smith, but you know or believe them to be the same person, all should be entered as JOHN S SMITH.
- List the entire business name as the payee or payor. For example: payments to Workman Forensics and Workman Forensics, LLC should all be entered as WORKMAN FORENSICS LLC

Part of the data processing process is to normalize payees, which involves review of payees upon completion of the processing to ensure that payee/payor names, locations, and merchant categories are entered exactly the same throughout the data set. Examination of the data sources is recommended prior to normalizing payees to determine if data sources will be combined in future analyses – such as the Source and Use Summary explained in Chapter 9. If data sources will be combined in the analysis step, it is recommended that payees are normalized across the data sources combined instead of individually for continuity.

 NOTE

1. Stephen Pedneault, *Need access to historical banking information? Better read the fine print, Fraud Magazine* (2014), accessed October 16, 2021, https://www.fraud-magazine.com/article.aspx?id=4294985046.

CHAPTER NINE

Standard Data Sleuth Analyses: Comparative Analysis and Source and Use Summaries

P RIOR TO THE DEVELOPMENT of the Source and Use Summary, I would use the filter and sorting functions in spreadsheet software to analyze and manipulate bank statement data and credit card statement data. I would look for anomalies within the data for which further investigation was needed. Having years of experience entering data into a spreadsheet, I was familiar with identifying unusual transactions based on the case strategy, but I had never stopped to specifically consider what made the transactions unusual. There was no defined process or methodology, and I struggled to communicate and train analysts to assist with the ever-growing caseload.

One afternoon, my only data analyst at the time asked me, "What does fraud look like? How do I know it when I see it?" These questions forced me, for the first time, to specifically pinpoint the steps I would take to find what was important in bank and credit card statement data for an investigation. At the end of the discussion, the analyst said, "So people commit fraud by writing checks to themselves?" Although it sounded too simple at the time, I discovered that she was absolutely correct. Through the identification of the ways in which someone has access and opportunity to divert funds for their personal gain and benefit, that is where fraud is found. Simplifying the analysis to highlight potential transactions of theft allowed me to build a team of analysts to assist with at least the initial analysis required in financial investigations. That is where the standard Data Sleuth analyses began to take shape.

The standard Data Sleuth analyses can be grouped into two categories:

- Analysis using two or more data sources
- Analysis of one data source

Analysis involving two or more data sources is comparative analysis. The framework for this analysis and its importance in forensic accounting and fraud investigations was explained in Chapter 6. Within this chapter, however, its practical application, and using spreadsheet software, is described in detail.

When data from one data source need to be analyzed for anomalies, several different analyses are used depending on the source of the data. A high-level summary of bank account and credit card account transactions, referred to as the Source and Use Summary, is explained within this chapter. The Source and Use Summary is a simple, effective tool to quickly identify transactions and types of transactions pertinent to the investigation priorities of a case.

 ## COMPARATIVE ANALYSIS

Forensic accounting engagements and fraud investigations often involve the comparison of two or more data sources or information that will uncover the answers to the questions "What happened?" and "What should have happened?" Comparative analysis is performed in Data Sleuth investigations by using the organizational benefits of a spreadsheet to compare information from two data sources in a side-by-side tabular format to identify discrepancies. It is within the collection of discrepancies that specific transactions are identified for further investigation, or the loss itself is quantified.

Analysis techniques and methods specifically used when analyzing bank statement and credit card statement data will be addressed in the following Source and Use Summary and Interesting Data Findings sections.

A side-by-side tabular comparative analysis requires one data source as the anchor by which other data sources will be used to compare. It is preferable if the anchor data source includes the entire data set, including information to confirm or deny the allegations and is retrieved from the source farthest removed from the subject. An example of comparative analysis is in the investigation of payroll fraud as described in "The Case of the Cash Back Payroll Scheme" in Chapter 3.

- **Anchor Data Source: Payroll report exports from the payroll processing company.** An export of payroll information for the relevant period provides information regarding "What happened?" and retrieving the information from the payroll processing company is most reliable as it would not involve the subject's access or risk alterations in retrieving it for the investigation.
- **Comparative Analysis: Payroll report exports versus timesheet entries.** Tabular timesheet entries, from which the payroll report exports should have been derived, can be connected to the payroll report exports by employee name, or identification number, and pay period. Combining the two data sets side by side allows for additional calculations to be performed in adjoining columns for each row identifying discrepancies between hours for which employees were paid and hours reported as being worked by the same employees.
- **Comparative Analysis Results.** The results of a comparative analysis, as described in the payroll fraud example, do not prove that fraud occurred but should be treated as a starting point for further investigation. In "The Case of the Cash Back Payroll Scheme" in Chapter 3, the overpayment of employees through the inflation of hours was confirmed through interviews of employees. Additionally, when the chief executive officer would inflate an employee's hours, she would enter the inflated portion of the hours into an unused field when entering the payroll information. This field was discovered to have been used only on time related to employees involved in the scheme.

THE CASE OF THE CASH FLOW FIASCO

Another example of the use of comparative analysis in an investigation is the case involving Lance Miller and his used auto dealership. Lance's family history was filled with stories of successful businessmen, and Lance was determined to be part of this legacy and, he hoped, create his own. His first auto dealership provided a nice living for his family and employees, and after a few years, he decided to expand into a neighboring town. Sadly, the new investment proved to be extremely costly as the duplication of his efforts in the original location were not profitable. For too long, he used cash from the lucrative dealership to try to keep the second location in business; ultimately, the second dealership was closed – but not before the once lucrative dealership was struggling to pay its bills on time. The operating of two used auto dealerships created a cash flow crisis, and Lance began looking to sell the lucrative dealership to a larger auto group.

As if things could not get any worse, the lender that had financed his used car purchases for years changed its repayment terms. Normally, when Lance wanted to purchase additional used car inventory, he would request an advance to pay for the vehicle and provide the lender with the title. When the car sold, he would remit the funds to the lender and receive the title to provide to the customer. The process of remitting the funds after the car was sold usually occurred within a week; however, the lender shortened this repayment turnaround to three days. With the cash flow crisis at hand, Lance contacted another lender requesting the same lending process but with better repayment terms. The lender agreed to extend Lance's dealership a loan with remittance of funds due no later than 14 days from the date of the sale to the customer. The negotiations with the larger auto group to purchase the dealership moved slowly, and Lance began to do everything he could to stay open, pay bills, and keep employees on the payroll.

A couple of months after the agreement with the new lender, the lender sent an auditor to perform an inventory count of all the vehicles for which the lender had advanced funds. For all of the advances that had not been repaid, the auditor requested that Lance identify the car for which funds were advanced or to provide a check from recent sales to remit to the lender to pay off the advance of the cars that had been sold. Reviewing the auditor's report, the loan officer identified that there were more checks provided by Lance to the auditor from alleged recent sales than the balance in the auto dealership's bank account. If the loan arrangement had been used properly, every time a car was sold, funds would have been deposited to the dealership's bank account. Then, a check to pay off the advance would have been written to the lender to pay off the corresponding advance. It was apparent that although the cars had been sold, Lance did not have the funds to pay the lender back.

The loan officer provided the investigator with a list of all advances that had not yet been repaid. The investigator requested a copy of all loan advance requests and copies of the checks Lance provided to the auditor for which the bank account did not have enough funds to process. Using this information, a comparative analysis was performed, as demonstrated in Table 9.1.

Using the list of advances from the lender as the anchor data source, the other supporting documentation of outstanding checks and loan advance requests were compared to the list of advances. "What should have happened?" is answered by identifying that the funds from vehicles that had been purchased and sold should have been returned to the bank. Therefore, the list of vehicles for which advances had not yet been repaid would have either been identified as remaining on the dealership's lot or a check returned to the lender by the auditor in which the check would have cleared the bank account. "What happened?" is answered by listing

TABLE 9.1 Comparative analysis illustration using data sources provided by the lender.

	Data Sources Provided by Lender/Client			
What should have happened?			What happened?	
Vehicles for which the amount advanced was outstanding.				
DATE OF ADVANCE	VEHICLE DESCRIPTION	AMOUNT ADVANCED	CHECKS RETURNED BY AUDITOR	INVOICE OR EMAIL SUBMITTED TO THE LENDER FOR ADVANCE
05/31/13	2014 JEEP COMPASS	$26,379.00		INVOICE
07/05/13	2011 JEEP GRAND CHEROKEE	$24,920.00		INVOICE
07/05/13	2011 JEEP GRAND CHEROKEE	$25,160.00		INVOICE
07/26/13	2012 CHEVY MALIBU	$13,225.00	YES	INVOICE
07/26/13	2009 TOYOTA CAMRY	$9,630.00	YES	INVOICE
07/26/13	2011 CHEVY MALIBU	$12,725.00		INVOICE
08/14/13	2014 JEEP CHEROKEE	$36,112.00	YES	EMAIL
08/19/13	2013 DODGE DURANGO	$45,514.00	YES	EMAIL
08/23/13	2012 JEEP PATRIOT	$14,460.00	YES	INVOICE
08/23/13	2013 RAM 3500	$47,082.00	YES	EMAIL
08/29/13	2012 RAM 2500	$44,852.00	YES	INVOICE
09/03/13	2012 JEEP GRAND CHEROKEE	$33,475.00	YES	EMAIL
09/04/13	2014 RAM 1500	$42,896.00	YES	EMAIL
09/05/13	2013 CHRYSLER 200	$13,655.00	YES	INVOICE
09/05/13	2010 JEEP PATRIOT	$8,325.00		INVOICE
09/05/13	2012 CHRYSLER	$49,516.00	YES	EMAIL
09/19/13	2013 RAM 1500	$46,277.00	YES	INVOICE
09/19/13	2013 JEEP GRAND CHEROKEE	$46,222.00	YES	INVOICE
09/23/13	2011 JEEP GRAND CHEROKEE	$24,140.00	YES	INVOICE
09/23/13	2005 RAM 3500	$17,000.00	YES	INVOICE
09/23/13	2006 JEEP LIBERTY	$7,145.00	YES	INVOICE
09/24/13	2014 JEEP CHEROKEE	$40,515.00	YES	EMAIL
09/24/13	2014 CHRYSLER T&C	$42,807.00	YES	EMAIL
09/24/13	2012 RAM 3500	$49,945.00	YES	EMAIL
	TOTAL	$721,977.00		

the known information for each vehicle on the lender's list by data source. The comparative analysis results regarding the 24 advances for vehicles with an outstanding balance remaining with the initial evidence included:

- **Two types of requests were used by Lance to advance funds on vehicles.** Lance submitted emails with invoices attached and email requests with no supporting invoice for which no invoice was ever provided.
- **All of the advances based on email requests were associated with outstanding checks.** None of the email requests for advances were associated with cars remaining on the dealership's lot but were instead represented by checks that would not clear the dealership's bank account. This finding from comparing the data sources indicated that perhaps the advanced funds were not used to purchase cars at all. Additional inquiry and analysis would be needed to confirm, but the comparative analysis provided a starting point.

By adding additional columns to the comparative analysis from related data sources at the dealership, such as bills of sale from the dealership and employee interviews, the schemes and related losses were determined.

- All email advance requests were not supported by an actual car purchase.
- Cars were purchased and sold for which no amount was remitted to the lender to repay the advance.
- Funds from the advance requests that were not used to purchase cars and car sales were determined to have been used to pay expenses of the business. The analysis performed to make this determination was based on the dealership's bank account statements using the Source and Use Summary.

 ## SOURCE AND USE SUMMARY AND ANALYSIS

The simplest and first step in analyzing bank and credit card statement data is through the Source and Use Summary. It is a high-level summary of all of the transactions in an account, or group of accounts, organized by the sources and uses of funds over a relevant period. The Source and Use Summary is structured to identify where money is coming from (i.e. sources) and where money was spent (i.e. uses) during the period. Before creating a Source and Use Summary, there are a few details that should be considered and completed to avoid inaccuracy, confusion, and performing the analysis repeatedly.

- As explained in more detail in Chapter 8, a relevant period should be established prior to processing the bank and/or credit card statement data. In this way, the Source and Use Summary can reference one complete, relevant period.
- Determine whether multiple bank and credit card accounts belonging to the same individual(s) or business(s) may be grouped together for the analysis. The decision should be based on the client questions and concerns to be addressed. If the analyst is uncertain whether to combine accounts, the most conservative approach is to analyze the accounts separately.
- If grouping accounts, bank accounts and credit card accounts should not be combined. Bank statements list payments to credit card accounts, and credit card accounts list charges for which the payments were made. In effect, credit card statement data are a subcategory to bank statement data, which is why it is recommended to analyze credit card statement data separately from bank statement data.
- If accounts are grouped together for this analysis, it is imperative to ensure that the data processed is complete for all grouped accounts for the relevant period and that the start dates and end dates are the same in each data set.

The Source and Use Summary process is similar for both bank accounts and credit card accounts; however, because of some differences, the explanation of the Source and Use Summary will be separated into sections specifically for bank accounts and credit card accounts.

 ## BANK ACCOUNT SOURCE AND USE ANALYSIS

For the purposes of this section, all steps will reference an analysis of one bank account; however, the same steps can be performed as a group of accounts keeping in mind the recommendations of the previous section. Table 9.2 illustrates a sample Source and Use Summary that will be further described throughout this section.

The Source and Use Summary is performed using spreadsheet software and its summarizing features such as pivot tables and subtotals. Before creating the summary, list the beginning balance as of the first date of the relevant period. This reference point will be used in reconciling the results to the underlying data at the completion of the summary.

TABLE 9.2 Sample bank account Source and Use Summary.

	Source and Use Summary – Bank Account			
	Account Name and Account Reference			
	For the Period: [Start Date] through [End Date]			
Name	**Related Account Numbers**	**Count of Records Summarized**	**Total Amount**	**Notes**
BEGINNING BALANCE			$ 82,557.69	
SOURCES (DEPOSITS/ CREDITS)				
Transfers & Wires				
TRANSFER	1234	15	300,500.00	
TRANSFER	9876	1	3,005.15	Unknown Account
WIRE FROM		1	8,813.50	Research source of wire
Other Deposits				
DEPOSITS		217	2,311,456.78	
OTHER CREDITS		6	47,377.92	
TOTAL SOURCES			$ 2,671,153.35	
USES (EXPENDITURES/ DEBITS)				
Withdrawals				
WITHDRAWAL		1	2,500.00	
ATM WITHDRAWALS		2	404.00	
Transfers and Wires				
TRANSFER	5678	10	50,555.25	
TRANSFER	2323	1	222.78	
Payments to Entities				
COMPANY CO.		7	13,962.57	
COMPANY CORP.		9	2,447.78	
COMPANY INC.		1	5,783.93	
COMPANY LLC		1	717.18	
Payments to Individuals				
JOHN DOE		3	1,750.00	
JANE DOE		14	23,997.00	

SUBJECT'S CHILD	1	1,416.00	Not an employee of company; research further
SUBJECT'S WIFE	16	23,150.00	Not an employee of company; research further
Credit Card Payments			
CHASE	2	33,735.00	Tie out to known statements
All Other Payments			
MISC PAYMENTS	275	966,756.36	
SERVICE CHARGES	5	5.40	
TOTAL USES		$ 1,127,403.25	
ENDING BALANCE		$ 1,626,307.79	

Sources (Deposits/Credits)

The detailed account transactions listed in a spreadsheet from data processing is then summarized based on whether the transaction is a source of funds or a use of funds. The section labeled "Sources" summarizes all of the deposits or credits to an account first by name, description, or type. Corresponding fields are used to list the total number of records and the sum of the records per summary line item. Then the sources are further summarized from highest to lowest risk of fraud to the client.

■ **Transfers from accounts within the same financial institution or wires from accounts at other financial institutions.** The data processing step should always include the identification of transfers and wires in a field. Identifying transfers of funds credited to an account is helpful in identifying all related bank accounts. Examples in which identifying the sources of transfers or wires are important are those in which the client or subject is unsure as to whether previously unknown accounts exist that may need to also be analyzed for identification of marital assets in a divorce matter, recoverable assets in an embezzlement, or additional shell companies in a ghost vendor scheme.

Additionally, the summary of transfers and wires can identify repayments of stolen funds, as in the "Case of the Mom of the Year" in Chapter 7.

Additional information regarding sending or beneficiary information for wire transfers can be obtained by request of the account holder or subpoena. Identifying the source of wires can be helpful especially if it is suspected that the subject has sold property or assets during the relevant period.

- **Counter, mobile, ATM deposits.** Counter deposits are deposits that are made at the counter or in the drive through of a financial institution with the help of a teller. Mobile deposits are those made using the financial institution's website or application through a mobile device. ATM deposits are those made using the ATM. Counter, mobile, and ATM deposits are reflected in the images section of a bank statement as a deposit slip, but the actual items deposited are not provided on the statement and must be requested by the account holder or through a subpoena. The decision whether to enter the payee from the individual checks deposited to the account depends on the client concerns and investigation priorities of a case.

  Not every case requires the data entry of deposit items, but if the client concerns include allegations in which knowing exactly from whom money was deposited by source, deposit items should be scheduled as part of the data processing step. If the data entered during the data processing step do not include the payor information from deposits, likely the sources section of the analysis will be limited.

- **Electronic deposits.** In the data processing step, sources of electronic deposits can usually be identified without a request made of the bank for additional documentation. These are also summarized as part of the sources section of the Source and Use Summary.

Total sources are calculated at the bottom of the sources section. Any items noticed by the analyst within this section as needing additional research should be flagged or noted for further investigation and research. Any items noted will also be considered in preparing the interesting data analysis to be explained in Chapter 10.

Uses (Expenditures/Debits)

The section labeled "Uses" summarizes all of the expenditures and debits to an account by name, description, or type. Corresponding fields are used to list the total number of records and the sum of the records per summary line item. If a client concern includes the quantification of missing money, and the subject had access to the bank account, then it is advantageous to understand the most common ways in which subjects steal money and the potential data indicators of the theft. Therefore, considering a subject's access to funds and systems is so important in the planning process, because when the analyst begins the Source and Use Summary and analysis, prioritization of transaction indicators can be considered based on the level of risk. The Data Sleuth Source and Use Summary in Table 9.2 is organized based on the most frequent ways in which subjects have stolen money in previous investigations.

- **Withdrawals and ATM withdrawals.** If a subject is a signer on an account or has access to a debit card, she can withdraw cash and/or obtain a cashier's check payable to a desired payee. If an account contains images of withdrawal slips, and if the subject would have been able to access to checking withdrawals in this manner, these items should be flagged with a request prepared by the account holder or by subpoena to obtain the supporting items from the bank, whether that be a cashier's check or cash out tickets. An example of the use of withdrawal slips to obtain cashier checks to purchase assets for personal use with company funds is provided in "The Case of the Man Cave" in Chapter 4.

- **Transfers to accounts within the same financial institution.** The identification of at least the last four digits of any account numbers to which funds were transferred is important in the Source and Use Summary in identifying undisclosed or unknown accounts, as discussed previously. By summarizing within the transfers section by the last four digits, comparison can be made between the Source and Use Summary and the account inventory to identify accounts for further inquiry, request, or examination. Typically, if an item is referenced as a transfer on a statement, it is referencing a transfer between accounts within the same financial institution.

- **Wires to accounts at other financial institutions.** A wire transfer refers to the sending of funds to an account at a different financial institution. Wires are helpful in identifying accounts held at other financial institutions because it lists the beneficiary's name, financial institution, and account number.

- **Payments to entities.** Creating a subcategory in the "Uses" section for payments to entities, which includes payee names ending in LLC, Inc., Co., and Corp, is helpful in identifying previously undisclosed related entities, shell companies, and fake vendors for example. By summarizing and extracting the payees that contain a reference to a type of entity or business name, then the subcategory of payments to entities can easily be reviewed. If needed, further research can then be performed to identify and confirm whether the payees are those that would be paid in the normal course of business or that benefited the client.

As demonstrated in "The Case of the Man Cave," Bill was able to steal funds by creating fake entities. Within the State of Oklahoma, registration of a new entity costs $100 with an annual renewal fee of $25. Registering entities with the state is inexpensive and allows the individual to create a bank account in the entity's name. If someone has discovered a method to steal funds from their employer and hide it as a vendor payment, the fees associated with registering an entity are not a deterrent.

- **Payments to individuals.** Creating a subcategory in the "Uses" section for payments to individuals is helpful in identifying individuals who received funds from the business, or even marital estate, who should not have received the funds. This subcategory is particularly helpful in divorce cases, to identify money that has been paid to a trusted friend or relative to hold until divorce proceedings have been finalized. This subcategory has also been used to identify payments to employee spouses who are not employed by the company but were paid directly from the bank account. With estate and trust matters, embezzlement is perpetrated by the trustee, caretaker, or personal representative simply by writing checks to themselves. Careful review of this subcategory may identify payments to the trusted individual that should not have occurred or that exceed an agreed upon amount.

- **Credit card payments.** Creating a subcategory of payments to credit cards may be helpful in identifying credit cards for which funds were spent by the client but they were unaware of the card or account.

- **All other payments.** The remaining subcategory of "All Other Payments" summarizes those transactions that were not previously categorized. Depending on the needs of the case, transactions summarized in this section may need additional research and analysis even though they do not fall into the standard subcategories.

In order to reconcile the Source and Use Summary to the underlying data, an ending balance calculation should be performed to match the ending balance of the last date of the relevant period to the supporting bank statement.

> Beginning account balance as of the first day of the relevant period
> + Deposits/Credits
> −Expenditures/Debits
> _____
> = Ending account balance as of the last day of the relevant period

How to Use the Bank Account Source and Use Summary Results

Using the Source and Use Summary as part of Data Sleuth analysis involves the following steps and considerations. The term "flagging" or "flagged" in the following sections refers to using the notes column in the Source and Use Summary to indicate further research, inquiry, investigation, or client feedback. The intention of the Source and Use Summary is to provide the analyst with a high-level perspective identifying where money came from and where it went within an account, allowing the analyst to flag potential items of interest. Anything the analyst believes the client should review is also noted to ensure its inclusion in the subsequent detail level Interesting Data Findings (IDF) analysis. Client feedback is obtained through the IDF first. To be certain that all findings are identified, the Source and Use Summary is provided in a second round of client review where the feedback from the IDF has been incorporated.

- **Transfers.** For all transfers in both the "Sources" and "Uses" section of the summary, the analyst should reconcile all account numbers listed on the summary to the account inventory. If any of the accounts for which transfers occurred involve accounts that are not listed on the account inventory or represent an account number for which the analyst does not have supporting documentation, that group of transfers should be flagged for client consideration and feedback and potential account requests made by the account holder or subpoena. This section represents transfers between accounts that are made electronically. Sometimes, funds are transferred between accounts using checks. As such, transactions grouped in other subcategories may need to be moved to the transfers section.
- **Deposits and deposit items.** If deposit items were entered into the underlying data set or spreadsheet, any deposits from payors relevant to the case investigation priorities, should be flagged for client feedback. Knowing the sources of deposits is helpful if the investigation involves comparing the expected deposits from sources to actual deposits by sources.
- **Wires.** Any wires that do not appear to be within the normal course of business or might potentially indicate that assets were sold or hidden or moved out of the control of our client, those transactions should be flagged.
- **Payments to entities.** All payments to entities for which the analyst is unaware should be flagged for at least client review. If the client is unable to review transactions, or if the client is unaware of certain payments to entities, then further research is performed by the analyst including but not limited to identifying registered agents and principals through public database

sources; locating supporting invoices; and comparing vendor information (i.e, addresses, phone numbers, and employment identification numbers) to similar fields in employee information reports.

■ **Payments to individuals.** Similar to the steps listed with regard to payments to entities, the list of individuals receiving payments during the relevant period are provided to the client for feedback and review. If the client is unable to identify the individuals, additional research may be performed such as trying to determine their relationship with a subject.

■ **Credit card payments.** Credit card payments should be flagged for client feedback and/or further review. The analyst should also compare the credit card companies identified in this section to the list of known credit cards in the account inventory. If any of the credit card companies to which payments were paid are not listed on the account inventory, the group of payments should be flagged for client consideration and feedback and potential account requests made by the account holder or subpoena.

■ **All other payments.** The payments not assigned to a subcategory should be reviewed and potentially flagged for client feedback especially if they are large individual payments or single even dollar payment amounts (i.e. multiples of 10 or 100).

CREDIT CARD ACCOUNT SOURCE AND USE SUMMARY

A credit card Source and Use Summary is set up similarly to that of the summary for bank accounts. The primary difference is the direction of the transactions in the data. For the transactions on credit card statements, purchases for which the credit card was charged are positive amounts, and payments to the credit cards are negative amounts. Table 9.3 illustrates a sample credit card Source and Use Summary that will be further described throughout this section.

Just as with the bank Source and Use Summary, begin by listing the beginning balance as of the first date of the relevant period. This reference point will be used in reconciling the results to the underlying data at the completion of the summary.

Sources (Payments/Credits)

The "Sources" section of the credit card Source and Use Summary lists payments to the credit card account as well as merchant credits or any other type of credit provided by the credit card company.

Uses (Purchases/Advances/Balance Transfers/Other Charges)

The "Uses" section of the Source and Use Summary for credit cards lists all of the charges during the relevant period, summarized by payee with subcategories similar to those on the bank account Source and Use Summary with a few differences:

- **Cash advances.** If a credit card is used to obtain cash, it is listed as a cash advance on the credit card statement. A subcategory to easily group and identify cash advances may be helpful depending on the case investigation priorities.
- **Balance transfers.** If a balance from one credit card is transferred to the credit card being analyzed, the analyst may want to determine from which account the balance was transferred and consider analyzing that credit card information as well if within the relevant period.

The purchases for which the credit card is charged are then summarized by payee. Depending on the case investigation priorities, it might be valuable to extract and review using subcategories, payments to entities and individuals as with the bank Source and Use Summary. Another feature of credit card data are the categories assigned to purchases by the credit card company. If the merchant categories are scheduled as part of data processing, subcategories could be created in the Source and Use Summary as well.

In order to reconcile the Source and Use Summary to the underlying data, an ending balance calculation should be performed to match the ending balance of the last date of the relevant period to the supporting bank statement.

> Beginning account balance as of the first day of the relevant period
> + Purchases/Advances/Balance Transfers/Other Charges
> − Payments/Credits
> _____
> = Ending account balance as of the last day of the relevant period

How to Use the Credit Card Source and Use Summary Results

Using the credit card Source and Use Summary results is similar to that of the bank account results, so considerations specifically for the credit card Source and Use Summary are explained in this section.

TABLE 9.3   Sample credit card Source and Use Summary

Source and Use Summary – Credit Card			
Credit Card Account Name and Account Reference			
For the Period: [Start Date] through [End Date]			
Name	**Count of Records Summarized**	**Total Amount**	**Notes**
BEGINNING BALANCE		$ 33,816.93	
SOURCES (PAYMENTS/CREDITS)			
Merchant Credits			
SECURITY SYSTEM COMPANY	15	4,288.15	
AUTOMOTIVE COMPANY	1	180.00	
ONLINE DATA STORAGE COMPANY	1	97.37	
TRAVEL INN	1	821.28	
Payments to Account			
PAYMENTS	45	115,544.83	Reconcile to known bank accounts
TOTAL SOURCES		$120,931.63	
USES (PURCHASES/ADVANCES/ BALANCE TRANSFERS)			
Cash Advances			
N/A		-	
Balance Transfers			
N/A		-	
Payments to Entities			
COMPANY CO.	41	20,990.15	
COMPANY CORP.	1	174.33	
COMPANY INC.	56	59,765.78	
COMPANY LLC	1	106.07	
Payments to Individuals			
N/A		-	
All Other Payments			
MISC PAYMENTS	3	4,733.60	
SERVICE CHARGES	3	1,344.77	
TOTAL USES		$ 87,114.70	
ENDING BALANCE		$ -	

- **Payments to account.** The payments to the credit card account should be flagged for additional analysis in the Interesting Data Findings analysis to reconcile the payments listed on the credit card statement to the corresponding payments in the bank account transactions. For any payments that are made to credit card accounts that do not reconcile to known bank accounts, the difference should be flagged for client feedback and to determine if additional bank or credit card statements should be requested.
- **Merchant Categories.** If merchant categories were scheduled with the credit card transaction data and used in the credit card Source and Use Summary as subcategories, the transactions within subcategories prohibited by policy or beyond the normal accepted use of a business credit card, such as clothing or shopping, those items should be flagged for further review.

Analysis of a credit card Source and Use Summary involves primarily reviewing the types of purchases charged to the credit card account. Review of the transactions is normally focused on delineating between the business-related purchases and non-business-related purchases. This delineation can often be performed on a summary by payee level from the Source and Use Summary by noting next to each payee group whether the charges fall into the buckets, described in Chapter 2, of:

- Business related
- Non business related
- Both business and non-business related
- Unknown

Any purchases within the "both business and non-business-related" or "unknown" designations should then be flagged for further detailed review in the Interesting Data Findings analysis and/or client feedback. Any payee group that is determined as non-business related will likely be included in the resulting loss amount.

CHAPTER TEN

Standard Data Sleuth Analyses: Interesting Data Findings, Risk Indicator Analysis, and Payroll Analysis

OST CLIENT CASES WORKED by Workman Forensics involve bank account and credit card account data and the Source and Use Summaries explained in Chapter 9. This provides a starting point to addressing client concerns and investigation priorities. However, a Source and Use Summary is only a high-level examination indicating where money came from and how it was used. It does not identify anomalies within the detailed underlying data. That is why the Interesting Data Findings analysis was created. It combines the power of data analysis with the intentionality and problem-solving of an investigation to answer the client's questions. The Interesting Data Findings is now a standard detailed analysis that allows investigators and analysts to perform what are now considered to be standard data analysis tests on client data for identifying outliers and anomalies.

Sometimes, especially when other supporting evidence is lacking, the best analysis requires identification of characteristics or specific indicators within the data. An analyst may not be able to confirm that a subject benefited at the expense of a client, but she may be able to organize and prioritize the transactions indicating the highest risk of fraud by identifying the fraud-risk characteristics of the data, or risk indicators. Risk indicator analysis has proven extremely helpful with investigating allegations of purchasing fraud and fake vendors.

An application of the comparative analysis, explained in Chapter 9, the data analysis tests from the Interesting Data Findings analysis, and the risk indicator analysis is in payroll investigations. All three analyses work well together when investigating allegations of ghost employees and payroll overpayments.

 ## INTERESTING DATA FINDINGS

Another Data Sleuth analysis to incorporate after the Source and Use Summary is the Interesting Data Findings (IDF) analysis. The IDF is a more detailed, granular analysis of specific transactions using data analysis tests to identify anomalies and the most common indicators within a data set, which might indicate fraud or attempts to hide assets or purchases of assets. There are standard data analysis tests that are performed on each data set; however, the analyst preparing the IDF also considers whether custom tests should be designed based on the client's concerns and investigation priorities.

Standard IDF Data Analysis Tests

The analyses described in this section are not necessarily useful in every case, nor is it all inclusive; however, the list is an excellent place to start. The IDF tests can be performed on any data set, including bank statement data, credit card statement data, payroll data, purchasing data, general ledgers, cash disbursement journals, and check registers – just to name a few. To create an IDF:

- Run data analysis tests on each data set in the case that are relevant to the client concerns and investigation priorities.
- Categorize the individual transaction results of the tests by type.
- Summarize the results in a simplified format for client feedback and or additional inquiry, research, or review.

Benford's Analysis

Benford's analysis is based on Benford's Law, which provides the expected distribution of a random population of numbers.[1] Using this law is helpful in spotting anomalies in data in investigations because deviations from the expected frequency distribution may indicate that the transaction was not a random occurrence but was influenced somehow. Benford's analysis works best on large data sets and can be run using spreadsheet software or data analysis software. As with any data analysis result, further research must be performed to decide if the anomaly is legitimate, erroneous, or fraudulent. Benford's analysis expected frequency deviations are explained through the following examples to illustrate Benford's analysis anomalies:

- **Legitimate.** Several partners in a medical practice were concerned that copays from their patients were being stolen by the office manager. One of the tests performed in the investigation was Benford's analysis. The analyses performed prior to Benford's analysis had determined that all cash payments recorded to the system had been deposited, which led to the analysis of bad debt write-off reports. The results of the analysis indicated a deviation from the expected frequency in the first digit for the number 1. All of the transactions for which the dollar amount began with a 1 were extracted and reviewed. It was quickly identified from the detailed transactions that the abnormal frequency of the payments with the first digit of 1 were due to normal insurance rates for the most common services. This category was still further researched by verifying the services were billed to the appropriate insurance agency and that the write-off was appropriate. Such verification was located, and for this client concern and investigation priority, no loss was identified. (See Figure 10.1.)
- **Unauthorized Expenditures, Fraudulent.** An employee was accused of using corporate funds for charitable contributions benefiting the executive personally and subsequently deducting the contributions on his personal tax return. A Benford's analysis was used on the bank account data. For all the first two digits within the data set that were abnormal to the expected frequency, additional research was performed and confirmed that all of the underlying transactions were charitable contributions not for the benefit of the company. (See Figure 10.2.)

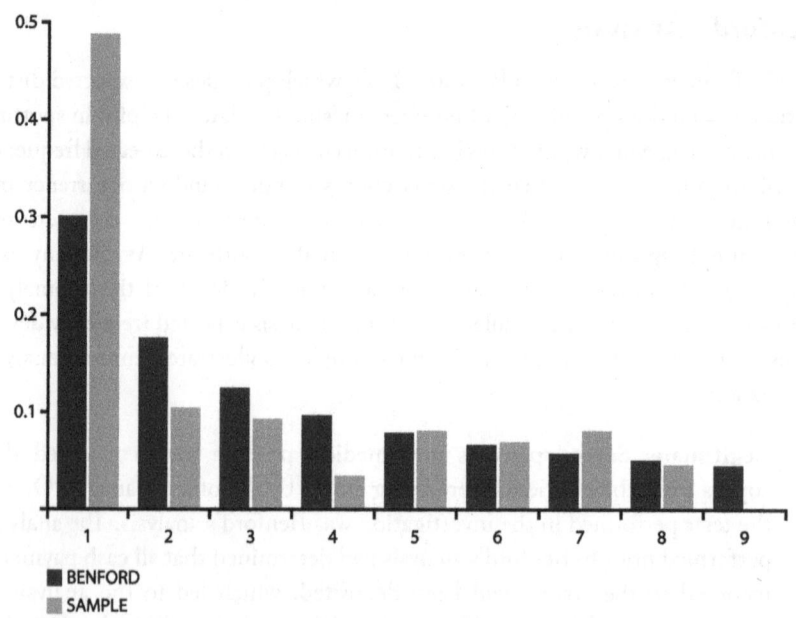

FIGURE 10.1 Benford's analysis graph of number of write-offs from patient accounts.

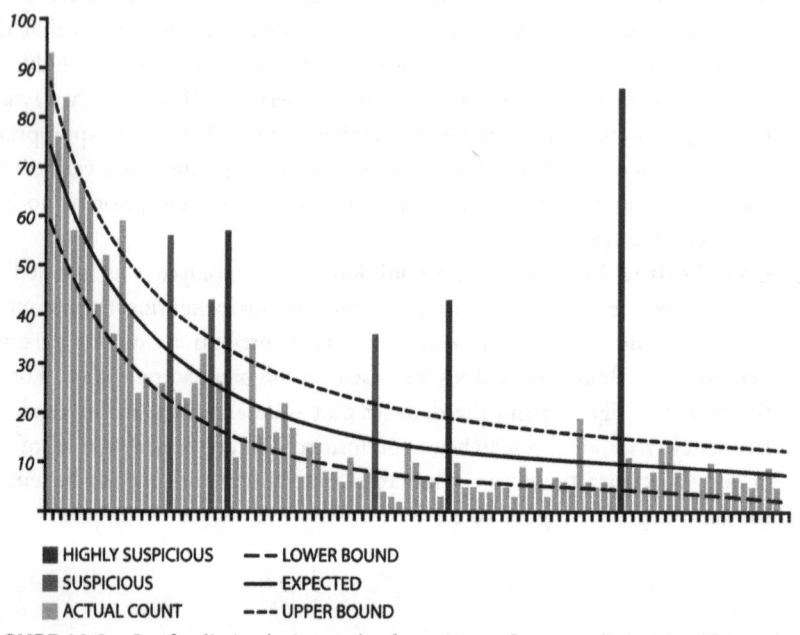

FIGURE 10.2 Benford's Analysis graph of suspicious first two digits identifying charitable contributions.

Even-Dollar Amounts

It is common that when individuals are stealing funds or moving money to hide in a divorce directly from a bank account or brokerage account, the payment amounts are multiples of 10 or 100 and are even in amount such as $3,500.00, $55,000.00, $205,000.00. Many data analysis programs assisting with Benford's analysis will provide a result for the last two digits for which even dollar payments can be exported. Additionally, filter functions within spreadsheet software can be used to filter for dollar amounts ending in ".00," "00.00," and so forth. When transactions of even dollar amounts are identified, additional research and inquiry can be performed to verify whether they were for the benefit of the subject or the client.

Large Individual Payments

Graphing expenditures in a data set may be helpful in identifying large individual payments or outliers in a data set. Graphing expenditures for this purpose could be used for all expenditures in certain general ledger accounts or for an entire expenditure report for the entire relevant period.

Month-Over-Month Pivot Table

For data in which regular monthly deposits or payments are made, a month-over-month pivot table may be helpful in identifying missing deposits that could include rental income or subscription income or debt payments. If the underlying data have payor information or if deposit items were scheduled, then a month-over-month pivot table can be created by payor identifying the total amount paid by payor by month and a total number of payments by month. For any months in which it appears a deposit was skipped, further research and inquiry should be performed to identify what happened, which could include that the payor simply did not pay; there was a catch-up payment in another month; or funds were diverted. An example of a month-over-month pivot table by customer is shown in Table 10.1. Conditional formatting in the spreadsheet was used to highlight the months for which no customer payment was received.

Pivot tables can also be used to evaluate month-over-month sales or expenditures by location or by sales employee or whatever other factor would help answer a client's concern or investigation priority. If check dates or transaction dates were scheduled as part of the data entry, pivot tables, similar to that of the month-over-month pivot table could be used to count the number of transactions occurring on certain days of the week.

TABLE 10.1 Illustration of month-over-month pivot table

Month-Over-Month Pivot Table by Customer – Sum of Customer Payments						
PAYOR NAME	2021-01	2021-02	2021-03	2021-04	2021-05	TOTAL
Adams	0.00	0.00	0.00	0.00	0.00	0.00
Andrews	3,951.04	3,904.04	3,904.04	4,880.05	3,904.04	20,543.21
Cole	13,973.88	4,060.00	4,495.00	5,053.00	0.00	27,581.88
Daughtery	4,004.04	4,004.04	4,165.04	4,959.05	4,065.04	21,197.21
Martin	3,904.04	3,904.04	3,904.04	4,880.05	3,904.04	20,496.21
Mason	0.00	0.00	0.00	0.00	1,450.00	1,450.00
Mitchell	0.00	0.00	0.00	0.00	0.00	0.00
Newton	7,960.00	4,060.00	4,495.00	4,210.57	4,495.00	25,220.57
Patterson	3,589.04	3,904.04	4,219.04	1,576.17	4,982.04	18,270.33
Williams	0.00	0.00	0.00	0.00	0.00	0.00
Workman	0.00	0.00	0.00	0.00	0.00	0.00

Month-Over-Month Pivot Table by Customer – Count of Customer Payments						
PAYOR NAME	2021-01	2021-02	2021-03	2021-04	2021-05	TOTAL
Adams	0	0	0	0	0	0
Andrews	1	1	1	1	1	5
Cole	3	1	1	1	0	6
Daughtery	1	1	1	1	1	5
Martin	1	1	1	1	1	5
Mason	0	0	0	0	1	1
Mitchell	0	0	0	0	0	0
Newton	2	1	1	1	1	6
Patterson	1	1	1	1	1	5
Williams	0	0	0	0	0	0
Workman	0	0	0	0	0	0

Extract Detailed Transactions from Source and Use Summaries

Any items that were flagged in the Source and Use Summaries, either from bank account or credit card account data, should be extracted from the underlying data source so that individual transactions can be reviewed for additional research, inquiry, or client feedback.

Using Accounting Records in the Interesting Data Findings Analysis

A helpful step in the IDF analysis, if valuable to the case, is joining transactions identified as anomalies with the general ledger or other report, that provides information about how the specific transactions were recorded in the accounting system. The corresponding general ledger account can be added as an additional field to the IDF summary for the client to help them identify whether the transaction was for the benefit of the client.

Create an Interesting Data Findings Summary

From the individual results of the data tests, categorize by finding type – not by general ledger account or a descriptive category. Then summarize the transactions by these categories explaining why the transactions are considered a finding. For example, common categories for an IDF summary are "Transfers to Unknown Accounts," "Wire Transfers," and "Even Dollar Payments." Another option is to summarize the findings based on the type of test performed. To avoid confusion, only one IDF category should be used per transaction or set of transactions. The best IDF category to use for a transaction that is a result from several tests should be the one that is the easiest to understand.

As part of the Data Sleuth Process, IDF summaries and detailed transactions are provided to the client for feedback. The analyst should take into consideration the end-client and use of the IDF in the client feedback step. This is important because the simpler the summary and understanding of its purpose, the better the information the analyst receives from the client to begin to piece the case, and ultimate loss calculation, together. This part of the Data Sleuth Process improves with experience. We have found it helpful if the data analyst performing the data analyses and IDF is not also the case manager – or the individual with client contact. This allows the two professionals to work together to ensure that the information provided to the client caters for the specific client and case needs. A sample Interesting Data Findings Summary is provided for reference in Table 10.2.

 RISK INDICATOR ANALYSIS

Clients will sometimes provide data from a data source and request that an investigator or analyst identify fraud within the data source based on a series of events. For our firm, these types of cases often involve larger companies with no internal audit department, but due to the size of the organization, more than one person manages the finances of the organization. The two most

TABLE 10.2 Sample Interesting Data Findings Summary

Interesting Data Findings Summary
For [Account Name, Account Number, Client Name, Etc.]
For the Period [Start Date] through [End Date]

Data Findings 1 | Transfers to Unknown Accounts

Date Range		Last Four Digits of Acct Number	No. of Recs.	Total Amount	Data Finding
From	To				
11/28/18	11/28/18	1234	1	250.78	Transfers to account not known to belong to the client.
09/12/19	05/08/20	5378	14	138,000.00	Transfers to account not known to belong to the client. Account may be associated with known LLC registered to subject.
06/05/20	06/05/20	1122	1	8,302.25	Transfers to account not known to belong to the client.

Data Findings 2 | Payments to Credit Cards Not Identified on Account Inventory

Date Range		Payee	No. of Recs.	Total Amount	Data Finding
From	To				
06/29/18	09/20/19	CREDIT CARD 1 PAYMENT	5	24,918.70	Credit card payments not matching account inventory list. Unknown if this is a personal credit card of the subject or belongs to the client.
01/05/18	01/14/19	CREDIT CARD 2 PAYMENT	32	125,349.97	Credit card payments not matching account inventory list. Unknown if this is a personal credit card of the subject or belongs to the client.

Data Findings 3 | Other Unusual Findings by Payee

Date Range		Payee	No. of Recs.	Total Amount	Data Finding
From	To				
04/03/18	09/20/19	SUBJECT WIFE	14	225,997.00	Large total payment amount to an individual.
02/21/18	01/28/19	UNKNOWN INDIVIDUAL	16	13,150.00	Large number of payments to an individual.
01/23/18	04/29/20	LAW FIRM	8	67,340.91	Large total payment amount and number of payments.
05/17/18	08/23/18	SUBJECT	2	20,000.00	Payments made to subject outside of payroll.
03/27/18	04/09/20	CONSTRUCTION LLC	13	71,294.67	Large total payment amount and number of payments.
05/09/19	01/09/20	SUBJECT REGISTERED LLC	7	27,230.50	Large total payment amount and number of payments.

common data sources involve purchasing and payroll records. This section will explain the risk indicator analysis involving purchasing records. The Payroll Analysis section will incorporate the use of the risk indicator analysis as part of testing for ghost employees.

Another use of the risk indicator analysis is in prelitigation investigations. Prelitigation investigations are performed when clients would like to sue another party, but they are not certain of the events that caused the loss. Usually, the clients do not have access to all of the evidence required for a full investigation, but they will be able to obtain what is needed through discovery or subpoena when the lawsuit is filed.

Risk Indicator Analysis Steps

- Identify data sets available for analysis and combine into one data set if possible.
- Perform data analysis tests, which can include those described for the IDF analysis, on the data set related to the client concerns and investigation priorities.
- For each transaction or data point that is identified as an anomaly from the individual data analysis tests, assign a value of at least 1. For all transactions that do not appear to be anomalies for a specific data analysis test, assign a value of 0.
- When all the data analysis tests are complete, sum the total values assigned for all data analysis tests by transaction.
- To prioritize additional research, inquiry, or client feedback, sort the risk indicator totals from largest to smallest.

Example for Using Risk Indicator Analysis

A client suspected fake vendors and/or purchasing fraud by at least one employee; however, no evidence documenting such had been obtained by the client. After preparing the case plan, a list of requested information was provided that would assist the investigator and analyst in both a comparative analysis and one data source analysis to confirm or deny the suspicions. The results of the data analysis were to be reviewed by the client and subsequent interviews performed.

As the client worked to gather the requested information, she discovered that many of the records and reports she originally believed she could export were not available and could not be created. The client, investigator, and analyst began to work together to determine data sources available to the client for which at least a risk indicator analysis could be performed. The following data sets and reports were obtained and combined into one table as applicable to begin performing a risk indicator analysis.

- Authorized vendor list
- Purchase order listing
- Vendor invoices (PDF and accounting system listing)
- Purchasing system user log listing submissions and approvals throughout the purchasing process
- Vendor payment listing

To combine information from the data sets, a matching primary key should be identified from the various data sets that can be used to link two data sets together.[2] For example, in the information listed previously, if each of the data sets reference a vendor identification number ("vendor ID"), then the vendor ID can be used to link the transactions between all of the data sets before performing the risk indicator analysis. Rarely is a primary key and join that simple between multiple data sets, so realistically, a few of the data sets will be joined together on one primary key, and then a different primary key will need to be identified in the combined data set and another data source, and so forth. Sometimes, not all the data sets can be combined, and some data sets may go unused or may require a separate analysis.

Data analysis tests performed on the combined data set included the identification of:

- Large individual payments/outliers as they related to the entire data set
- Large individual payments/outliers as it related to the corresponding individual general ledger accounts
- Even-dollar payments
- Vendor addresses that matched employee addresses
- Payments for which no purchase order was assigned
- Payments for which no purchase order was approved
- Payments for which no invoice was on file

For each transaction with a positive result from the data analysis tests, a value of 1 was assigned to transaction. If the data analysis test returned a negative result for the transaction, a value of 0 was assigned. All the data analysis test results were totaled and sorted from largest to smallest to identify the vendors and payments of highest risk. The results of this analysis were then reviewed by the client to narrow the results further. The resulting list of high-risk vendors was used in the interview process of personnel. An example of a risk indicator analysis worksheet is provided in Table 10.3.

TABLE 10.3 Example of a risk indicator analysis involving purchasing records.

Example of a Risk Indicator Analysis Involving Purchasing Records

Payment Date	Vendor	Amount	Overall Outlier	Account Outlier	Even-Dollar	Vendor Employee Address Match	No Invoice	No PO Number	No Approval of PO	No. of Risk Factors
01/16/19	ABC LLC	107,100.00	1	1	1	0	1	0	0	4
01/17/19	TRUCK COMPANY INC	46,818.00	1	1	1	0	1	0	0	4
01/16/19	ABC LLC	56,317.50	1	1	0	0	1	0	0	3
01/28/19	CONSTRUCTION COMPANY INC	596,964.00	1	0	1	0	1	0	0	3
02/07/19	MANUFACTURING LLC	27,041.18	1	1	0	0	1	0	0	3
02/07/19	CONSTRUCTION COMPANY INC	596,964.00	1	0	1	0	1	0	0	3
02/15/19	MANUFACTURING LLC	43,245.68	1	1	0	0	1	0	0	3
02/28/19	CONSTRUCTION COMPANY INC	60,939.00	1	0	1	0	1	0	0	3
01/28/19	CONSTRUCTION COMPANY INC	115,600.50	1	0	0	0	1	0	0	2
01/29/19	CONSULTANT LLC	30,606.24	1	0	0	0	1	0	0	2
02/07/19	CONSTRUCTION COMPANY INC	150,259.50	1	0	0	0	1	0	0	2
02/28/19	CONSTRUCTION COMPANY INC	75,436.50	1	0	0	0	1	0	0	2

PAYROLL ANALYSIS

Payroll analysis uses both analysis of one data source as well as comparative analysis. Using only the data provided in a payroll report, anomalies regarding payroll to employees, including expense reimbursements or benefits, can be identified. When working with one data source analysis, the most meaningful results are those when the data set is complete and includes all employees – or at least all employees from a department or all employees in a certain pay grade or position. It is difficult to find anomalies when a client has edited the data set prior to providing the information. In order for anomalies to be discovered, there must be a benchmark or a way to identify what is normal to the data set.

Although most payroll providers are able to export any data collected from payroll into a tabular format, if clients are using older versions of the software that have not been updated, sometimes it is not economically feasible to convert payroll data for all employees to a tabular format for one data source analysis. Sometimes, clients will request that only one employee's records be reviewed. When either of these situations occur, the payroll analysis immediately becomes a comparative analysis as other data sources will need to be used to identify any discrepancies or unauthorized disbursements of funds through payroll. Note: if a client requests that only one employee's records are to be reviewed and there is little supporting documentation, be sure to exercise professional skepticism about the client's intentions behind the engagement. The following analyses assume a complete data set of all employees and involve the analysis of one data set at a time and then comparative analysis as a second step.

Ghost Employees

Ghost employees is the term most commonly used when individuals are paid through payroll but either never worked for the company or whose status remained active after leaving and was used to issue additional paychecks to someone in the company. There are several different indicators an analyst will want to test for in a data set to identify ghost employees. The data analysis tests explained in this section can be applied to most data sets involving employee information. Custom tests can also be designed, depending on the data provided by the client and the client's concerns and investigation priorities.

The term "indicators" when referring to data analysis looking for ghost employees is intentional because if the indicators are discovered in a data set, fraud is not certain to have occurred. The indicators are used to flag data points within employee records for which further research may be warranted. If an employee record is flagged for one or more indicators that may imply a ghost employee, then payment records need to be reviewed to see if that specific employee record was in fact paid. If indicators of potential ghost employees exist, but no payment is actually made to the employees, then fraud has not occurred; however, the client will need to consider either deleting or updating the employee records with indicators to prevent unauthorized payments in the future.

As explained in the previous section, for each of the data analysis tests described to identify ghost employees, assign a value of one for each indicator a test identifies. At the end of the testing, the risk indicators will be totaled and sorted from greatest to smallest to prioritize the next steps in the investigation.

Data Analysis Test: Number of Employees

Using a tabular export of employee information from the client's system, identify the number of employees with separate active employee records and compare the total to the expected number of employees currently active. If the number of employee records listed as active in the system export is greater than the number of employees actually working for the company, there are likely duplicate records, which could be an indicator to consider when identifying ghost employees.

Data Analysis Test: Duplicate Social Security Numbers

Using a tabular export of employee information and spreadsheet functions, identify duplicate social security numbers (SSNs). A simple method to identify duplicate social security numbers is to use the conditional formatting function for duplicate values within a selected column, such as the social security number column. The conditional formatting function will highlight all cells with identical duplicate values. Then using the filter function, the same column can be filtered by the highlighted color. This will identify all employee records with duplicate social security numbers. For all duplicate social security numbers, assign a value of one to each employee record. (See Table 10.4.)

Data Analysis Test: Employee Records without Addresses

Using a tabular export of employee information, spreadsheet functions can be used to identify all employee records without addresses. Spreadsheet functions helpful in performing this test include conditional formatting or even filtering for blank address fields. (See Table 10.5.)

TABLE 10.4 Illustration of identifying employee records with duplicate social security numbers.

	Data Analysis Test: Employee Records with Duplicate SSNs				
Employee No.	SSN	Address	City	State	Zip Code
1	###-##-#335	716 W 1st St	A Town	STATE	55555
2	###-##-#768	1514 S 2nd Ave	A Town	STATE	55555
3	###-##-#642	1514 S 2nd Ave	A Town	STATE	55555
4	###-##-#879	3145 W. Victory St	A Town	STATE	55555
5	###-##-#879	3145 West Victory Street	A Town	STATE	55555
6	###-##-#366	336 E 106th Pl S	A Town	STATE	55555
7	###-##-#347	107 S 286th E Ave	A Town	STATE	55555
8	###-##-#389	5555 E 39th St	A Town	STATE	55555
9	###-##-#268	601 E. 31st Place	A Town	STATE	55555
10	###-##-#540	336 E 33rd Pl	A Town	STATE	55555
11	###-##-#506		A Town	STATE	55555
12	###-##-#464	4910 E El Paso St	A Town	STATE	55555
13	###-##-#048	2619 E. Albany	A Town	STATE	55555
14	###-##-#547	8495 S School Blvd	A Town	STATE	55555
15	###-##-#689	22 Oak Ln	A Town	STATE	55555
16	###-##-#415	1518 S 193 Ave.	A Town	STATE	55555
17	###-##-#984		C Town	STATE	52555
18	###-##-#413	600 E 9th St	D Town	STATE	53555
19	###-##-#640	505 N Oak Trail	D Town	STATE	53555
20	###-##-#965	15960 South 120 Road	D Town	STATE	53555

↓

	Data Analysis Test: Employee Records with Duplicate SSNs					
Employee No.	SSN	Address	City	State	Zip Code	Risk Indicators Duplicate SSN
4	###-##-#879	3145 W. Victory St	A Town	STATE	55555	1
5	###-##-#879	3145 West Victory Street	A Town	STATE	55555	

TABLE 10.5 Illustration of identifying employee records without addresses.

Data Analysis Test: Employee Records without Addresses

Employee No.	SSN	Address	City	State	Zip Code
1	###-##-#335	716 W 1st St	A Town	STATE	55555
2	###-##-#768	1514 S 2nd Ave	A Town	STATE	55555
3	###-##-#642	1514 S 2nd Ave	A Town	STATE	55555
4	###-##-#879	3145 W. Victory St	A Town	STATE	55555
5	###-##-#879	3145 West Victory Street	A Town	STATE	55555
6	###-##-#366	336 E 106th Pl S	A Town	STATE	55555
7	###-##-#347	107 S 286th E Ave	A Town	STATE	55555
8	###-##-#389	5555 E 39th St	A Town	STATE	55555
9	###-##-#268	601 E. 31st Place	A Town	STATE	55555
10	###-##-#540	336 E 33rd Pl	A Town	STATE	55555
11	###-##-#506		A Town	STATE	55555
12	###-##-#464	4910 E El Paso St	A Town	STATE	55555
13	###-##-#048	2619 E. Albany	A Town	STATE	55555
14	###-##-#547	8495 S School Blvd	A Town	STATE	55555
15	###-##-#689	22 Oak Ln	A Town	STATE	55555
16	###-##-#415	1518 S 193 Ave.	A Town	STATE	55555
17	###-##-#984		C Town	STATE	52555
18	###-##-#413	600 E 9th St	D Town	STATE	53555
19	###-##-#640	505 N Oak Trail	D Town	STATE	53555
20	###-##-#965	15960 South 120 Road	D Town	STATE	53555

↓

Data Analysis Test: Employee Records without Addresses

Employee No.	SSN	Address	City	State	Zip Code	Risk Indicators Duplicate SSN	No Address
11	###-##-#506		A Town	STATE	55555		1
17	###-##-#984		C Town	STATE	52555		1

Data Analysis Test: Employee Records with Duplicate Addresses

Using a tabular export of employee information and spreadsheet functions, identify duplicate addresses. A simple method to identify duplicate social security numbers is to use the conditional formatting function for duplicate values within a selected column similar to the test for duplicate social security numbers; however, because addresses may be keyed in various ways with abbreviations, the duplicate values conditional formatting function will identify only exact matches.

One simple way to perform this test despite the inconsistencies in addresses is to extract the street numbers from the address field and use a concatenate function to join the street numbers with the zip code numbers. Then, conditional formatting can be used to highlight duplicate values. Then using the filter function, the same column can be filtered by the highlighted color. Using this method will likely identify false positives in that it is possible for the same street numbers to exist on more than one address in a zip code. All duplicates highlighted in the concatenated field will need to be compared to the address field to ensure they are in fact duplicates. For all confirmed duplicate addresses, assign a value of one to each employee record. (See Table 10.6.)

It is possible that employees who work at the client organization live with each other or are related and live with each other. This is where providing risk indicator values to positive test results is helpful because although there may be duplicate addresses, if the social security numbers are not duplicated, it could be that employees live at the same address. This could also happen if employees live in the same apartment complex. As demonstrated in Table 10.4, employee numbers four and five have duplicate addresses and duplicate social security numbers, so payments to these two employees will have a higher priority in the next step than the remainder of the employees in Table 10.4.

Another great use of this test is in relation to company nepotism policies. The data analysis test regarding duplicate addresses could be helpful in identifying family members who live at the same address and work within the same department or otherwise.

Data Analysis Test: Total Risk Indicators and Comparing to Payroll Records

When the risk indicators are totaled for the tests performed in the data set, the total column can then be sorted largest to smallest to determine the highest risk records that may warrant further investigation. As demonstrated in Table 10.7, employee numbers four and five have the greatest total number of indicators

TABLE 10.6 Illustration of identifying employee records with duplicate addresses.

		Data Analysis Test: Employee Records with Duplicate Addresses					
Employee No.	SSN	Address	City	State	Zip Code	Address No.	No. + Zip
1	###-##-#335	716 W 1st St	A Town	STATE	55555	716	71655555
2	###-##-#768	1514 S 2nd Ave	A Town	STATE	55555	1514	151455555
3	###-##-#642	1514 S 2nd Ave	A Town	STATE	55555	1514	151455555
4	###-##-#879	3145 W. Victory St	A Town	STATE	55555	3145	314555555
5	###-##-#879	3145 West Victory Street	A Town	STATE	55555	3145	314555555
6	###-##-#366	336 E 106th Pl S	A Town	STATE	55555	336	33655555
7	###-##-#347	107 S 286th E Ave	A Town	STATE	55555	107	10755555
8	###-##-#389	5555 E 39th St	A Town	STATE	55555	5555	555555555
9	###-##-#268	601 E. 31st Place	A Town	STATE	55555	601	60155555
10	###-##-#540	336 E 33rd Pl	A Town	STATE	55555	336	33655555
11	###-##-#506		A Town	STATE	55555		55555
12	###-##-#464	4910 E El Paso St	A Town	STATE	55555	4910	491055555
13	###-##-#048	2619 E. Albany	A Town	STATE	55555	2619	261955555
14	###-##-#547	8495 S School Blvd	A Town	STATE	55555	8495	849555555
15	###-##-#689	22 Oak Ln	A Town	STATE	55555	22	2255555
16	###-##-#415	1518 S 193 Ave.	A Town	STATE	55555	1518	151855555
17	###-##-#984		C Town	STATE	52555		52555

(continued)

185

TABLE 10.6 (*Continued*)

Data Analysis Test: Employee Records with Duplicate Addresses

Employee No.	SSN	Address	City	State	Zip Code	Address No.	No. + Zip
18	###-##-#413	600 E 9th St	D Town	STATE	53555	600	60053555
19	###-##-#640	505 N Oak Trail	D Town	STATE	53555	505	50553555
20	###-##-#965	15960 South 120 Road	D Town	STATE	53555	15960	1596053555

Data Analysis Test: Employee Records with Duplicate Addresses

Employee No.	SSN	Address	City	State	Zip Code	No. + Zip	Risk Indicators		
							Duplicate SSN	No Address	Duplicate Address
2	###-##-#768	1514 S 2nd Ave	A Town	STATE	55555	151455555			1
3	###-##-#642	1514 S 2nd Ave	A Town	STATE	55555	151455555			1
4	###-##-#879	3145 W. Victory St	A Town	STATE	55555	314555555	1		1
5	###-##-#879	3145 West Victory Street	A Town	STATE	55555	314555555	1		1
6	###-##-#366	336 E 106th Pl S	A Town	STATE	55555	33655555			n/a
10	###-##-#540	336 E 33rd Pl	A Town	STATE	55555	33655555			n/a

TABLE 10.7 Illustration of sorting by total risk indicators.

| | | | | Total Risk Indicators | | | |
| | | | | | Risk Indicators | | |
Employee No.	SSN	Address	No. + Zip	Duplicate SSN	No Address	Duplicate Address	Total Indicators
4	###-##-#879	3145 W. Victory St	314-5555	1		1	2
5	###-##-#879	3145 West Victory Street	314-5555	1		1	2
2	###-##-#768	1514 S 2nd Ave	1514-5555			1	1
3	###-##-#642	1514 S 2nd Ave	1514-5555			1	1
11	###-##-#506		-5555		1		1
17	###-##-#984		-2555		1		1
1	###-##-#335	716 W 1st St	716-5555				0
6	###-##-#366	336 E 106th Pl S	336-5555			n/a	0
7	###-##-#347	107 S 286th E Ave	107-5555				0
8	###-##-#389	5555 E 39th St	5555-5555				0
9	###-##-#268	601 E. 31st Place	601-5555				0
10	###-##-#540	336 E 33rd Pl	336-5555			n/a	0
12	###-##-#464	4910 E El Paso St	4910-5555				0
13	###-##-#048	2619 E. Albany	2619-5555				0
14	###-##-#547	8495 S School Blvd	8495-5555				0
15	###-##-#689	22 Oak Ln	22-5555				0
16	###-##-#415	1518 S 193 Ave.	1518-5555				0
18	###-##-#413	600 E 9th St	600-3555				0
19	###-##-#640	505 N Oak Trail	505-3555				0
20	###-##-#965	15960 South 120 Road	15960-3555				0

resulting from the three data analysis tests. It is recommended that the payroll records for at least employee numbers four and five be examined further, which may include:

- Identify if payroll was paid to employee numbers four and five in the same pay period for the same work (i.e. review the payments to identify whether they are duplicate payroll).
- Identify if payroll and benefits paid to employee numbers four and five are consistent with employee agreements and reconcile to W-2s.
- Identify if expense reimbursements to employee numbers four and five are substantiated by supporting documentation.

The Case of the Limited Payroll Records

The president of a company called an investigator because he had been notified by an employee that the human resources (HR) director had asked the reporting employee for a loan. Because the HR director was responsible for the payroll for the entire company, he wanted his payroll information reviewed for a relevant period of two years and an examination of their payroll records for any ghost employees. The investigator requested payroll data for the two years to include all employees, but the president advised that the payroll company was able to provide only printed payroll reports and requested that the tests be performed on only the HR director's payroll and the employee information reports listing employee social security numbers and addresses. Data analysis tests included:

- Comparison of payroll registers to W-2s to authorized salary agreements for the HR director
- Recalculation of benefits for the HR director
- Testing of employee information reports for duplicate or missing social security numbers, duplicate or missing addresses, and duplicate or missing direct deposit account numbers

Some strange activity was discovered in the pay records of the HR director, including the maximizing of exemptions, thus reducing his tax withholdings to almost nothing. The investigator discussed this finding with the client; however, no evidence supporting unauthorized payroll, unauthorized payments of benefits, or ghost employees was identified. Within the final report, the investigator listed the data analysis tests performed and documented the strange withholdings finding. She also reiterated her initial conversation with the president that had all of the pay data for all employees been reviewed, ghost employees and overpayments to other employees may have been uncovered. The president advised they did not want to expand the scope of the investigation, and the investigation ended.

 ## OVERPAYMENTS OF PAYROLL

Using data from payroll reports, indicators of payroll overpayments within the payroll report data alone can be identified using the data analysis tests explained in this section. As with any other data analysis test of one data source, any of the findings from the analysis should then become a comparative analysis to verify the purpose of the indicated overpayment.

Data Analysis Test: Pay Date Review

A quick, high-level review using payroll data to identify anomalies includes the following steps:

- Summarize total payments to employee by pay date and graph the total payments by pay date, using perhaps a scatter graph, to identify outliers including payments to employees for off-cycle payroll.
- Plot on a scatter graph every payment paid to every employee over the relevant period to identify outliers such as individuals whose pay was considerably higher and lower than other employees.

A pay date review may also identify bonus payments, appearing as off-cycle payroll. Further review of the payments should include identifying the employees receiving the off-cycle payroll and the payment frequency. It is possible the payments were for all employees as a company-wide bonus at the end of the year. It is also possible that the person responsible for payroll is providing himself and friends, or co-conspirators, with unauthorized bonus payments.

Data Analysis Test: Even-Dollar Payments of Net Pay and Expense Reimbursements

If someone is stealing funds through payroll, finding net pay disbursements or expense reimbursements in multiples of 10 or 100 and are even in amount such as $3,500.00, $55,000.00, $205,000.00, may be an indicator of fraud. An employee's net pay is rarely an even-dollar amount because of taxes and other withholdings. Additionally, it is less common that an employee will need to be reimbursed for an even-dollar amount than a non-even-dollar amount. Any even-dollar net pay, or expense reimbursement, should be flagged for further investigation.

Data Analysis Test: Days of the Week

Converting pay dates in the payroll data to days of the week using spreadsheet formulas can be helpful to identify payroll payments paid on non-workdays or off-cycle payroll. If payroll is paid every other week on Friday, and several payroll payments are paid on a Monday, those payments should be flagged for further review. If a business is closed on the weekends, and payroll is never run on weekends, then any pay dates representing a Saturday or Sunday should be flagged for further review.

Data Analysis Test: Large Individual Payments

Graphing payments for payroll may assist in identifying large individual payments or outliers in a data set. When testing for large individual payments, the test can be run on gross pay, net pay, expense reimbursements, and/or benefits. Any large individual payments should be flagged for additional review – with greater emphasis if they are always paid to the same employee during the relevant period.

Data Analysis Test: Number of Payments to Employees Per Month

Using a pivot table or subtotal feature in a spreadsheet or data analysis software, summarize the number of payments to each employee by month. If the expected number of payments per month is two, for pay dates of the 15th and last day of the month, any employees with three or more payments should be flagged for further review.

Risk Indicator Analysis and Comparative Analysis

When any of the aforementioned data analysis tests result in flagged transactions, risk indicator analysis and comparative analysis are great investigative next steps. For each transaction with a positive result from the data analysis tests, a value of 1 can be assigned to the transactions. If the data analysis test returned a negative result for the transaction, a value of 0 can be assigned. All the data analysis test results should then be totaled and sorted from largest to smallest to identify the employees and payments of highest risk. Then from the list of prioritized risk, copies of employment agreements, employee handbooks, expense reimbursement documentation, and any other supporting documentation of company bonuses and how they should be calculated can then be compared to what was paid to employees.

The Case of the Overpaid Administrator

Sandy was the administrator for a business owned by two business partners whose business was organized into three different companies: operations company, retail company, and a company that owned the building to house the other two businesses. Sandy was told that she would be paid a salary of $75,000 a year as an employee. However, one day in reviewing financial information to send to the accountant to prepare taxes, one of the partners thought that the total amount of payroll for the year seemed larger than he expected. The partnership hired a forensic accountant to investigate the issue further before confronting Sandy. The payroll records for the operating company were examined, including data analysis tests such as large individual payments and number of payments to employees per month. The results of these two tests identified that Sandy was the highest paid individual in the entire company – receiving more pay than even the two partners. The total payments to Sandy for the two-year relevant period were compared to her agreed-upon salary of $75,000, which identified she had overpaid herself by $100,000 over the two years examined.

Knowing that Sandy managed two other companies on behalf of the partners, the bank statements were examined, which resulted in the identification of payroll being paid out of the building management company. The building management company did not have any employees, yet payments to a payroll processing company were found in the bank account data. Total payroll paid to Sandy out of the building management company exceeded $50,000 for the two-year period, resulting in a total loss to the partners of $150,000. Sandy resigned and agreed to repay the $150,000 to the partners over three years, and the partners decided not to file criminal charges.

 NOTES

1. J. Carlton Collins, "Using Excel and Benford's Law to detect fraud," *Journal of Accountancy* (April 1, 2017), accessed October 15, 2021, https://www.journalofaccountancy.com/issues/2017/apr/excel-and-benfords-law-to-detect-fraud.html.
2. Dave Fowler, "JOIN Relationships and JOINing Tables" (Data School, 2021), accessed October 15, 2021, https://dataschool.com/learn-sql/joins/.

CHAPTER ELEVEN

Findings, Reports, and Testimony

FOR A FORENSIC ACCOUNTANT or investigator working in the private sector as a consulting or testifying expert, the value created in an investigation is not realized until the results and findings from the investigation are communicated. There are three levels of communication of findings used in our Data Sleuth process that will be explained in this chapter:

- **Findings Summary.** The Findings Summary with corresponding tables, charts, and graphs is prepared for all of our clients. For some clients, the engagement ends here as the Findings Summary is sufficient for the investigative goals.
- **Report.** A formal report is prepared based on the Findings Summary and attachments, but it is not prepared for all client engagements.
- **Testimony.** Testimony is the least common work product in an investigation as not all cases go to trial or have hearings where an expert is needed testify.

FINDINGS

Early in my career, I prepared a report for every engagement. I found this step helpful in connecting findings and articulating conclusions – especially in anticipation of a hearing or trial at which I would be testifying. However, as the Data Sleuth Process began to expand beyond just a data processing and data analysis solution, I realized that a report is not always necessary. Reevaluation of this step in the process allows us to now proactively ask the client about the intended purpose of a report or desired recovery avenue. If the client does not require a final, signed report, we instead provide the client with a Findings Summary.

For each of the analyses listed on the case plan, a corresponding work paper is prepared containing:

- A description of the client's concern and the corresponding investigation priority
- A description of the analysis task to be performed
- A description of the purpose of the analysis to be performed
- A detailed description of all investigative and financial analysis findings considered for the Findings Summary

By requiring these items in the analysis work papers, when the analysis is complete, the analyst drafts the findings as if they will be sent to the client. In this way, the findings are prepared contemporaneously rather than in a report writing step just before a deadline. Not all of the analyst's findings for each analysis are used in the Findings Summary and report, but the use of work papers in this manner allows for multiple analysts and investigators to work on the same case with the same goals.

From the results of each analysis, after detail and case manager review, the findings from the analyses are compiled in the Findings Summary with attachments resulting from the analysis accompanying the findings. An example of a Findings Summary is provided in Table 11.1.

For each finding, the investigation priority determined in the case planning step is listed along with the relevant period, finding description, amount of the loss, and a reference to the attachment table, chart, or graph for each finding. The attachments are prepared as if they will be included with a report or with the expert's testimony. The Findings Summary is then reviewed by the case manager and then with the client prior to the preparation of the final report. Encouraging a meeting with the client to review the Findings Summary provides an opportunity to ensure that the client and investigator are on the same page, that nothing was overlooked by the investigator, and that there will be no surprises for the client if a report is issued. Additionally, if any of the findings or corresponding attachments are confusing to the client or the client's attorney, adjustments can be made prior to the finalization in a report.

TABLE 11.1 Example of a Findings Summary.

FINDINGS SUMMARY
<Case Name> Matter
For the Periods: As Specified Below

INVESTIGATION PRIORITY	PERIOD EXAMINED	FINDING DESCRIPTION	AMOUNT	ATTACHMENT REF.
Employee versus Vendor Relationships and Payments	FY 2010–2015	1. Employee records were reviewed for duplicate addresses and SSNs to identify potential "ghost" employees. Information to date did not identify any known issues. 2. Vendor records were compared to employee records to identify potential employee-owned businesses. This test identified 14 potential employee-owned businesses. Payments to employee-owned businesses totaled $64,522.98 during FY 2010 through 2017. 3. Employee and vendor records in system contain duplicate entries and information.	N/A	ATTACHMENT 1
Quantify amount of bank account funds used not for the benefit of the client	01/01/10– 12/31/15	Using transactions from bank statements, net expenditures totaling $423,921.36 were identified by the client as unauthorized and not benefitting the business. In addition, expenditures totaling $35,200.00 were identified by the client as bonuses.	$459,121.36	ATTACHMENT 2
Quantify disbursements to bank accounts owned by subject	01/01/10– 12/31/15	Transaction data was examined to identify whether or not client funds were transferred to any of the five accounts that belonged to the subject. No such activity was discovered.	N/A	ATTACHMENT 3

REPORTS

As explained in Chapter 4, the most common recovery methods for a victim of embezzlement or corporate fraud are through criminal prosecution, civil proceedings, and/or insurance reimbursement. A final, signed report is recommended when a case is being referred for criminal prosecution and/or insurance reimbursement. In expectation of a trial or as if criminal charges will be filed, best evidence is the basis of the findings, and specific items as opposed to estimates are used to quantify the loss. Such a strategy in the analysis steps and loss calculation creates an opportunity to maximize the preparation and use of one report for the various recovery avenues. To this point in my career, every report that was prepared according to this methodology, which was submitted to both law enforcement and the client's insurance company, has initiated criminal charges and assisted our clients in obtaining insurance reimbursement.

Not only is issuing one report that can be used in all three recovery avenues efficient for the client, but it also promotes continuity and reduces confusion in any future expert testimony. In my experience, there seems to be prevailing strategies by attorneys for litigating cases involving financial investigations. These may not be immutable strategies, but they are what I have noticed to be most common:

- A prosecutor or plaintiff's attorney works to simplify the facts of the case and make it simple for the judge or jury to understand to eliminate doubt as to what happened.
- A defense attorney works to find areas within the prosecutor's or plaintiff's theory to exploit and cause confusion in hopes of creating reasonable doubt. When possible, the exploitation of the theory is simplified by the defense attorney to create even more doubt as to the validity of the prosecution or plaintiff's theory.

Either side, however, is looking to reinforce their theory through making even the most complicated of stories involving financial transactions as simple as possible. This is why minimizing confusion within a report is of utmost importance. Not only should the contents of the report be clear and concise but also the organization of files, correspondence, and report versions. Creating multiple versions of final work products is not advisable. If all versions become accessible in discovery, it is an area for the opposing counsel to potentially create confusion. As an example, if an opposing counsel is able to obtain a copy of the expert's working file and finds that multiple reports were issued, the expert incurs the risk that she may be questioned about each report in a deposition, or hearing, or trial in an effort to confuse the decision maker(s). With every report issued, it is also possible to have contradicting opinions, analysis results, or calculations. Although it is possible for an expert to recover if a mistake is found in a work product, it is an unnecessary risk to issue multiple reports with the same types of findings.

One exception to not issuing multiple reports is that if, for some reason, a particular analysis performed does not create value in the respective recovery avenue. When this occurs, the removal of that analysis is the only difference between the reports. This makes the removal simpler to explain.

 ## A REPORT FOR CRIMINAL CHARGES

If an investigation finds that laws have been broken for which criminal charges may be filed, a report is helpful in presenting the client's case to law enforcement. A forensic accountant or investigator is not required to refer cases to law enforcement, and we always obtain written permission from clients before referring a case on their behalf. Not all clients want their cases referred to law enforcement and prefer to settle either through civil court or even just a simple agreement with the subject. There are numerous investigative agencies who will review complaints from citizens regarding crimes for which a case may be opened, and understanding the purposes of these agencies and the crimes they are authorized to investigate is advantageous to the client's case being successfully prosecuted.

Not all law enforcement agencies will be addressed in this chapter, but the ones we work with most often for financial crimes have been listed for reference starting with federal law enforcement agencies:

- **Federal Bureau of Investigation.** The FBI has the authority to investigate all types of fraud. The cases referred most commonly by our team are those involving bank fraud, wire fraud, mail fraud, identify theft, and money laundering.
- **Internal Revenue Service Criminal Investigation Division.** IRS-CID investigates tax fraud, money laundering, and Bank Secrecy Act violations, including structuring.
- **Secret Service.** The Secret Service agents investigate financial crimes particularly focusing on credit card and debit card fraud.
- **United States Postal Inspection Service.** Postal inspectors can investigate financial crime particularly when the scheme involves the use of the mail.

At the local and state levels, investigative agencies with the authority to investigate financial crimes include:

- **Local Police Departments.** In Tulsa, the local police department has a financial crimes unit that will investigate financial crimes within the city of Tulsa.
- **County Sheriff's Office.** Fraud cases that occur within the county may be investigated by a county sheriff's office.
- **State Investigation Agencies.** In Oklahoma, the state law enforcement agency is the Oklahoma State Bureau of Investigation, which will work fraud investigations as requested by the state auditor or other statutory requestor.[1]
- **State Auditor's Office.** The state auditor's office in the state of Oklahoma is not a law enforcement agency, but if petitioned by citizens, they can open investigations into public service entities. If crimes are discovered, they will refer the criminal investigation to the Oklahoma Attorney General's office or the Oklahoma State Bureau of Investigation.

By identifying the possible investigative agencies, it is helpful to understand the crimes committed by the subject in order to refer the case to an agency that has the authority to investigate the crime. If a client's case results in a large loss amount, and the crime committed is one that federal law enforcement can investigate, we refer to federal law enforcement because there are typically more resources available for white-collar investigations with federal law enforcement than with state and local law enforcement. Because of the usual nonviolent nature and first-time offender factors of embezzlement and corporate fraud, cases that are charged at the local level tend to be pled down to misdemeanors.

Clients will often ask for assistance in presenting their case to federal law enforcement for embezzlement; however, embezzlement is not a federal crime. It violates state statutes – unless it involves embezzlement from a federal agency or organization. To have a case prosecuted federally, for what would be charged as an embezzlement at the state level, a federal crime must be identified in the scheme. For example, a controller stole funds from his employer because he was convinced he was making payments to unlock an inheritance from a long-lost relative. The controller received emails from someone he did not know advising that he was to inherit a multimillion-dollar inheritance. To claim the inheritance, the controller needed to send them money. When the controller began to send money, the scammer continued to create excuses as to why the controller had not sent enough money to "unlock" the inheritance. In reality, the controller was a victim of an inheritance scam that involved stealing from his employer while giving hundreds of thousands of dollars to a con artist.

The investigation was performed for law enforcement referral, the investigator identified that the funds had been paid via wire from a local bank to a bank whose headquarters were in another state. Because of the use of a wire as the payment method and the funds crossing state lines, the subject was charged with wire fraud, and the case was able to be prosecuted federally instead of embezzlement by local law enforcement.

 ## REPORT RECOMMENDATIONS FOR LAW ENFORCEMENT REFERRAL

If the goal of the expert is to help their client's case to be investigated by law enforcement, then making this process simple for the agent or detective is key. To do so, consider preparing a report and supporting documentation with law enforcement in mind. Avoid providing them a report of every procedure performed and the result of the procedure, whether it created a finding or not. Simplify the report to communicate the findings of the investigation, the analysis used in the investigation, and the data relied on in the investigation. Create tables and charts to illustrate the results of the findings, removing any extraneous information. An example of a commonly used format when presenting findings and the resulting loss to law enforcement is provided in Table 11.2.

After law enforcement has reviewed the report and supporting attachments, they may request additional information from the files. With written permission

TABLE 11.2 Example of a table provided to law enforcement as attachment to report.

Example of Table Provided to Law Enforcement	
Attachment 1 **Nonbusiness Uses of Company Funds** **For the Period 01/01/14 through 10/15/16**	
Cash Withdrawals	**Total**
Cash withdrawals	4,848.50
Meals for family	8,067.93
Travel not for business purposes	41,184.57
Unsupported personal expenditures	32,093.66
Personal credit card payments	8,293.94
Total nonbusiness uses of company funds	$ 94,488.60

by the client, we provide organized files with a corresponding copy of the Document Inventory so they can easily navigate the evidence in our possession and then obtain the remaining information they need.

Within the report, the findings should communicate to the agent or detective the reasons supporting why a subject's benefit was unauthorized or at the expense of the client using employment agreements or emails documenting intentions. Clearly identifying a subject's unauthorized benefit through an intent to deceive assists law enforcement in taking their next steps with the investigation.

The goal behind a criminal investigation is successful prosecution. This can be obtained on the federal level through two primary avenues for which assisting law enforcement in building a simple, concise case is important:

- The subject cooperates with the investigation, resulting in an information to be filed listing the charges. This type of filing often occurs if the person does not intend to go to trial.
- The subject is not expected to cooperate with the investigation, resulting in a potential indictment being filed. The subject could plead guilty or could decide to go to trial.

It is important when working with law enforcement that accounting details are used for context or to provide evidence of the intentions of the subject and is not the basis for understanding the scheme altogether. This is one of the primary reasons the Data Sleuth Process is built on the foundation of focusing financial investigations on cash coming into or leaving financial accounts. Sometimes, obtaining specific evidence is limited when financial accounts have to be subpoenaed and the client is not filing a civil lawsuit. This is when the strategy of the report still focuses on cash as much as possible but sets up the agent or detective to subpoena the related accounts, confirm the finding in the expert's report, and identify possible assets purchased with stolen money, using the subject's bank account.

 ## AN EXPERT REPORT FOR CIVIL LITIGATION

An expert report is prepared outside of the courtroom and as such is typically not admissible as evidence because it is considered hearsay.[2] In Oklahoma state courts, an expert report is not required; however, in federal court, an expert report is required even though it is not admissible as evidence. Prior to preparing a report for civil litigation, the attorney for the client should be consulted to determine if the report is necessary. Sometimes, if a report is being prepared for civil litigation only and not the other recovery avenues, a brief report summarizing findings with corresponding attachments may suffice. In my experience, civil litigators have different approaches to how they work with experts – especially if the case is in state court.

My personal preference is to prepare a report and all attachments intended for use with my testimony to provide a logical approach to a settlement. Because the reports we prepare are data driven and follow a logical investigation process, I have found that providing a summary of our findings and corresponding detailed attachments reduces the need for unnecessary arguments, depositions, and expert witness duels. The cases in which only a couple of summary attachments were prepared without any explanation have resulted in tedious, unfruitful depositions and trial testimony full of confusion.

When preparing an expert report for civil litigation for any venue, it is recommended to follow the Federal Rules of Civil Procedure, Rule 26(2)(B)[3] by including the following with the expert report:

- A curriculum vitae listing all qualifications, certifications, licenses, relevant work experience, prior testimony, opinions, publications, and presentations
- A list of all information relied on in preparing the findings, conclusions, and opinions within the report and expected testimony
- All attachments that will be used to summarize or support the testimony
- A statement of compensation for the analysis and testimony in the case

AN EXPERT REPORT FOR INSURANCE REIMBURSEMENT

An expert report prepared for an insurance reimbursement is helpful in obtaining reimbursement in a timely manner. Insurance companies will use the services of a forensic accountant to review claims submitted by customers. Having both submitted reports to insurance agencies and reviewed reports for insurance claims, the use of an experienced investigator in this process is invaluable. If the claim is unclear and poorly documented, and I am working for the insurance company, I will not recommend payment of a claim that is not substantiated. In preparation of a report, I want the reviewing forensic accountant to be able to follow the logic of the analysis based on best evidence and understand the findings to maximize the substantiated reimbursement for the client.

If a report will be used by the client to submit a claim to an insurance company, the insurance company typically requests that the customer file a case with law enforcement. This allows the insurance company to potentially receive restitution payments to subsidize the payout to the customer. When I volunteered at the local police department, the detectives advised that they do receive inquiries from insurance companies verifying that customers did file a police report. Knowing this, I think it is helpful that the same report submitted for insurance reimbursement also be provided when filing a police report.

 ## REPORT ORGANIZATION RECOMMENDATIONS

When preparing a report for any audience, less is more, and simplicity is key. Most readers of forensic accounting or fraud investigation reports want to be able to read a report once and digest the important information in a quick and efficient manner. Every report issued by our team includes a section labeled "Background" in which we state the purpose of the engagement, the background pertinent to the engagement, the relevant period, and a summary of information reviewed.

The sections following the "Background" section use the Findings Summary as it serves as an outline to guide the order of the final report. A brief explanation of the analysis performed and the findings from the Findings Summary are copied directly, as applicable, to maintain consistency between the Findings Summary and final report.

Consider creating sections of the report where the analysis is grouped by client concern and/or investigation priority. Within the concerns and priorities, consider grouping the findings by method, transaction, or payment type. One of the strategies my mentor at the FBI taught was if listing a transaction, use bullet points and the same format for each item. In this way, the reader does not have to read every word on every line to understand the information. For example:

- On 10/19/21, check number 1234 payable to John Doe cleared BANK5454 in the amount of $5,000.00.
- On 10/20/21, check number 1238 payable to John Doe cleared BANK9898 in the amount of $2,500.00.

The use of "BANK5454" and "BANK9898" in the example refers to the use of account references as explained in Chapter 8. The account reference provides a shortened name for the financial institution and the last four digits of the account. This simplifies references to bank accounts within the body of the report for which details can be obtained by consulting the Account Index.

As findings are communicated, any evidence supporting intentions of the subject to deceive a custodian or owner of the funds stolen are incorporated. A simple example is in the investigation involving a fire chief. The fire chief was using the fire department's debit card for personal expenses. He would then record the purchases in QuickBooks in general ledger accounts that hid the true purpose behind the expenditure. In an interview with his assistant, she advised that the fire chief was the only individual with access to QuickBooks. We were able to confirm this statement when we had to obtain the QuickBooks from the fire chief. In the section of the report where the debit card purchases were explained, the incorporation of the assistant's statement and our confirmation was also listed to provide supporting evidence of the fire chief's intention to hide the personal purchases from the board.

For every calculation or list of transactions resulting in a loss, we create both a detailed and summarized table to include with the report. We refer to the tables, charts, example emails, or flowcharts as attachments instead of exhibits. These attachments are prepared with the intention that they may be used in a hearing, deposition, or trial testimony. As such, the referencing of exhibits to the report in testimony can get confusing because the plaintiff has exhibits and the defendant has exhibits as well and depending on which side is using one of our tables, it will be given an exhibit number. Labeling and referencing the table as "attachment 1 to the report" is less confusing in a hearing, deposition, or trial setting.

TESTIMONY

After I earned the Certified Fraud Examiner's credential, I joined the local chapter and volunteered on the board of directors. Anxious to learn all I could about fraud investigation, I attended every training event and met as many of the speakers as possible. One of the speakers at the local conference was a litigation attorney who had worked with countless expert witnesses and shared tips about testifying as an expert. The primary recommendation from his presentation I have carried with me throughout my career – to work on cases for both plaintiff and defendants. Since that day, I have encountered many experts who share this philosophy, and as I began to testify, I understood why.

There are several questions that are typically asked of expert witnesses on cross-examination that are intended to make the expert appear unqualified, biased, or paid to testify to a desired result of the attorney.

- Are you a Certified Public Accountant (or whichever credential opposing counsel considers missing from your curriculum vitae)?
- How many cases have you worked with this law firm or attorney?
- Do you normally testify only for the plaintiff (or defendant)?
- How much were you paid for your testimony today?

When responding to questions like this, an expert wants to be honest, and I try to answer the question from a place of neutrality and to not take offense or make it personal. The attorney is doing his job for his client and testifying is part of mine. It is not uncommon that an attorney who questions me on cross-examination later refers a client or hires me to consult on a case. Keeping this in mind reminds me that we are not actual enemies in life; we are both doing a job.

The question, "How much were you paid for your testimony?" is designed to trick an expert into appearing as if she was paid to testify to a specific result – which is not accurate in the cases I work. My response to this question is, "I am not paid for my testimony (or for a report or answer). I am paid for my time." Every report I issue reiterates this policy with the language, "Workman Forensics' fees for this engagement are based upon our normal hourly billing rates and are in no way contingent upon the results of our findings."

Testimony advice I have learned from attorneys and also experience in the courtroom includes:

- Breathe. The calmer I can remain on the stand, the greater difficulty opposing counsel will have in confusing me and, in turn, the judge or jury.
- If I do get confused, I ask if I can clarify or restate my response. The judge may not allow it, but it never hurts to ask.
- Listen to the question in its entirety and only answer the question that is asked. This requires practice and discipline. It is natural to want to help someone finish sentences or understand a concept, but on cross-examination, this instinct needs to be ignored.
- An attorney told me before my first deposition, "Leah, it may feel slow to listen to the question completely and to pause to think about it before responding, but the transcript does not reflect the pauses. Just take your time." Take your time in understanding the question and contemplating your response.
- If I don't understand the question, I let the attorney know and ask her to restate or rephrase it. Sometimes the response of opposing counsel is to make an expert feel as though she is dense, but once again, do not take it personally. Ignore feelings of inadequacy and admit that you do not understand the question so that you can provide a confident answer to a question you understand.
- Testifying requires patience and can feel as if the attorneys' questions will never end. Slow down, try to relax, be professional, answer with confidence, and be yourself.

Recently, I was asked to testify to a calculation I performed during a bench trial, and my testimony began one afternoon, and I was asked to return the following morning to complete my testimony. The opposing counsel asked the judge if I would send him some of my work papers the following morning. The judge did not order that I do so, but he did advise that he thought it would be helpful. After dinner, I worked to organize the work papers until 2:00 a.m. so they could be printed and presented the following morning in a simple fashion. Sitting on the stand that next morning, opposing counsel was asking questions about the work papers but the questions were not making sense to me – especially with such little sleep. I responded to one of his questions saying, "I'm sorry, Mr. Attorney, but I don't believe we're communicating very well this morning." The judge echoed, "I agree," and the opposing counsel actually moved on to another line of questioning. When I first began testifying, I was rigid and wanted to be so exact all the time. I have noticed that by intentionally practicing the recommendations previously explained, I enjoy testifying more, and I am a much more effective witness in presenting the findings from the financial investigation or forensic accounting component of the case.

 NOTES

1. Oklahoma State Bureau of Investigation, accessed October 19, 2021, https://osbi.ok.gov/.
2. WomensLaw, "What Is Hearsay?" accessed October 19, 2021, https://www.womenslaw.org/laws/preparing-court-yourself/hearing/hearsay/what-hearsay.
3. Cornell Law School Legal Information Institute, "Rule 26. Duty to Disclose; General Provisions Governing Discovery," accessed October 19, 2021, https://www.law.cornell.edu/rules/frcp/rule_26.

CHAPTER TWELVE

Practice the Data Sleuth Process

THE MOST EFFECTIVE STRATEGY to executing the Data Sleuth Process is through working investigations and engagements. Listening to client concerns, converting concerns into investigation priorities, understanding the subject's access to systems creating misappropriation of funds opportunities, and identifying the analysis and data necessary to answer the client questions takes practice. Practice provides the investigator with confidence that no matter the situation, if money is missing, he or she can find it. At the same time, the investigator can use the process to find the missing money to answer the client's questions regarding the method used by subjects to steal, divert, or hide funds. Using the Data Sleuth Process from the initial client inquiry to the final report, the investigator maintains objectivity, organization, and clarity when explaining the findings to the end-client and target audiences.

Working a variety of numerous cases per year may not be practical for all forensic accountants and fraud investigators, so within this chapter are two case studies with worksheets and corresponding solutions to begin the implementation of the Data Sleuth Process.

 ## REVIEW OF THE DATA SLEUTH CASE PLAN

As a recap, the Data Sleuth Case Plan works in the following order as described in detail in Chapter 6:

- Translate the client's concerns into investigation priorities
- Understand the subject's access to systems and information through risk-based analysis

- Create a Data Analysis Plan
- Identify best evidence data sources
- Request and process relevant data
- Perform relevant analyses
- Perform additional research, investigation, review, or obtain client feedback
- Consolidate and simplify findings
- Prepare a report for the target audiences

 ## REVIEW OF DATA SLEUTH DATA PROCESSING

The Data Sleuth data processing step begins with defining a relevant period so that information is as complete as possible before beginning the processing of data. As client information is received, contemporaneously record and update the information in the Document Inventory and Account Index. Review the received information to determine what data should be included with in the scheduling of financial accounts or other data sources. When processing the data, attention to detail is encouraged to ensure consistency in the data to be used in the following analysis step.

 ## REVIEW OF THE DATA ANALYSIS PLAN AND STANDARD DATA SLEUTH ANALYSES

To create a Data Analysis Plan, select the type of analyses that most appropriately address the client's investigation priorities. Possible analysis options to consider for the Data Analysis Plan include the following and are described in greater detail in Chapters 9 and 10:

- **Comparative analysis.** Comparison of two data sets or two data sources that answer the questions "What happened?" and "What should have happened?"
- **Source and Use Summary.** Summary by data source, or combination of data sources, providing high-level information regarding where money came from and how it was used by payee, payor, or other description.
- **Interesting Data Findings (IDF) Analysis.** The use of standard and custom data analysis tests based on the client's concerns and investigation priorities such as:
  - Benford's analysis
  - Even-dollar amounts

- Large individual payments
- Month-over-month pivot tables
- Detailed transactions extracted from the Source and Use Summary
- Incorporating accounting records related to the IDF results
- **Risk Indicator Analysis.** The use of providing values to the results of data analysis tests to prioritize further research, inquiry, or client feedback.
- **Payroll Analysis.** The combination of data analysis tests for one data source, risk indicator analysis, and comparative analysis related to employee information and payroll data. Data analysis tests for payroll analysis can include testing for:
  - Number of employees
  - Employee records with duplicate social security numbers
  - Employee records without addresses
  - Employee records with duplicate addresses
  - Graphing of pay date payments
  - Even-dollar payments of net pay and expense reimbursements
  - Days of the week
  - Large individual payments
  - Number of payments to employees per month

CASE STUDY 1: THE CASE OF THE DISAPPEARING BUSINESS

Eric owned a consulting business that required his exclusive expertise and time, but a few years prior, he had an opportunity to open a retail store. What started out as a small operation, which he just hoped would break even, was soon more successful than he had imagined. So successful, in fact, that it was too much for him to manage in addition to his consulting business. On July 15 of year two, he hired Mandy to run the storefront, but Eric soon realized that the operations were falling apart under her management. Eric met with Mandy to discuss terminating her employment, but Mandy detected the hints from the beginning of the conversation and suggested that her mom, Denise, manage the store so that Mandy could be demoted to a clerk position. Eric agreed to give the arrangement a try after interviewing Denise and learning about her extensive retail experience. From that day forward, the mom-daughter duo ran the store.

To keep Eric in the loop, Denise would email Eric daily with the sales for the day and attach any supplier invoices for inventory that needed to be paid. The responsibilities of the financial management of the store were delegated to Denise including:

- Daily sales deposits
- Cash drawer reconciliation
- Inventory management
- Providing timesheets to Eric for time worked by Denise and Mandy

The financial management responsibilities delegated to Eric and an external bookkeeper included:

- Payroll processing
- Vendor payments
- Bank reconciliations
- Financial statements

Denise's daily sales emails boasted of great sales almost daily, but something strange kept happening. When it was time for Eric to pay payroll, he reviewed the timesheets, entered the time to be paid into the payroll provider's website, and then double checked the retail store's bank balance online and in the accounting system prior to final authorization of payroll. He began noticing in December of year 5 that the cash balance in the bank account was barely covering payroll every two weeks, which was their normal payroll cycle. He transferred money from the consulting business to cover the deficit the first time as he believed it was a timing difference.

Although the business had some corporate clients that they billed rather than collecting payment immediately at the point of sale in the store, this was a small percentage of the normal revenue; therefore, a timing difference resulting in an inability to pay payroll would have been doubtful. The bookkeeper prepared the clothing store financial statements on a cash basis, so revenue was recorded when received. Additionally, the financial statements were prepared from the recording of deposits and expenditures listed on the bank statements, so because of all of these things, a timing difference between the recording and collection of revenue was even more unlikely.

After transferring money to cover payroll for several pay periods, and with his consulting business taking even more of his time, Eric told Denise that he was going to close the store at the end of the month. Denise responded to the news by asking him to sell the store to her family. Wondering why Denise would want a business that was not paying all the bills, he agreed to sell the store anyway. Denise was to pay a total of $150,000 to Eric over several months. With a signed letter of intent, dated February 28 of year six, Denise provided Eric with three postdated checks for $5,000 each dated one month apart. The letter of intent was signed, and Eric deposited the first check, or so he thought. He was notified by the bank the following day that the check he deposited from Denise had been returned due to insufficient funds in her account. Eric called Denise, who apologized, saying that she forgot to move funds over from their savings account. She assured him the next one would clear her account. The next day, Eric tried to deposit the second check, and it was returned due to insufficient funds as well. Frustrated, Eric called Denise again about the returned check. She apologized again and delivered a replacement check to Eric the same day. Thinking the third time would be the charm, Eric was beyond frustrated when the check was returned for the final time.

Eric drove to the store directly from the bank after depositing the third and final insufficient funds check to evict Denise and to shut down the store for good. He could liquidate the merchandise over the next month and be finished with the unprofitable operation and drama for good. However, when he arrived, the store was uncharacteristically dark. There were no customers or any movement inside. The once carefully arranged window displays were empty. Eric cautiously approached the front door. It was locked. Pulling out his keys to open the door he saw through the front door windows what looked to be the leftovers of a robbery. Frantically, he opened the door and pulled out his phone to call Denise. The call went straight to voice mail. He did not want to believe it, but after three bounced checks, he knew in his gut – Denise had stolen the merchandise. As he walked around the disheveled space with only the rickety racks and off-season merchandise remaining, he was at a loss for words.

A couple of days later, through a series of texts from friends, Eric learned that Denise had opened a retail store just a couple blocks south of the original store. He could not believe it, but driving past the new location, it was true. The new retail store display windows were fully stocked and carefully assembled with Eric's merchandise and displays.

The next morning, Eric filed a police report and hired an attorney. Within a couple of days, a civil lawsuit was filed, and a forensic accountant was hired. Eric wanted to know if Denise was willing to buy a failing store and steal all of the inventory, what was really going on the entire time? More specifically, Eric wanted to know:

- If the sales were as great as Denise reported to him daily, why was there not enough money in the bank account to cover payroll?
- If Denise stole money during the period, how much had she stolen?
- How much inventory was stolen by Denise for her new store?

Case Study 1: Exercise 1

Using the details from Eric's story, and The Case of the Disappearing Business Worksheet in Table 12.1, for which a downloadable worksheet is available at www.datasleuthbook.com, identify the questions Eric wanted answered by the forensic accountant. Using information provided about Denise's responsibilities in the business, list her access to funds and systems giving her the opportunity to steal money. Eric's questions and Denise's access combined will be used to translate Eric's questions into investigation priorities. The investigation priorities will the analyses needed, which in turn narrows the data sources needed to answer Eric's questions. Finally, make sure to identify the relevant period for which all data will need to be requested.

The following section will provide guidance as you prepare a case plan for Eric. The appendix contains the recommended solution to this exercise.

- In an interview with any client, remember to inquire as to when an employee/subject was hired and when the final event or termination of employment occurred. This will often be used to determine the relevant period with occasional limitations due to the inability to obtain bank statements going back to the hiring date, the statute of limitations, or the number of years a court allows.

- Using Denise's financial management responsibilities, what opportunities to steal funds did Denise's access to systems provide? What opportunities to steal funds might exist with a mother and daughter duo running the store?

- To translate Eric's questions into actionable investigation priorities, consider the answer that you will provide assuming Eric's allegations of theft are true. It may be helpful to formulate the investigation priorities as big picture tasks. For example, if Eric wants to know how much Denise may have stolen from the business, an actionable investigation priority could be "Quantify funds the business should have received from sales."

- When describing the analysis required to perform the investigation priority, consider the brainstorming process with a comparative analysis. The filing of a civil lawsuit provides what additional analyses opportunities?

- Finally, list the data sources needed to perform the analysis. How were sales tracked? What data sources exist that the analysis, previously identified, will answer "What should have happened?" and "What happened?" What data sources became possibly available with the filing of the civil lawsuit?

TABLE 12.1 Case planning worksheet example for Case Planning Exercise 1.

©2020, Workman Forensics, LLC.

CASE OF THE DISAPPEARING BUSINESS PLANNING WORKSHEET EXERCISE 1

RELEVANT PERIOD: _____

CLIENT QUESTIONS	SUBJECT'S ACCESS	INVESTIGATION PRIORITY	ANALYSIS	DATA SOURCES

 ## CASE STUDY 2: THE CASE OF THE SNEAKY CFO

XYZ Co. was made up of three partners who all made cash investments at the origination of XYZ. Scott was a long-time friend of one of the partners who was recommended to hire as chief financial officer. The partners agreed to hiring Scott as CFO. Scott wanted to be a partner in XYZ, but he was still recovering from significant financial issues and could not afford to purchase shares. Knowing his desire to become a partner, as part of his employment agreement, Scott was offered the position of CFO with the opportunity to earn ownership in the company. A 25% ownership was promised to be given to Scott when all of the other partners recovered their initial investments. Scott signed the employment agreement, and XYZ began serving its customers and earning revenue.

The three partners' roles became that of investors as they were unable to run the operations of the business due to other various business interests. Scott assumed the role of chief operating officer as well as CFO. This role assumption was never formalized with an agreement, but the partners trusted Scott and knew he was incentivized to make the company succeed if he wanted to become a partner. XYZ operated with Scott at the helm for five years, and the partners were happy with his performance.

One afternoon, Jack, one of the founding partners, received a phone call from the bank used by XYZ informing him that their line of credit was maxed out and that it was time to renew the loan. The loan officer wanted to know how they would like to renew or if they were looking to pay off the balance. Jack did not have an immediate response for the loan officer. When he did respond, he advised that there must be a mistake because XYZ had never advanced funds on the loan. When the company opened, Jack offered to be the guarantor on the loan as it was just a backup plan to supplement during emergency cash flow crises. It was common in XYZ's industry that customers would be slow to pay outstanding invoices because of the massive sizes of the companies comprising XYZ's customer list. To Jack, and the other partners' surprise, however, customers were paying on time, and Scott had advised in several partnership meetings that the line of credit remained untouched. The loan officer assured Jack that the line of credit had been drawn down and had an outstanding balance of $1.5 million. Jack asked the loan officer to renew the line of credit for one more year to give them time to sort out what was really happening at the XYZ.

Jack left his office immediately to drive to the offices of XYZ to talk to Scott in person. Scott had plenty of explanations, but Jack could not understand them. At first, he thought that maybe the finances of XYZ were more complicated than his other businesses because none of Scott's reasons as to using the line of credit made sense. Jack called his attorney and explained the situation. The attorney told Jack that the confusion he felt was warranted; something was not right at XYZ. The attorney recommended that Jack and the other founding partners hire a forensic accountant to discover what was truly happening. Jack told the forensic accountant that he wanted answers to the following questions:

- What was happening to all of the revenue being reported to the partners by Scott to necessitate the use of the line of credit?
- Where are other financial issues negatively impacting the company's cash flow?

Case Study 2: Exercise 1

Because the founding partners were not involved in the daily operations of the company, they were unaware as to how money would be stolen – or if it was stolen at all. Use the information obtained from interviewing Jack about Scott's access and responsibilities provided in the following interview memo to complete the Data Sleuth Fraud Detection Worksheet in Table 12.2 and Table 12.3, for which a downloadable worksheet is available at www.datasleuthbook.com.

TABLE 12.2 Data Sleuth Fraud Detection Worksheet example for Case Study 2: Exercise 1 – Money In.

©2020, Workman Forensics, LLC.

Data Sleuth Fraud Detection Worksheet Example for Case Study 2: Exercise 1
MONEY IN
Source of Funds Payment Type: Checks

People who touch the payment from the origination to bank deposit	When and where do these people touch the payment?	If this person stole funds, where could it happen?	If funds were stolen, how would you know?

Sources of Funds Payment Type: ACH

People who touch the payment from the origination to bank deposit	When and where do these people touch the payment?	If this person stole funds, where could it happen?	If funds were stolen, how would you know?

Initial Client Meeting with Jack

In the interview of Jack, one of the founding partners of XYZ Co., Jack advised that since learning about the fully exhausted line of credit, he discovered that Scott's access and responsibility concerning the operations and financials of XYZ

TABLE 12.3   Data Sleuth Fraud Detection Worksheet example for Case Study 2: Exercise 1 – Money Out.

Data Sleuth Fraud Detection Worksheet Example for Case Study 2: Exercise 1 MONEY OUT Use of Funds Payment Type: Checks			
People who authorize the expenditures	Who releases the funds to pay the expenditure?	If this person stole funds, where could it happen?	If funds were stolen, how would you know?

Use of Funds Payment Type: ACH			
People who authorize the expenditures	Who releases the funds to pay the expenditure?	If this person stole funds, where could it happen?	If funds were stolen, how would you know?

over the five years of business included everything – from the invoicing of customers, to the receiving of payments, preparation of payroll, and paying vendor invoices. Information regarding how funds came into the business and the most common expenditures include the following.

- Sources of funds for XYZ Co. included payments from customers who are invoiced monthly for services provided. Payments are received via check and ACH.

- Primary uses of funds for XYZ Co. included:
  - Payroll through ACH using a payroll processor and checks out of bank account.
  - Distributions to owners using checks and ACH payments.
  - Loan payments using transfers from the XYZ Co. bank account to the loan account.

Case Study 2: Exercise 2

Using the details from Scott and Jack's story, and The Case of the Sneaky CFO Planning Worksheet in Table 12.4, for which a downloadable worksheet is available at www.datasleuthbook.com, identify the questions Jack wanted answered by the forensic accountant. Using information provided about Scott's responsibilities in the business, list his access to funds and systems giving him the opportunity to steal money from XYZ. Jack's concerns and Scott's access combined will be used to translate Jack's questions into investigation priorities. The investigation priorities will determine the analyses needed, which in turn narrows the data sources needed to answer Jack's questions. Finally, make sure to identify the relevant period for which all data will need to be requested.

The following section will provide guidance as you prepare a case plan for Jack. The appendix contains the recommended solution to this exercise.

- Using Scott's financial management responsibilities, what opportunities to steal funds did his access to systems and funds provide?
- To translate Jack's questions into actionable investigation priorities, consider the answer that you will provide, assuming Jack's suspicions are true that Scott stole funds. Formulate the investigation priorities as big picture tasks such as "Quantify deposits diverted by subject, if applicable."
- Which of the standard data sleuth analyses might be helpful in answering the client's concerns and completing the investigation priorities?
  - Comparative analysis
  - Source and Use Summary
  - Interesting Data Findings Analysis
  - Risk Indicator Analysis
  - Payroll Analysis
- Finally, list the data sources needed to perform the analysis. What systems or third-party data sources will identify the amounts that should have been received? What data sources exist that the analysis, previously identified, will answer "What should have happened?" and "What happened?"

TABLE 12.4 Case of the Sneaky CFO Planning Worksheet example for Case Study 2: Exercise 2.

CASE OF THE SNEAKY CFO PLANNING WORKSHEET CASE STUDY 2: EXERCISE 2

RELEVANT PERIOD: _____

CLIENT QUESTIONS	SUBJECT'S ACCESS	INVESTIGATION PRIORITY	ANALYSIS	DATA SOURCES

CHAPTER THIRTEEN

The Cases that Went Wrong

THIS BOOK WOULD BE incomplete if I did not allocate at least a few pages to those cases that did not go as planned or advised. These are most common when little to no findings are uncovered when the client insists they were wronged and those when the client's decisions hinder the effectiveness or completion of the investigation. Engagements like these are incredibly challenging because when a client shares their story in the initial client meeting, they are convincing. They are certain that they have been wronged, stolen from, that money has been hidden from them, or that their sibling has taken more than her fair share. If the investigator listening to the story is remotely empathetic, she relates to the client and wants to help him or her find a solution that ultimately feels like justice to him or her. Everyone leaves the meeting energized to uncover what happened and help this client take his or her next steps.

THE CLIENT WHO BELIEVES HE WAS WRONGED

It is in the case planning stage that the difficulty begins. The case manager will prepare the list to request information from the client, and then something strange happens. The client is either not responsive, or they do not have access to the information they claimed to be able to provide. It is not that they should have access and find out they do not – for instance, a business owner who used to be a signer on all accounts is no longer a signer on the main operating account and has to work with the bank to prove that he should have access. No – this client actually knows that he does not have the information requested at all; it does not exist. The client often minimizes the information request and instead wants the forensic accountant to work *CSI* magic by entering keywords into a database that does not exist in the reputable, court-admissible world and put someone in jail – or at least help him file an insurance claim. But using inadmissible evidence to put a subject in jail at the direction of a client is not the role of the forensic accountant or investigator. The role of an investigator is to uncover what actually happened. If evidence does not exist from which analysis can be performed to identify what happened, then the client's problem cannot be solved. No one is going to jail, and no insurance claim will be filed by the ethical forensic accountant or investigator if the data do not lead to a finding of fraud.

One interesting observation in client situations like this is that if the scenario was reversed, and our clients were the defendants, as they sometimes are, they would be arguing with everything they had that they were not being charged fairly because of insufficient evidence. They would be outraged if the evidence proving the allegations did not exceed a preponderance of the evidence or beyond a reasonable doubt. If someone would not want to be charged with a crime based on insufficient evidence, then it should not be permissible either when someone is the victim.

It should always raise a red flag in an investigator's mind if someone is convinced something happened, but they are not willing to let the evidence and investigation run its course. This red flag should alert an investigator that professional skepticism is required in evaluating whether the client knows evidence does not support their allegations and that the hiring of an investigator is fueled by an agenda. Although I may want to believe my client, I must maintain professional skepticism and objectivity, so that I do not get caught up in their story where I cannot see that I am being tricked. It does not feel good to have to tell someone, "I'm sorry. We've reviewed your allegations and the available evidence, and based on this evidence, you don't have a case where we can help you." However, the role of an investigator is not to create something from nothing but to uncover what happened from real, best evidence.

The Case of the Inaccurate Insurance Claim

Frank inherited an appliance retailing business from his father and had worked to add multiple locations across the United States. Negotiating contracts for retail space, marketing, and opening new successful stores were Frank's areas of strength, which is why he hired Nolan to run operations. As Frank discovered the secrets to opening new successful locations, Nolan was constantly playing catch-up and did not have time to adequately set up the inventory systems and controls that he knew were necessary. Frank had opened 10 locations over a period of a few years and needed a break. Nolan was thankful so he could properly begin tracking inventory and implement consistent policies, procedures, internal controls, and security systems at each location.

A site audit was performed at each location, including an inventory of all appliances. This was a challenging audit for Nolan's team because no one had counted the appliances when received to ensure what was ordered was delivered. With the potential for discrepancies known, Nolan instructed his team to perform an inventory count of what existed as of the day of the audit. The results of the count would be compared to the inventory ordered for that location with a reduction for sales. It was not perfect, but Nolan felt they could get a reasonable count. For the first few stores, there were a few discrepancies but not so large a difference that it caused alarm. The day after the fourth store's audit, the manager for the on-site audit called Nolan in a panic. After counting and double checking their calculations, the team had uncovered a discrepancy totaling over $100,000.

Nolan called Frank with the news, and Frank immediately reviewed his insurance policy and called his agent to begin filing a claim. The insurance company advised that for a loss of this magnitude, they would need to provide certain evidence supporting the claim and that a forensic accountant would review the claim and evidence. Knowing that this was more detailed than what Nolan had time for, Frank hired an investigator.

Having learned about Frank's situation, the forensic accountant prepared a case plan and a document list requesting the following information for the relevant period:

- Detailed information regarding inventory purchases
- Inventory count worksheets
- Inventory discrepancy work papers
- Point of sale exports for sales and returns
- Payroll reports and timesheets
- Security system access records

Nolan began providing the information requested, but the investigator quickly recognized that although the inventory discrepancy appeared to be well documented, the client lacked the information to identify the individual responsible for the theft. No security system access records were available because they had not yet installed the security system. Timesheets and sales records were available, but because there was no periodic inventory count, or reliable perpetual inventory tracking, during the relevant period, it was unknown when the discrepancies occurred to narrow down the theft to the employees working those dates.

Frank contacted the investigator weekly to see how the investigation was progressing. The investigator consistently told him that without additional data or information clearly identifying who was working when the theft occurred, the only findings for the report were the analysis and confirmation of the total dollar amount missing from inventory. The investigator would follow up the phone call with an email listing the information needed to identify which employees, if any, had stolen the appliances. Frank was concerned that this would not be sufficient for the insurance company and pressured the investigator to connect the theft to one of the employees. The investigator suggested that she visit the site to see if any of the employees would talk about what they might have witnessed during the period of alleged theft. Frank agreed; however, when the investigator arrived to perform interviews, she discovered that Nolan told a few employees the investigator was coming and was going to get confessions. Needless to say, the employees who agreed to meet with the investigator would not answer any questions of significance. Nolan talked with the investigator at the end of the interviewing day and claimed he knew who had been stealing the appliances because he had been gathering intelligence while performing the audit. He provided the investigator with the employees' names.

The investigator did not trust the information provided by Nolan. She was aware that if she had been pressured by Frank to connect the loss to an employee, he had likely probably pressured Nolan even more intensely. The data provided were reviewed one more time in an effort to identify any other potential anomalies that would indicate a connection between the loss and employees, but no indicators were found. The investigator updated a frustrated Frank and advised that she would prepare a report documenting the loss totals that could be used to make a claim with the insurance company; however, no employees would be accused or connected to the theft. The report was completed, and the investigator never heard from Frank again.

If a client is stolen from and has an employee dishonesty policy or a fidelity bond, although the purpose is to help the policyholder recover from theft, the insurance company may have restrictions and limitations regarding types of theft for which claims will be paid. When this happens, the victim of the theft risks becoming a possible subject in a fraud investigation himself. Being stolen from is not justification for committing insurance fraud – or any other type of fraud.

There is an unexplainable pressure when a client has paid the investigation fees and the results they desired are not attainable because an investigator has refused to promote an unsupported conclusion. I have found that although the client was not thrilled with the result of the investigation being less than he hoped, by providing the results that could be substantiated, I was able to offer some value and not entirely lose the client relationship.

The Case of the Unreconciled Cash Drawer

A doctor's office hired an external bookkeeper to handle all of the accounting responsibilities for the busy practice. As the practice grew, so did the doctor's business opportunities, and the doctor asked the bookkeeper to also handle the bookkeeping for the side businesses in addition to the practice. Eventually, the doctor brought the bookkeeper on full time, and his family embraced the bookkeeper as one of their own. She was so integrated into the family that she would watch their kids and even joined them on annual vacations.

The bookkeeper had some recurring health problems after a few years and needed time off for a surgery. While she was out, payroll needed to be paid, so the doctor logged in and noticed in clicking between screens on the payroll provider's client portal that her paid time off (PTO) balance was zero as of the three months prior, but he was certain that before this surgery was scheduled last month, she said she had PTO available to cover the time off. He submitted payroll to be paid without applying her vacation hours, but he could not shake the feeling that something was wrong. His concern about her seemingly trivial lie grew as he remembered how frequently she visited casinos and always seemed to be shopping online and having packages delivered to the office.

Although it was not a normal practice, he insisted the receptionist count the cash at the beginning of the day the following week. It totaled $200 in various denominations. The doctor had decided he was going to monitor her more closely. The bookkeeper did not suspect anything had changed while she was gone and resumed her normal duties of preparing the deposits for the doctor's practice. However, as she was completing the deposit slip, the doctor asked her if she would leave $200 in the drawer each night and then deposit the remainder. She agreed, wrapped up her tasks, and went to the bank.

After a couple of busy days with patients, the doctor compared the daily deposit report in the system with the deposit made to the bank. The system report listed total cash payments of $500 for the day, but only $400 had been deposited to the bank. The doctor counted the cash drawer. His count confirmed that the $200 from the beginning of the week was still in the drawer. Convinced the bookkeeper had the missing $100, he confronted her the following day. She cried, yelled, and resigned, but she never would admit to taking the missing cash.

Outraged, the doctor called an investigator wanting a full investigation of all deposits and payroll. His theory was that if she was willing to steal cash, then she was probably overpaying herself through payroll too. The investigator asked baseline questions of the doctor to better understand her access to systems and funds.

- What is the normal balance of the cash drawer?
- Is the cash drawer reconciled daily?

- Is the bookkeeper the only employee with access to the cash drawer?
- Does the bookkeeper submit timesheets and paid time off requests?
- Are the bookkeeper's timesheets approved prior to payment?
- Who submits the payroll to the payroll provider?

In response to the questions, the doctor advised that they normally did not count the cash drawer at the end of the night. The normal practice was to leave $200 in the drawer and put the remaining cash in a small lockbox to use as petty cash. The $200 in the drawer was counted only by the bookkeeper, but the cash in the lockbox was never counted. Additionally, multiple employees were able to take payments during the day, which sometimes included the bookkeeper. As for payroll, the bookkeeper was supposed to submit a timesheet, but she never did as there was no one designated to approve her time. The bookkeeper input everyone's time, including her own, into the payroll provider's client portal for the practice. The doctor advised that she was supposed to work 30 hours per week and received two weeks of paid time off per year – none of which could roll over. The doctor ended the conversation by expressing his sense of betrayal and resulting anger at the bookkeeper. He wanted the investigator to put the case together quickly and help him work with law enforcement to have her arrested and sentenced to jail.

Because of the lack of internal controls, and the number of people who had access to the cash drawer, the investigator advised the doctor that likely there would not be enough evidence to prove she stole the cash. The investigator recommended verifying cash, check, and credit card deposits for a short relevant period of a month to see if there was any data evidence of the theft. As it related to payroll, once again because of the lack of internal controls surrounding the bookkeeper's timesheet, payroll submission, and no employment agreement, the investigator emphasized that there could be a chance she would not be prosecuted if the evidence did not support the allegations – especially if the best evidence was his word against hers.

The doctor still insisted on hiring the investigator, so the investigator prepared a case plan reiterating his concerns about the lack of documentation and information available. He specifically requested copies of system deposit reports, carbon-copy deposit slips, bank statements with deposit items, payroll reports, and any timesheets and calendars that existed.

The analysis results identified in cash deposits, a total of $1,000 was not deposited to the bank. No discrepancies were identified for other deposit types. From the payroll analysis comparing the information provided by the doctor to actual payroll paid, it appeared the bookkeeper had been overpaid by $1,500; however, when the number of hours worked on her timesheets were compared to her payroll, there was no discrepancy.

The investigator called to tell the doctor about the analysis findings. The investigator reluctantly had to tell him again that although he believed the loss to be $50,000, the information provided did not support the same. Although it was possible the cash discrepancy found in the one-month relevant period was due to the bookkeeper removing cash from deposits, it would be impossible to prove beyond a reasonable doubt because it was also possible that the cash was placed in the petty cash lockbox. As for the alleged overpayments of payroll, because the timesheets supported the hours the bookkeeper was paid, it was going to be a tough case to support that she should not have been paid those hours because there was no way to prove that she did not work the hours recorded to the timesheets. The doctor was furious that the investigator did not have the proof he believed existed supporting a loss of over $50,000. When asked how the doctor determined the loss was $50,000, he explained that he based it on what he presumed the balance of the petty cash lockbox should have been and on verbal agreements as to the bookkeeper's time and PTO.

The investigator closed out the case by releasing a report of the findings to the doctor disclosing the lacking information surrounding the findings.

Clients who are victims of theft tend to believe that the wrong committed against them must be avenged by having the subject arrested and put in jail at any and all cost. However, this approach is dangerous because a client will start looking for loopholes and avenues to force a situation in which the goal is no longer the truth or the facts surrounding what actually happened, but instead to punish the subject. A client's emotional response to the breach of trust in financial investigations is expected and warranted, but it does not permit the creation of evidence, facts, or situations just to obtain an outcome they believe fitting for the subject.

When an investigator notices the red flags from a client's behavior shifting from "I want to know what happened," to "This is what happened," but no new evidence has surfaced, it is imperative to maintain objectivity, professional skepticism, and to scrutinize the information being provided by the clients. Remain faithful to the investigation and allow it to work rather than forcing a result a client wants. Integrity in investigations promotes future repeat referrals; being a "hired gun" or always advocating for a client no matter the facts is successful only in the short run.

THE CLIENT WHOSE DECISIONS AFFECT AN INVESTIGATION

Sometimes an investigator can follow all the right processes and uncover the most convincing findings from a financial investigation, but the client may still decide to ignore the findings. A client may decide, as in "The Case of the Nonexistent Inventory" in Chapter 4, to not prosecute a financial crime for fear of public exposure or reputation repercussions.

In learning to separate client decisions from our value as professionals, we try to recognize that we are valuable regardless of someone's response to our findings. No matter the action or inaction taken by a client, we will continue to organize, analyze, and present findings with care because we want to help people uncover the truth; what they do with the findings is their responsibility.

The Case of the Overworked Office Manager

Jim owned a manufacturing business. He admitted repeatedly that he didn't understand "all of this accounting stuff," but he knew something was wrong with his cash balance at the bank. He explained to an investigator that his office manager, Jenny, was "great." He trusted her, but he was beginning to worry about her honesty.

The Office Manager

Jenny ran the office and had worked for Jim for eight years. She was responsible for almost everything in the office, including invoicing customers, making deposits, and paying bills. Jenny had been responsible for paying payroll for a long time. However, when an additional office employee was hired, she began to manage the payroll tasks. Jim made sure to let the investigator know that making the payroll change had resulted in quite the fight as Jenny was extremely reluctant to give up her duties. He also noted that Jenny was always stressed. She worked a lot, and she made sure Jim and everyone else who worked for the company knew how stressed she was about working so much. Despite how vocal she was about being overworked, she consistently called off or left early most workdays. Jim was fairly certain she was taking days off and not using her paid time off allotment, but he decided to ignore it. Jenny was great and made his life so much easier. Jim advised the investigator that he reviewed the bank statements each month and had not noticed any check payments being made that did not benefit the company. Additionally, he signed all of the checks.

After finishing his explanation to the investigator of his concerns about Jenny, Jim said, "You know what? I'm just paranoid. That's it. She's probably not doing anything she shouldn't be." The investigator assured him that in her experience, if the cash balance in an account does not appear to be correct, and if the client has a bad feeling, then the client should at least look to be certain there is no theft.

The Analysis

From the risk-based analysis, the investigator determined that the expenditures and payroll paid from the company were a lower fraud risk than the deposits because Jim paid all expenditures and the new employee managed payroll. The investigator recommended that the top investigation priority focus on revenue and deposits. The investigator knew that the manufacturing plant site was operated by a state-of-the-art computer system specific to the industry. The employees in the plant could not place an order for a customer and begin manufacturing without the computer recording the details of the order and printing order tickets. The order tickets were gathered at the plant and delivered to Jenny at the end of each day. Jenny would then use the order tickets to prepare customer invoices within a week of the order ticket's date.

When the investigator learned about the computer system controlling the manufacturing of products but that the invoices were prepared from a separate, accounting system, the investigator asked Jim if the two systems had ever been reconciled. The investigator specifically wanted to know if Jim was certain that the product being ordered and shipped to customers was actually being invoiced, collected, and invoiced by Jenny. Jim thought about his response longer than expected and said, "No. I cannot confirm that."

The investigator prepared a case plan for Jim including a comparative analysis between the computer export of order tickets to the invoices in the accounting software. Depending on the results of that analysis, the second step of the analysis would compare the deposits in the accounting software to the deposits on the bank statements. Jim approved the plan, but he wanted to limit the relevant period to only one month.

The investigator started discreetly reconciling the plant computer order reports to the invoices in the accounting system. The primary reason for working behind the scenes was that Jim wanted to avoid upsetting Jenny. If she was not stealing from the company, Jim did not want her to know he had ever doubted her. Comparing the units of finished goods shipped to the invoices prepared by Jenny, the investigator realized immediately that Jenny did not have a consistent process when invoicing customers. Jenny was a very inconsistent bookkeeper, which made the comparative analysis more difficult than it should have been. The investigator knew that if Jenny was not stealing money, there were going to at least be errors discovered. The comparative analysis should have been simple in matching order ticket numbers to invoices; however, Jenny did not consistently log the order ticket numbers on the invoices. If she had recorded this information, the investigator could have simply joined the two data sets using the primary key of the order ticket number. However, the inconsistency resulted in the need to perform a more manual comparison.

After manually comparing the one month's worth of data between the order ticket export and the invoices in the accounting system, the investigator identified a large number of transactions exceeding $20,000 that did not reconcile. The plant computer system showed $20,000 more ordered than Jenny had invoiced. The investigator called Jim to explain the results of the analysis. Jim responded, "That's impossible. I can't be missing $20,000 from one month. It's just a timing issue. Isn't that a thing?" Despite the numerous attempts to explain the investigation's results, Jim argued with the investigator and refused to consider that there was a problem.

The investigator provided Jim two options:

- End the engagement, or
- Allow the investigator to talk with Jenny.

He surprisingly chose option number two.

The Interview

Jim told Jenny the investigator was going to be arriving to ask her questions about a reconciliation. So, when the investigator arrived, Jenny was not happy to see her. Jenny bluntly said, "I am way too busy for this. I don't have time for an auditor." While the investigator sat at Jenny's desk, Jenny made herself appear busy shuffling papers, answering phones, yelling and chatting with neighboring employees, and kept stating how she was overworked.

Finally, the investigator calmly advised of the purpose of her visit and began to ask questions regarding the invoicing anomalies. For each one, Jenny would respond with one of the following reasons:

- "I'm just so busy, sometimes I make mistakes. Tell me what they are, I'll make notes and go fix them later."
- "Oh, that's no big deal."
- "I'll research it and get back with you."

After listening to Jenny's responses repeatedly, the investigator presented her with the largest anomaly she had found in the comparative analysis. The investigator showed Jenny an invoice and the corresponding order ticket revealing a $7,000 discrepancy between the two items. "Oh my!" Jenny exclaimed, "Let me look at that. What is the invoice number? What was the difference?" The investigator waited for her to research the invoice in the accounting system when she finally said, "I'm not going to be able to look into this today. I don't know what happened.

More than likely it was a mistake, but I'll need to get with the salesman. He's not here, and I need to leave to pick up my kids."

And that was it.

The Client's Decision

The investigator reported her findings one more time to Jim incorporating Jenny's responses from the interview. The investigator asked Jim if he wanted her to expand the case plan to analyze another month's worth of data. He never responded to the investigator's question. He simply said, "It will cost me too much to replace her," and he paid the investigator's invoice. The investigator believed a possibility existed that the salesman and Jenny were being paid directly by customers. Yet despite the discrepancy, Jim decided Jenny was too valuable to his company as his office manager, even if she was stealing, to fire her and to find a replacement.

When clients make decisions like Jim did, it is frustrating to the investigator—especially when long hours and care have been poured into uncovering what actually happened, but the ultimate decision is in the client's hands. If he does not want to make a decision based on the facts presented, an investigator will not convince him otherwise.

Client actions, or inactions, should not change who we are as analysts, forensic accountants, fraud examiners, auditors, or Data Sleuths. A client's response is not a reflection of our purpose, skills, or talents. When we have a client experience like this one, it does not mean that we are irrelevant, insignificant, or invaluable. Although it may be difficult to compartmentalize Jim's seemingly negative response to the investigator's work, he is not criticizing her directly. He has to make the decision whether to acknowledge or to ignore Jenny's actions to do what he deems best for his company. This is something we cannot do for him.

CHAPTER FOURTEEN

Data Sleuth Expansion

WHEN ASKED IN 2013 WHAT I hoped Workman Forensics would accomplish in the future, I responded with the first idea that came to mind, "To make forensic accounting accessible to more people." Now that simple answer has matured into the Data Sleuth Process of today, expanding into an even greater vision. Today the vision of Data Sleuth is threefold:

- To bring the problem-solving capabilities intrinsic to the Data Sleuth framework to clients and industries of all sizes by creating a reliable, systematic, technologically advanced process to investigations.
- To expose the fraudulent activities once concealed under the camouflage of being "too immaterial" or "too complicated to prosecute" or "too difficult to know for sure."
- To empower professionals interested in joining the investigation profession that translates fraud investigation theories into practical, scalable skills.

This vision is not linear but circular. As empowered professionals in turn bring the problem-solving capabilities of the Data Sleuth Process to more clients and industries, they will uncover more fraudulent activities that were previously concealed. With each revolution of the cycle, the Data Sleuth Process becomes more applicable, more accessible, more user friendly, more technologically advanced, more efficient, and simpler, amplifying its usefulness to a broad user group in both private and public sectors. (See Figure 14.1.)

The Data Sleuth Process is the future of financial investigations. It is a convergence of forensic accounting, fraud investigation, and data analysis

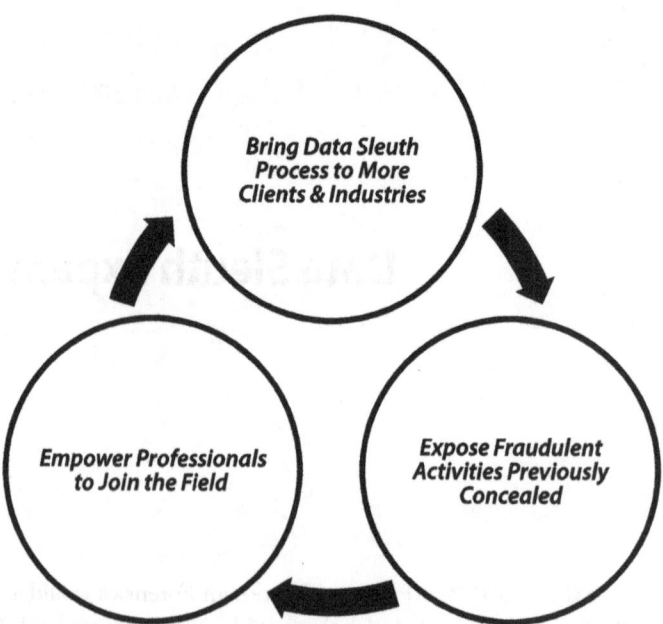

FIGURE 14.1   Illustration of the Data Sleuth Process vision.

that transforms theoretical complexity into clear, actionable discovery. (See Figure 14.2.) The Data Sleuth Process empowers everyone, from an accountant to a spouse in a divorce, to understand the foundational data sources and logical analyses that can be used to quantify losses and find undisclosed assets. The process also provides tremendous opportunities for the establishing of Data Sleuth divisions within public accounting firms, consulting and advisory firms, and law firms to expand service offerings, improve client satisfaction, and generate new revenue streams.

DATA SLEUTH EMPOWERS THE CURIOUS

The Data Sleuth Process provides a roadmap for those who are not familiar with accounting, to be able to quantify losses in embezzlement or find hidden assets using financial information. Even though the Data Sleuth Process explained in this book focuses on the forensic accountant or financial investigator, many investigations can be worked by non-accountants. It is through the combination of the most common data sources (i.e. bank statements, credit card statements, and payroll reports) and the standard Data Sleuth analyses that fraud is uncovered

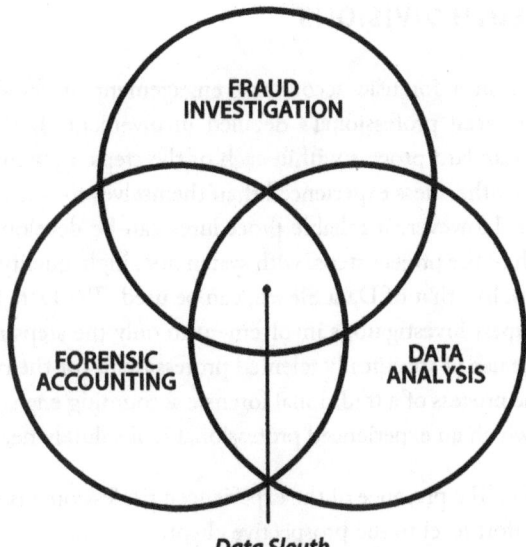

Data Sleuth

FIGURE 14.2　The Data Sleuth convergence.

and assets unhidden. Demystification of financial investigations is possible with the Data Sleuth Process. Victims no longer have to wonder "What if someone is stealing from me?" They can discover for themselves.

The primary data sources of most financial investigations addressed in this book rely on the use of bank statements, credit card statements, and payroll reports. The understanding of what these data sources represent and applying the appropriate analysis to quantify losses are the core elements of many financial investigations, and to perform these steps does not require experience in accounting. The Data Sleuth Process is not just for the forensic accountant. This means that private investigators, paralegals, attorneys, data analysts, and any other curious individuals can use logic, guided by the Data Sleuth Process, to discover what actually happened in financial data.

The part of an investigation that necessitates the use of a forensic accountant, or financial investigator, is in expert testimony. A forensic accountant, or financial investigator, is able to testify to the nuances of financial information such as normal business practices, explaining how someone stole money using the context and evidence of intent supported by accounting records, or referencing tax returns to explain the discovery of hidden assets in a marital dispute. A forensic accountant, or experienced financial investigator, with testifying experience can also communicate confidence and legitimacy as a third party when testifying before a judge or jury, which can be extremely valuable to a client's case.

DATA SLEUTH DIVISIONS

Not all the steps in a forensic accounting engagement or fraud investigation require an experienced professional's detailed involvement. If the professional does not have a standard process within each of the steps, they may not be confident in allowing others less experienced than themselves to work on the various parts of the case. However, if reliable procedures can be developed and implemented into each of the project steps, with systematic, high-quality review, then a replicable process, like that of Data Sleuth, can be used. The Data Sleuth Process minimizes the expert investigator's involvement to only the steps most necessary and promotes the use of specifically talented professionals for the other areas.

Consider the process of a traditional forensic accounting engagement and the critical steps in which an experienced professional is absolutely necessary:

- **Client intake.** The presence of the experienced professional is helpful in providing a comfort level to the prospective client.
- **Case planning.** Because the experienced professional will be required to take responsibility for the resulting work product, that professional should be involved in planning each engagement.
- **Document inventory.** This step does not require the involvement of an experienced professional. Review of the document inventory by the professional, once compiled, may be necessary to determine if additional document requests should be made of the client prior to performing analysis.
- **Data processing.** This step does not require the involvement of an experienced professional. If the professional can communicate what data need to be processed and in what resulting format, the professional's time and performance of this step are not vital to the case results.
- **Analysis of data.** If the experienced professional is proficient at data analysis, this step may be performed by the professional. However, if the professional can communicate the purpose of the analysis to a data analyst, the professional may not need to perform the actual analysis itself.
- **Analysis and findings review.** If the professional will be using an analysis in the resulting work product, his or her review of the analysis is necessary.
- **Report.** At a minimum, the experienced professional should carefully review the report explaining the analysis performed and resulting findings.
- **Testimony.** If testimony is pertinent to the case, the experienced professional will be needed to testify to the findings.

This foundational, simple structure provides opportunities for scalability through the reduction of decisions required to be made based on judgment and experience. Such a process allows the expert investigator's time to be spent only in the areas required, which may include business development, training the team, and ideation of other uses. At the same time, a higher-quality work product and solution for the client is being produced. With a process easily replicated from investigation to investigation, then professional services firms and law enforcement agencies can create Data Sleuth divisions to further improve investigations for clients and the public at large.

PUBLIC ACCOUNTING FIRMS

Through the adoption of the Data Sleuth Process, public accounting firms have an opportunity to create a Data Sleuth division that could operate seamlessly with other service offerings. What once may have felt like the Wild West, which would necessitate reliance on a professional's experience in investigation decision making, using the Data Sleuth Process, forensic accounting and fraud investigation workflows can be structured similarly to those of tax preparation and external audit engagements.

- Client intake
- Project planning and procedure development or improvement
- Tax preparation or audit procedures
- Detail review
- Final review and release of tax return or audit report

The Data Sleuth Process gives management a starting point to bring structure to forensic accounting engagements. It provides a bridge between fraud investigation theories and their practical application and execution. This bridge empowers all members of the team to make decisions, pertaining to their area of involvement, in a logical, methodical manner guided by the prioritization of best evidence and application of reliable analysis procedures that promote consistency in work products and the ability to conduct a quality review of the analysis of other team members prior to issuing a report.

Integrating the Data Sleuth Process into a public accounting firm also allows professionals interested in this type of work to allocate their time across a variety of interesting projects. Because forensic accounting and fraud investigation engagements cannot be predicted or structured with deadlines, reluctance to add a forensic accounting service offering is understandable. However, dividing forensic accounting tasks across team members allows everyone to fulfill their primary work responsibilities while applying their skills to a unique consulting engagement without negating or creating a backlog in other annual, deadline-driven services. When there is a process in place, planning can happen, where client expectations, client deadlines, court deadlines, and the process in between can be scheduled around other annual, recurring client projects.

The integration of the Data Sleuth Process is not limited to just the standardization and expansion of consulting engagements, but it could also be incorporated into existing, recurring client engagements. It is a common discussion between external auditors and fraud investigators that external audits are not designed to find fraud, but what if external audit procedures could be updated to detect fraud without interfering with the traditional workflow? By performing a fraud risk assessment regarding how money is received and spent by an organization, data analysis tests, machine learning, and automation could be incorporated into interim reviews and annual audits to detect the most common fraud schemes.

Finally, from a revenue perspective, as a consulting engagement, forensic accounting and fraud investigation projects typically bill at a higher realization than annual services. The incorporation of the Data Sleuth Process in these engagements should improve the realization because of the confidence in the system and the resulting work product. Additionally, within the same budget, the value created for the client provides more detailed, accurate, and complete answers to clients' questions. Where samples of data may have been examined before the integration of the Data Sleuth Process, now entire data sets can be reviewed in the same amount of time. The value of useful, practical solutions for clients generates future referrals, which is critical for project-based, nonrecurring engagements.

 ## CONSULTING AND ADVISORY FIRMS

Consulting and advisory firms often provide many diverse service offerings to clients creating a perfect opportunity to establish a Data Sleuth division to support the numerous specialized consultants. Many large consulting and advisory firms have been adding forensic accounting and fraud investigation to their list of client services by employing professionals with financial investigation experience. The firm may provide support personnel to handle administrative duties, but most of the work is performed by the professionals in the manner preferred by that professional. The client services from professional to professional vary in execution because the professionals have differing opinions on the best way to serve each client. Clients generally accept varying results from financial investigators and forensic accountants, but there is a better way.

Consistency in the investigation process, using the Data Sleuth Process, would allow consulting firms to offer reliable, scalable financial investigation services in which revenue from the services is not dependent on the varying methods of independent professionals and capped by their individual availability. Additionally, the risk of unsatisfied clients would also decrease as there would be greater quality control throughout the entire project.

Implementing the Data Sleuth Process within a consulting firm allows the collaboration of forensic accountants, investigators, and other subject matter experts, such as open-source intelligence, surveillance, due diligence, and other expertise to provide complementary services to clients. Some of my favorite investigations are those we have worked jointly with other specialized investigators to provide a comprehensive solution to the client's concerns.

THE CASE OF THE PHONY PROFESSIONAL

Professional Engineers Oil and Gas, Co. (PEOG) provided professional engineering and programming services for oil and gas construction projects. It was a customary practice for companies, like PEOG, to bid on jobs with the intention to collaborate and hire subcontractors. PEOG was awarded a large project, and in order to provide a cost-effective and timely completion for their client, they subcontracted to a small engineering firm owned by Caleb. The managing partner of PEOG had been introduced to Caleb a year earlier by a mutual contact. Caleb provided his resume to PEOG, which stated he had earned a PhD in two engineering disciplines. The resume also indicated that Caleb held a professional engineering license.

PEOG and Caleb prepared an estimate for the client's project in the amount of which Caleb's budget would consist of 40% of the total project hours. However, only one month after the project began, Caleb exceeded his budget and billed PEOG for all of the hours allotted to both Caleb and PEOG combined. Two months into the project, PEOG's client placed a hold on the invoices and all payments as the allotted hours far exceeded the scope and agreed upon budget. PEOG met with Caleb to discuss the budget overrun and to strategize about how to complete the project. Caleb insisted that his time was accurate and that he would not discount his future time on the project. In fact, if the PEOG's client demanded a discount from him, Caleb would quit the job entirely. Oddly, Caleb continued to work on the project and to send excessive billings to PEOG for three more months even though he knew the client was refusing to pay outstanding invoices. After the third invoice, PEOG demanded to exercise their contractual right with Caleb to audit his company's books and records, but on the same day, Caleb issued a payment demand letter to PEOG. After many phone calls between PEOG's managing partner and Caleb, a mutual agreement was reached. If Caleb allowed the audit, depending on the outcome of the audit, then PEOG would consider paying the outstanding invoices.

PEOG hired a forensic accountant to perform the contractual audit, but after multiple requests for information from Caleb, the forensic accountant knew she should recommend the use of other specialized investigators. The client agreed to the collaborative assistance of a private investigator to perform surveillance and an open-source intelligence investigator. PEOG was concerned that Caleb would not actually cooperate with the audit and would instead begin shredding all pertinent information. To address this concern, the private investigator specializing in surveillance began monitoring Caleb's home and office locations. At the same time, the open-source intelligence investigator began researching Caleb's history.

Caleb's business website listed all kinds of engineering services and boasted pictures of a beautiful office and engineering team, but from surveillance activities, the team discovered that Caleb did not actually occupy an office but rather did all of the work from his home. This caused serious doubt about the existence of an actual team. Further online research uncovered evidence that Caleb had been outsourcing the engineering work overseas and was not performing the work himself. Thus, an unlicensed individual from another country was producing the work Caleb claimed to be his. A search of the Secretary of State website identified that the company Caleb claimed he owned and represented was delinquent in its registration by several months and was never current while working on this large project.

The investigation team noticed that representations made by Caleb to PEOG were not supported by evidence uncovered through the research. Contacting each school on Caleb's resume, one of the investigators requested to verify Caleb's purported degrees. None of the schools were able to verify his attendance as he had never attended any of the universities. Using public records and investigative databases, the team also discovered that two years prior, Caleb had been charged with multiple counts of "obtaining property under false pretenses" for making unauthorized purchases of tires and sporting goods for his personal use with his previous employer's funds. Then in the following year, he had been charged with one count of "obtaining property under false pretenses," because he had purchased computers under his employer's name, for which he did not have authorization to represent or to make purchases. The computer vendor billed the employer, but Caleb never returned computers.

While researching and surveilling, the client advised that when cleaning out a temporary office they had loaned Caleb, the client discovered a professional engineering stamp in his desk drawer. The stamp listed his full name and a license number. Using the state licensing website for engineers, a search for the license number was run revealing another person's name. Caleb had ordered a fake professional engineering stamp listing his name using an actual licensed professional engineer's license number.

The evidence that Caleb had been defrauding PEOG and PEOG's client kept mounting, and by interviewing individuals connected to open-source intelligence findings, it became increasingly apparent that Caleb was a serial fraudster. A police report was filed about the incident, as PEOG had to absorb the payments they had paid to Caleb. Law enforcement advised PEOG that because Caleb's relationship to them was as a contractor and because of the use of a fake professional engineering license that the case should be filed civilly instead of charging criminally. A report of the surveillance and research findings was provided to the client, should they decide to file a civil case, but the most effective use of the report was to stop the incessant demands of Caleb to pay the outstanding invoices.

Once the financial investigator realized that the client was not going to receive the requested documentation for the audit, collaboration among a team of specialized investigators provided an opportunity for the client to still gain valuable evidence and information despite the inability to perform the audit-like procedures as initially hired.

 ## LAW FIRMS

When a client hires an attorney to assist in a potential civil litigation matter, research and investigation may be performed by the law firm to determine whether the client's case is one that can be litigated. Sometimes, attorneys refer cases before a lawsuit has been filed to identify, based on evidence available, what claims might be asserted in the petition. The ability to perform the analysis in a timely matter is often very important to the client wanting to file a lawsuit, and Workman Forensics is able to do so with the use of the Data Sleuth Process. Once the lawsuit is filed and more information is obtained through discovery or subpoena, the full investigation can begin, which may result in future testimony.

The investigative measures performed for prelitigation purposes by attorneys and paralegals would be greatly amplified by the incorporation of the Data Sleuth Process. Using the process as part of a prelitigation strategy would improve the reliability of the results in determining whether to take a case. Additionally, to minimize exposure on contingency fee cases or class action lawsuits, data and evidence pertinent in determining the validity of a client's claims could be performed in house using the Data Sleuth Process as a guide.

Even though the attorney or paralegal cannot testify to their findings, they are able to prepare the briefs and petitions containing previously verified facts. Then if the use of an expert is needed in the future, the analysis and findings resulting from the use of a reliable process could help in clarifying the scope of the expert's testimony.

LAW ENFORCEMENT

Some law enforcement agencies have created financial crime units and task forces to investigate financial crimes; however, because of the size and complexity of some of the cases, and the ever-growing workload, analyses of the information can take months if not years. The Data Sleuth Process would allow even nonfinancial investigators to perform much of their data analysis without solely relying on the limited capacity of financial analysts. Additionally, the Data Sleuth Process could improve the efficiency of financial analysts and support personnel to work through outstanding cases more quickly. The support of financial investigations provided through a Data Sleuth division would increase the timeliness of help to victims of financial crimes and better serve the public at large.

THE FUTURE OF DATA SLEUTH

The Data Sleuth Process is just the beginning of addressing clients' concerns with accuracy, specificity, and consistency. Advancement of the Data Sleuth Process uncovers facts that answer client questions by connecting the power of data analytics with the curiosity that drives investigations. As Data Sleuth grows, it will continue to look for ways to seamlessly connect fraud investigation theories and practical application. Using the standardized data analysis process that leverages technological improvements, investigators everywhere can implement the Data Sleuth Process to provide data-supported answers to the clients in their communities. As more professionals embrace and implement the Data Sleuth framework, we will continue to invest in the technology that will further improve the way the Data Sleuth Process can be sued by professionals. As more people use the process and benefit from the results, more clients will trust the process and will see the benefits of incorporating it as a preventative solution to detect fraud before a fraud loss is astronomical.

DATA SLEUTH AS PREVENTION

Whether an organization has a robust fraud prevention program or not, the Data Sleuth Process can be adapted as an ongoing fraud detection measure. If an investigation can be performed using data within the Data Sleuth Process to uncover what happened, then that same process can be used on a regular basis to test for the same anomalies and findings – preferably before the loss closes a business, causes layoffs, or results in a family losing their investment.

Fraud prevention in a business is typically supported through a well-crafted system of internal controls and segregation of duties limiting one's access and control of a system. However, internal controls and segregation of duties are ineffective when two or more people collude to commit fraud. Just as inventory shrinkage in a retail environment cannot be prevented 100% of the time, occupational fraud will not be successfully prevented 100% of the time. Early fraud prevention has its limits; therefore, a fraud prevention program must be paired with a fraud detection program. Fraud detection early in the life of the fraud scheme is the best result for everyone. No matter when in the life of a scheme fraud is detected, trust has been broken, and likely an employee will need to be replaced. But recovering the loss from a scheme that occurred over a year or two versus five or more years is much easier.

LICENSES, CREDENTIALS, AND PROFESSIONAL DEVELOPMENT

Fraud investigations, in several states across the country, must be performed by licensed private investigators, attorneys, or Certified Public Accountants. Expanding the offerings of the Council on Law Enforcement Education and Training to include a Data Sleuth license would not only advance private investigation into the digital age, but would also allow professionals, such as Certified Fraud Examiners, who are not private investigators or accountants to meet the statute requirements without the inapplicable training classes required to become a private investigator. Currently, in the state of Oklahoma, the classes required to obtain a private investigator's license are still based on investigative techniques and methods that are becoming increasingly obsolete. Although continuing education courses for private investigators may support more cutting-edge skills, the course to obtain the license does not, which makes it less desirable for those professionals who would like to work financial investigations but are neither a private investigator, an attorney, nor an accountant. The creation of a license for private investigators and professionals alike would also improve the quality of investigative training by developing relevant curriculum and would increase funding for the state.

A certification program providing the Certified Data Sleuth credential would teach and empower professionals how to implement strategy when approaching client cases and incorporate data analysis as the basis to their findings and loss calculations, resulting in more reliable investigative results and referral sources.

Within the areas of licensing and credentialing opportunities, the Data Sleuth framework provides a standardized, data-first approach to the forensic accounting and fraud investigation professions by equipping professionals to raise the quality and efficiencies of financial investigations. Data analysis training is more widely provided within the internal audit profession, for which the use of data analysis, machine learning, and automation will likely become a standard practice for internal audit departments. Data analysis in the forensic accounting and fraud investigation niche should be no exception; however, the investigation industry currently lacks professional development and training regarding the use of data, financial or otherwise, in investigations.

Appendix: Case Study Exercise Solution Recommendations

CASE STUDY 1: EXERCISE 1 – SOLUTION RECOMMENDATIONS

The case plan for "The Case of the Disappearing Business" addressed three of Eric's primary questions concerning Denise and the missing money. For each question, Denise's access to funds and systems should have been considered in determining the investigation priority for the investigator. To complete the planning, the analyses required to address the investigation priorities must be determined followed by the identification of the best available data and evidence to be requested for the relevant period of **July 15, Year 2 through February 28, Year 6**.

If the sales were as great as Denise reported to Eric, why was there not enough money in the bank account to cover payroll? If the deficit in the bank account was due to theft, how much did Denise steal?

- **Denise's Access to Funds and Systems.** Denise had access to the point-of-sale software, which gave her the ability to control the recording of the funds in the system.
  - She could choose to record some, but not all, of the sales.
  - She could skim cash payments, or remove cash from deposits before they were recorded, taking only the checks to deposit to the bank.
  - Denise could open a bank account in a tradename similar to that of the retail store name, (i.e. Denise doing business as Retail Store Name), which would allow her to divert check payments.
  - She could set up a separate credit card processing account to process credit cards instead of using the account connected to the point-of-sale software.
  - Not only did Denise have full control over the sales and collections process, but because of the mother/daughter relationship of Denise and

Mandy, the risk of the theft of funds from sales was not mitigated by any segregation of duties between employees.

■ **Investigation Priority.** Quantify any losses related to deposits and revenue. This investigation priority could be further categorized by type of payments such as cash, check, or credit card because the business was a retail store, and all types of payments could be at risk.

■ **Analysis.** Compare sales recorded to the point-of-sale software to the deposits to the bank account. The analysis could be divided by payment type: cash, check, and credit card.

■ **Data Sources.** The investigator should request point-of-sale sales reports and bank statements with deposit items.

How Much Inventory Was Stolen by Denise for Her New Store?

■ **Denise's Access to Funds and Systems**. Denise had complete access and control of the inventory management for the store. She had a key to the store.
  ■ She could purchase extra inventory and sell it on the side.
  ■ She could purchase extra inventory once she knew she would be taking the merchandise to her new location.
  ■ She managed the inventory counts – when they were performed and the totals recorded to the point-of-sale software.
  ■ She could choose to record some, but not all, of the sales.

■ **Investigation Priority.** Quantify the loss due to theft of inventory.

■ **Analysis.** Determine the value from the last reliable inventory count, add all purchases since the date of the inventory count from invoices paid by Eric, and subtract cost of goods sold to determine expected ending inventory. Compare the expected ending inventory to the actual ending inventory to estimate the loss related to inventory.

■ **Data Sources.** The investigator should request point-of-sale inventory records and cost of good sold reports, evidence of the last inventory count and value, vendor invoices for merchandise purchases, and the value of the inventory remaining in Eric's store after Denise stole the merchandise.

CASE STUDY 2: EXERCISE 1 – SOLUTION RECOMMENDATIONS

The Data Sleuth Fraud Detection Worksheet prepared for "The Case of the Sneaky CFO" found the following risk areas needed to be further examined and incorporated into the case plan.

Money In

- **Scott's access to systems and funds.** Scott invoiced the customers, retrieved the payments from the mail, recorded the invoices to the accounting system, and deposited the payments to the bank account.
- **If Scott stole check payments, how could it have happened?** With Scott controlling the entire process, the risk of theft existed in that he could delete invoices when payments were received and deposit the checks to a bank account that only he could access. He could also invoice outside of the system and have payments mailed to a post office box or his home and avoid the company altogether.
- **If Scott stole the ACH/electronic payments from customers, how could it have happened?** Whether Scott used the XYZ accounting system to invoice customers or not, he could have stolen ACH, or electronic payments, by directing customers to send payment to a bank account to which he alone had access.
- **If funds were stolen, what are the data sources that would help confirm or deny Jack's suspicions?** A user audit log from the accounting system may identify if invoices and/or customer payments were recorded to the system and then subsequently deleted. A comparative analysis of hours worked by employees on each customer's job in a month could be compared to the hours invoiced to the customer. If a customer was not invoiced and should have been, further investigation may be warranted. For all invoices for which payments were recorded to the system, the bank account should be examined for subsequent deposits.

Money Out

- **Scott's access to systems and funds.** Scott was a signor on the operating bank account for XYZ Co. As part of his responsibilities, he initiated all payroll disbursements whether through a payroll processor ACH/direct deposit or via check. He paid all vendor invoices using both checks and ACH. He also initiated all distribution payments to the partners using check and ACH payments.
- **If Scott stole money using the payroll process, how could it have happened?** With Scott controlling the entire payroll process, the risk of theft existed in that he could pay himself more than the agreed upon salary, bonuses, or through unsubstantiated expense reimbursements.
- **If funds were stolen through the payroll process, what are the data sources that would help confirm or deny Jack's suspicions?** Payroll reports for the

entire period should be requested from the payroll processor and examined for additional payments to Scott through salary, bonuses, or unsubstantiated expense reimbursements.

- **If Scott stole money using checks or ACH payments from the bank account, how could it have happened?** Scott could simply write checks or send ACH payments to himself or LLCs he fully controlled disguised as vendor payments.
- **If funds were stolen, what are the data sources that would help confirm or deny Jack's suspicions?** Bank statements and supporting information for ACH/electronic payments could be requested from the bank and reviewed for expenditures not benefiting XYZ Co.
- **If Scott stole money using line of credit advances, how could it have happened?** Scott could have advanced funds to a bank account he controlled that had a similar account name to that of XYZ Co. Then he could have spent the advanced funds from there for personal expenditures.
- **If funds were stolen using loan advances, what are the data sources that would help confirm or deny Jack's suspicions?** Loan activity or history statements could be requested from the bank. All advances could be compared to the known XYZ Co. bank accounts to confirm whether all the loan advances were deposited to the operating account.

Although there are many areas of fraud risk for XYZ Co. with such little oversight, the paths of least resistance are the areas given the highest risk and investigation priority.

CASE STUDY 2: EXERCISE 2 – SOLUTION RECOMMENDATIONS

The case plan for "The Case of the Sneaky CFO" addressed two broad concerns for the client, Jack. For each question, using the findings from the Data Sleuth Fraud Detection Worksheet evaluating Scott's access to funds and systems, preparing a case plan should identify the analyses required to address the investigation priorities. Then to perform the analyses, the identification of the best available data and evidence will need to be requested for the relevant period of **five years.**

What was happening to all of the revenue being reported to the partners by Scott to necessitate the use of the line of credit?

- **Scott's Access to Deposits from Customers.** As identified in exercise 1, Scott controlled this entire process, so the case planning for this client concern should prioritize the areas of fraud risk from simplest to most complicated method(s).

- **Investigation Priority.** Determine if revenues are being diverted to bank accounts controlled by Scott. Quantify any findings.
- **Analysis.** Review user audit logs for deleted invoices and/or deleted customer payments. Compare the expected revenue from customers to actual revenue deposited to the operating account. Compare hours worked on jobs to hours invoiced to customers.
- **Data Sources.** The investigator should request an accounting system backup if available. Otherwise, request the specific reports listing detailed customer accounts receivable, user audit logs, and invoices. A report listing employee hours by job should be obtained as well as customer contracts. Bank statements with deposit items should be requested.

Where are other financial issues negatively affecting the company's cash flow? Expenditures.

- **Scott's Access to XYZ Co. Funds to Pay Expenditures.** As identified in exercise 1, Scott managed everything about the payroll and purchasing processes.
- **Investigation Priority.** Determine if Scott overpaid himself through payroll or directly from the bank account. Quantify any findings.
- **Analysis.** Using data analysis tests and risk indicator analyses for payroll, identify any anomalies in the employee information and payroll payments. Compare all payments to Scott to his employment contract. For all expense reimbursements, compare to supporting documentation, if it exists. Using a Source and Use Summary and Interesting Data Findings (IDF), identify any payments not benefiting XYZ Co. that may have benefitted Scott personally. Any IDF results should be compared to the accounting system to determine the way in which the transaction was recorded by Scott.
- **Data Sources.** The investigator should request an accounting system backup, if available. Otherwise, request the specific reports listing cash disbursements, payroll, and a general ledger. Payroll reports should be requested from the payroll processor, and bank statements with check images and ACH supporting documentation should be requested from the bank.

Where are other financial issues negatively affecting the company's cash flow? Loan funds.

- **Scott's Access to Loan Funds.** As identified in exercise 1, Scott was able to advance loan funds from the line of credit without any authorization from the founding partners.

- **Investigation Priority.** Determine if Scott diverted loan funds to an account he controlled. Determine if Scott advanced loan funds to cover deficits in the bank account. Quantify any findings.
- **Analysis.** Using comparative analysis, compare the advances from the line of credit to the deposits to the bank account. If advances were made that were not deposited to XYZ's account, request additional information from the bank. Compare the timing of loan advances to the daily balances in the bank account and/or the check register balance in the accounting system.
- **Data Sources.** The investigator should request a loan activity/history statement for the line of credit and bank statements for XYZ.

About the Author

L EAH WIETHOLTER, CFE, PI, CPA, is a modern-day Sherlock Holmes and is an expert in following patterns to find money through financial investigations. Beginning her career as a student trainee with the Federal Bureau of Investigation under the direction of a forensic accountant, Leah has worked on more than 150 cases in her career. She is the chief executive officer and founder of Workman Forensics, LLC in Tulsa, OK, where she uses the Data Sleuth® Process to build a team that provides data-driven results to assist with client disputes including embezzlement, corporate fraud, divorce, financial institution fraud, and criminal defense.

About the Website

D ATA SLEUTH® WORKSHEETS AND resources have been made available for download to readers of *Data Sleuth: Using Data in Forensic Accounting Engagements and Fraud Investigations* at www.datasleuthbook.com.

- **Chapters 6 and 7: Sample Data Sleuth® Fraud Detection Worksheet:** The sample Data Sleuth Fraud Detection Worksheet provides investigators with a tool to begin performing a risk-based analysis for organizations as part of the case planning step in the Data Sleuth Process. This tool provides the investigator with a framework to facilitate the identification of cash sources and uses and the level of risk associated with the internal controls (or lack thereof) relating to each.
- **Chapter 12: Case Study 1 – Data Sleuth® Case Planning Worksheet:** The Case Planning Worksheet is provided as a downloadable template to facilitate practicing the case planning step of the Data Sleuth Process for the case study "The Case of the Disappearing Business" and corresponding Exercise 1. The template provides investigators with a guide to organize a case plan that specifically answers client questions, specifies the priorities of the investigation, identifies the analyses required to complete the investigation priorities, and lists the corresponding data sources necessary for the analyses.
- **Chapter 12: Case Study 2 – Data Sleuth® Fraud Detection Worksheet:** The Case Planning Worksheet is provided as a downloadable template to facilitate practicing a risk-bases analysis in the case study "The Case of the Sneaky CFO" and corresponding Exercise 1. The sample Data Sleuth Fraud Detection Worksheet

provides investigators with a tool to practice performing a risk-based analysis in this case study to identify cash sources and uses, and the level of risk associated with the internal controls (or lack thereof) relating to each.

- **Chapter 12: Case Study 2 – Data Sleuth® Case Planning Worksheet:** The Case Planning Worksheet is provided as a downloadable template to facilitate practicing the case planning step of the Data Sleuth Process for the case study "The Case of the Sneaky CFO" and corresponding Exercise 2. The template provides investigators with a guide to organize a case plan that specifically answers client questions, specifies the priorities of the investigation, identifies the analyses required to complete the investigation priorities, and lists the corresponding data sources necessary for the analyses.

Index

Page numbers followed by *f* and *t* refer to figures and tables, respectively.